outing to Cromer 1986

Clickers, Walter Edwards & Son Ltd, 1925

The Story of the Norwich Boot and Shoe Trade

The Story of the Norwich Boot and Shoe Trade is published by Norwich Heritage Projects which is a totally independent non-profit making organisation with the simple aim of encouraging an appreciation of the heritage of our beautiful City of Norwich.

The Story of the Norwich Boot and Shoe Trade
Published by Norwich Heritage Projects
Norwich Heritage Projects
5, Cringleford Chase
Norwich
NR4 7RS
www.norwich-heritage.co.uk

Norwich Heritage Projects is a small group of enthusiasts who combine local historical resource and expertise with modern technology to take a fresh look at the rich and varied heritage of Norwich.

ISBN 978-0-9566272-3-0

Edited, designed and brought to production by Norwich Heritage Projects.
Printed and bound in the UK by
Barnwell Print Ltd, Dunkirk Industrial Estate, Aylsham, Norfolk, NR11 6SU

Front cover photographs (left to right):
Top Row
(L to r) Princess Elizabeth and Geoffrey Holmes, Edwards & Holmes, 1951
Kaye Sisters and Martin Miller (front right), 1958
(L to r) Pamela May, Margot Fonteyn and Len Waspe, c1952
Middle Row
Conveyor belt , Riverside, Norvic, 1961
Norvic, St George's Plain, 1946
Stockroom, Start-rite, c1975
Bottom Row
Closing room, Sexton, Son & Everard, 1959

Title page: See pages 92 and 97

Image Credits.
We are very grateful to all who have allowed us to reproduce images including:

- Our contributors (see pages v to vii)
- Shoe firms especially: Bobcol, Bowhill & Elliott, Broadland Slippers, the Florida Group, Freed of London and Start-rite. These firms have allowed us to reproduce images from their archives and also to take photographs of their current operations.

Additionally the following individuals and organisations have permitted us to reproduce images. Where accreditation is not made in the text, we have listed the page number where the image is located:

Archant Newspapers: 20 (CWS), 27, 31, 34 (Sexton & Norvic), 35, 36, 46 (Bally & Kirbys), 55, 79, 83, 88 (mechanical), 123, 146 (CWS), 164 (Mag. Shoes), 168 (Croxford & trimming), 171 (clicking room & factory), 178 (machine room), 179, 185, 195, 197 (outing), 202, 213, 214 (stock room), 223, 235, 243.

Philip Armes: 18,105, 132, 133, 184 (Sultzer's Court), 215.

Mike Dixon All photos of shoes in the Bridewell Museum Collection. All interior 2012 photographs of Florida's Dibden Road factory. All exterior shots of former factories and factory sites taken in 2012.

Norfolk County Council Library & Information Service: 146 (Boulton & Paul), 173 (George White),184 (Palace Works), 193, 197 (St Mary's Works), 227 (c1963).

Norfolk Museums & Archaeology Service: The Bridewell Museum: iv, 3 (shoeworkers), 4, 20, 39, 51,52, 64 (Band), 76 (Executive), 82 (conveyor), 88 (CAD), 91, 127, 147, 156 (post 1990), 176, 178 (teenage council), 182, 200, 221 (factory).

Norfolk Record Office: All photographs of Walter Edwards & Son Ltd, 45, 47, 64, 206, 207.

Ordnance Survey Department: 174.

George Plunkett (permission from Jonathan Plunkett): 65,166 (factory, 1936), 187, 201 (Colman House 1936), 203 (54, Pottergate, 1968), 222, 227 (1938), 234, 236.

Contents

Foreword

Charabanc outing, Howlett & White, 1920

After completing our book on Norwich Pubs and Breweries in 2011, we were looking for a new project when Vic Hopes, a veteran of the industry, suggested that we might like to take on the Norwich boot and shoe trade. We soon found that since Wilfred Sparks wrote 'Shoemaking in Norwich' in the 1940s, other books had concentrated their efforts on the history of specific firms rather than the industry as a whole. It therefore seemed an ideal subject to research.

From the start we were amazed at how little had been recorded about the industry, particularly about the period since WWII. This was despite the fact that it was very clear from the response to the excellent oral project on the subject completed by the Costume & Textile Association (between 2006 and 2008) that there was massive interest in the subject.

In our previous undertakings we have aimed to bring history alive by including personal stories and images, but these have been mainly used to add colour to written sources. For the boot and shoe trade they have often been used as our starting point. Therefore, great thanks have to be given to all who have shared their memories and lent us their family photographs. Collectively our contributors had vast experience in the shoe trade, having cumulatively clocked up well over a thousand years of service.

ARCHANT

Our next major source of material was from Archant, who very kindly gave us access to their extensive newspaper and photographic archive. This enabled us to chart the final years of many of the major firms as headline after headline reported their demise. Their reports also gave a contemporary view of local opinion at the time.

Then of course there was the question of the shoes. To fully understand the industry it is important to see the beautiful footwear that was made in Norwich. Throughout the book we have shown the lovely shoes that were manufactured in the City. Here we have to give particular thanks to the Bridewell Museum who allowed us access to their fabulous collection.

Nor must we forget the Norwich footwear firms that are still operational. Start-rite, the Florida Group, Freed of London, Broadland Slippers and Bowhill & Elliott all welcomed us into their workplaces, enabling us to bring the story right up to date.

These are just a few of the many people and organisations that have given us permission to use their material, for which we are very grateful. Further information on all who have contributed can be found in the bibliography, acknowledgements' page and photo credits.

Although this is by no means a text book, elements of the trade can be somewhat confusing. To clarify the situation we have included the following:

- Brief details of the contributors who shared their memories can be found on pages v to vii
- An explanation of the company names as used in the text is on page viii
- A glossary which explains the various terms used throughout is provided on page 254.

Contributors

Many thanks to the following whose memories of the Norwich boot and shoe trade have been included throughout the narrative:

Janet Abbott: In 1894 Janet's great grandfather founded the firm of John F. Kirby. The business remained in the family until 1963.

Betty Barnard: Betty started work at Shorten & Armes in 1940 when she was aged 14. She subsequently worked at Meadows until 1956.

John Barrett: John's father, Geoffrey, was MD at Shorten & Armes where John joined the board in 1962. Subsequently the family were involved in Trimfoot and also took over Meadows Shoes. After these businesses closed down John went on to form Meadows Bridal Shoes.

Mike Batson: Batson & Webster was formed by Mike's paternal and maternal grandfathers. He joined the business in 1950 when he was 15. In 1962 the business was taken over by the Liverpool Shoe Group. He continued to work there until 1965.

Glenda Bradford: Glenda started working at the Florida factory in 1984 in the machine room. Since then she spent eight years working as a clicker. She was still working there in 2013.

Margaret Brawn-Meek: Margaret's grandfather Frederick Waspe started work in the shoe industry around 1922, her father Len began in the trade in 1931. Len made his name as a designer at Barfield & Richardson. Subsequently he became a director at Trimfoot.

Avis Brown: Avis started working in the shoe room at Edwards & Holmes in 1957, when she was 15 years old. In the years that followed she also worked at Sextons and Trimfoot before joining Start-rite in 1974, where she stayed until 2003 when the factory closed.

Nigel Brown: Nigel started in the making room at Start-rite in 1974. He later transferred to an administrative job and was still working for the firm in 2013.

Peter Buckinghham: Peter Buckingham was the sixth generation of his family in the footwear trade. He joined the family retail business, J. Buckingham & Sons, in 1958 where he rose to the position of MD. In 1981, with no one in the family wanting to carry the business on, Peter sold the company's chain of shops to Clarks.

Ray Carpenter: Ray started working at Norvic in 1960. He later moved to Edwards & Holmes and then on to Florida when the two firms merged. He still makes shoes at the Dibden Road factory in 2013.

Mike Copland: Mike started working in Bowhill & Elliotts' slipper factory in 1963 where he stayed for 42 years, eventually rising to the position of manager. He has since set up Broadland Slippers, which he runs with Shaun Cubitt.

Billy Critten: Billy started work at Bally from school before he went to fight in WWII. After his return he trained as a clicker. He went on to become an officer for the Norwich branch of the National Union of Footwear and Leather and Allied Trades, eventually rising to the position of President. He retired in 1989.

Muriel Critten: Muriel worked in the shoe industry for 17 years. She first worked at Edwards & Holmes in 1942. After a break she returned to the trade in the 1970s when she worked at W. H. H. Clarke.

Ken Cutting: Ken worked at Mansfields Box Company as a delivery driver from 1948 until 1992.

Bob Drake: Bob started work at the last makers Mobbs & Lewis in 1960. He subsequently worked for a number of firms including: Sextons, H. B. Cares (last makers owned by Bally) and Freeds. In 1995, together with Colin Gibson, he set up Bobcol. The firm, which still trades in 2013, manufactures a range of items including: heels, wedges, platforms, shoe-trees and lasts.

Peter and Jane Gascoyne: Peter's father, Reginald, joined the firm of Ponds in 1919 and in 1945 he became the joint owner of the shop on Castle Meadow. Peter joined the firm in 1947, taking over from his father c1960. Peter sold the shop in 2004, when he was 77.

Professor Ian Gibson: Ian was the Labour MP for Norwich North from 1997 to 2009. In the 1970s he was on the National Executive of the Association of Scientific, Technical and Managerial Staffs, which represented supervisors in the shoe factories. In 2001 he initiated a debate in Parliament about the collapse of the Norwich footwear industry.

Elizabeth Glover: Elizabeth started work at Bowhill & Elliott as an assistant in the 1980s, since when she has become the shop manager.

Simon Goodman: Simon's grandfather, Adelman Goodman, founded the Florida shoe factory in 1936. Simon joined the family firm in 1972 and is now the chairman of the Florida Group.

Bernie Grant: Bernie Grant's grandfather, Alf Grant, came to Norwich to manage a shoe factory run by a Mr Herschel. In 1936 it was sold to Adelman Goodman, and became Florida's first factory.

Ron Green: Ron was employed in the shoe trade from 1949 to 1978. During this time he worked at both Bally and W. H. H. Clarke.

W. E. Hastings: In 1966 Mr Hastings wrote about his time at Bowhill & Elliott. He worked there from 1904 until 1965.

Steve Hewitt: In 1969 Steve Hewitt started work at C. J. Clarks in Somerset. Six years later he joined the Footwear, Leather and Fur-Skin Industry Training Board. In 1977 he started his career at Florida. Since 1983 he has worked in a selling role, and now looks after new business sales.

Arthur Holmes: Arthur worked as Start-rite's cost accountant from 1950 until 1986.

Audrey Holmes: Audrey worked in a number of departments at Start-rite whilst her husband Arthur (see above) was the firm's cost accountant.

Peter Holmes: Peter's grandfather, Sir Henry Holmes, founded Edwards & Holmes in 1891. Peter joined the firm in 1949, and in 1957 he became the sales director before taking on the roles of MD and chairman. In 1987 he oversaw the sale of the business to Florida.

Sarah Hopes: Sarah's father, Arthur Nobbs, taught shoemaking skills for many years at Norwich City College (under its various guises).

Vic Hopes: Vic worked at Sexton, Son & Everard as Assistant Production Manager in the late 1950s.

Mollie Howes: Mollie's husband Derrick took over from his father Richard as MD of Wards in 1973. From 1977 until his retirement in 1991 he worked at Start-rite.

Graham Howlett: Graham's grandfather Frederick Webster founded the company Batson & Webster Ltd where his father, Arthur Howlett, was also a director. In the mid-1950s Graham became a director of Arthur Howlett Ltd, which he ran with his brother, Eric. In 1968 the brothers sold Howletts to Norvic. Subsequently Graham worked for Norvic until 1980.

Kris Hunt: Kris's mum, Annie Vines, worked at Haldinsteins from 1918 until 1932. From the 1960s she organised reunions for the Haldinstein 'old girls'.

Reg Kilbourn: Reg's career in the shoe trade stretched from 1949 to 1999. During this time he worked at Barfield & Richardson, Batson & Webster, Sexton, Son & Everard, Norvic, R. Roberts and Start-rite.

Lenford Laband: Lenford started as an apprentice at the Standard Engineering Company in 1946. In 1959 he was appointed as manager. He supplied goods to all the major shoe manufacturers.

Brian Lambert: Brian started working for Bally in 1953 when he was 15. In the years that followed he undertook a number of roles including those of technical and factory manager. From 1974 he headed the technical department. He left in 1982 to set up Rombah Wallace where he was a director until 1993.

Peter Lamble: Peter is the chairman and MD of Start-rite, which has been run by his family since 1792. He joined the firm in 1990 as its finance director.

Jason Larke: Jason is the Head of Marketing at the Florida Group.

John Lincoln: John started his career in the Norwich shoe trade in 1948 at Howlett & White Leather Merchants, a subsidiary of Norvic. From 1968 to 1981 he was a sales manager at Kiltie Shoes, part of Norvic.

Michael Martin: Michael joined Norvic straight from school. In 1983 he started work at Magdalen Shoes. He stayed on when it was bought by Freed of London in 1990, and today manages the Norwich factory.

Janet Metcalf: Janet started at Start-rite in 1959 when she was 15. Eight months later she moved to Florida where she worked in the shoe room. After a break, from 1968-1978, she returned to Florida, to the same department, where around 1980 she was appointed as the forewoman. She retired in 2004.

Peter Metcalf: Peter joined Edwards & Holmes in 1960 when he was 15. When he was 17 he was appointed as the under foreman in the clicking room and less than a year later was appointed as quality manager. In the early 1970s Peter successfully applied for the job of quality manager at Florida where he remained until 1998. After that he worked for six years at Howard & Hallam Ltd, who were a Leicester-based shoe manufacturer.

Barbara Miller: Barbara has been a Blue Badge Guide, in its various guises, since 1963. She has a vast knowledge of Norwich's heritage and is a renowned speaker on the subject.

Martin Miller: Martin worked in Norvic's sales department from 1948 until 1969.

Walter Moll: Walter's father, Paul, moved from Switzerland to Norwich in 1934 to set up the partnership between Haldinsteins and Bally. Walter joined Bally in 1944. In 1955 he was appointed to the company's board and subsequently undertook a variety of roles including that of personnel director. He retired in 1988.

Ray Newman: Ray joined Kirbys to train as a clicker in 1953. Over the next three years he worked at Florida, Clarkes and Bally, and then left to work as a bus conductor.

Jean Palmer: Jean's father, Victor Scarlett, started work at Haldinsteins in 1927 as the 'run about' for George Haldinstein. He continued working for the firm after it was taken over by Bally, eventually retiring in 1974.

Jenny Perry: Jenny's mother, Trixie Bussey, worked at Bally from around 1942 to 1986.

Mike Quinton: In 1951 when Mike started at Norvic he became the first arts graduate to be employed in the Norwich shoe industry. In 1966 he was appointed sales director. He left in 1975 after which he moved to Bally where he was appointed to the board of directors c1980. He worked here until his retirement. Mike passed away in 2013.

Bruce Rampley: In 1945, at the age of 14, Bruce started work at Edwards & Holmes. He originally trained as a pattern maker before progressing to be a pattern cutter. In the 1960s he started photographing shoes for the firm's catalogue and other factory scenes for pamphlets. In 1967 Bruce left to become a full-time photographer. Bruce died in 2012. We are very grateful to his family for allowing us to reproduce his comments and also many of his lovely pictures.

Richard Ramsbottom: Richard's grandfather, Arthur, founded Ramsbottom Brothers Ltd in 1892.

Keith Richardson: Keith joined Start-rite in 1982 as a trainee clicker. At the time at least 14 members of his family worked at the firm. Around 1997 he started working on the resource side of the business and he still works there in 2013.

Edward Roberts: Edward's grandfather Robert Roberts founded R. Roberts Ltd in 1926.

Nigel Rudling: In 1970 Nigel started work at the CWS footwear factory as a work-study engineer. As a manager he was responsible for instigating many changes in working practices. In 1987, after the factory closed, Nigel set up a new shoe manufacturing company called Rudards which he sold in 1989.

Derek Rye: Derek started as a trainee clicker at W. H. H. Clarke in 1964 and continued to work there after the firm was taken over by K Shoes. He was still there in 1992 when the Norwich factory closed.

Jean Rye: Jean joined Sextons straight from school in 1964. For the next five years she worked in the shoe room after which she left to start a family.

Henry J. Sexton: Henry J. Sexton started his career in the shoe industry working for H. Sexton & Sons Ltd which was founded by his grandfather c1886. In 1913 he founded Sexton, Son & Everard Ltd. In 1952 he gave a fascinating insight into his life when he spoke to the Norwich Boot & Shoe Managers' and Foremen's Association about his 'Fifty Years in the Shoe Trade'.

Jean Smith: Jean started work as a machinist at Edwards & Holmes in 1948 when she was 15. She subsequently moved to Meadows. In 1963, after a short break, she started work at Norvic, subsequently working as a trainer on a government scheme. She left the industry in 1980.

John St Quintin: John's career in the shoe trade started in 1948. In the years that followed he worked for a number of firms, including Barfield & Richardson, J. F. Kirby and Shorten & Armes, where he designed many beautiful shoes. He left the trade in 1981.

John Thain: John started working in the shoe trade in 1966 at Norvic, where he trained in the pattern room. In the years that followed he worked at a number of factories, including Shingler & Thetford and Pells. Since 1970 he has worked at Start-rite where he is now head of fitting.

Christine Thorpe: Christine Thorpe's father, Harold Peace Johnson, joined Edwards & Holmes in 1932 as a pattern cutter. In 1977 he was appointed to the board as factory director.

David White: David's family have run Start-rite since 1772. David first worked at Start-rite in 1957. In 1978 he was appointed chairman of Start-rite, and in 1985 he also became chairman of James Southall & Co. David retired in 2002.

Jean Woods: In 1956 Jean started work at Norvics' closing room at Gressenhall. Subsequently she worked at a number of Start-rite factories including the closing room at Wymondham, Arthur Howletts' old premises on Fishergate, and the Crome Road factory. She left the industry in 1995.

Company Names Used in the Text

The names of many of the companies covered in this book have changed over time. Additionally a large number are better known by their 'local' names rather than their official titles. This can cause some confusion. In the text we have used the name we judge to be most appropriate, but for guidance please see the notes below.

The following are the main companies which, due to mergers and takeovers, had significant name changes:

- Howlett & White Ltd: In 1935 the firm was renamed the Norvic Shoe Company Ltd
- James Southall & Co. Ltd: In 1966 the name of Start-rite was officially adopted as the firms trading name
- Magdalen Shoes Ltd: In 1990 the company was taken over by Freed of London
- Osoeasie Slipper Company Ltd: In 1960 the firm was purchased by Bowhill & Elliott Ltd
- P. Haldinstein & Sons Ltd: In 1946 the company became Bally Shoe Factories (Norwich) Ltd
- Sexton, Son & Everard Ltd: In 1972, after the firm entered into receivership, the company's assets were transferred into a new company called Sexton Shoes Ltd
- Shingler & Thetford Ltd: In 1988 the firm had a name change when they became part of the Burlington International Group
- S. L. Witton Ltd: In 1934 the firm was taken over by the Norvic Shoe Company Ltd
- W. H. H. Clarke Ltd: In 1961 Clarkes became a wholly owned subsidiary of K Shoes Ltd, but it did not change its name until 1976 when it was called K Shoemakers Ltd.

The following firms are sometimes referred to by their local names, which are given in italics in the table below:

Arthur Howlett Ltd	*Howletts*
Bally Shoe Factories (Norwich) Ltd	*Bally*
Co-operative Wholesale Society Ltd	*CWS*
Barfield & Richardson Ltd	*Barfields*
James Southall & Co. Ltd	*Southalls*
John F. Kirby	*Kirbys*
Norvic Shoe Company Ltd	*Norvic*
Pell Footwear Ltd	*Pell*
P. Haldinstein & Sons Ltd	*Haldinsteins*
P. Segger (Norwich) Ltd	*Seggers*
R. Roberts (Norwich) Ltd	*Roberts*
Sexton, Son & Everard Ltd	*Sextons*
Shingler & Thetford Ltd	*Shinglers*
S. L. Witton Ltd	*Wittons*
Thomas Bowhill & Hubbard Ltd	*Bowhill & Hubbard*
Trimfoot Shoes (Norwich) Ltd	*Trimfoot*
W. H. H. Clarke Ltd	*Clarkes*
W. Hurrell Ltd	*Hurrells*
Ward Shoe Company Ltd	*Wards*

A full review of more than 30 firms (including all of the above) is given in chapter eight.

1. History of the Norwich Boot and Shoe Industry

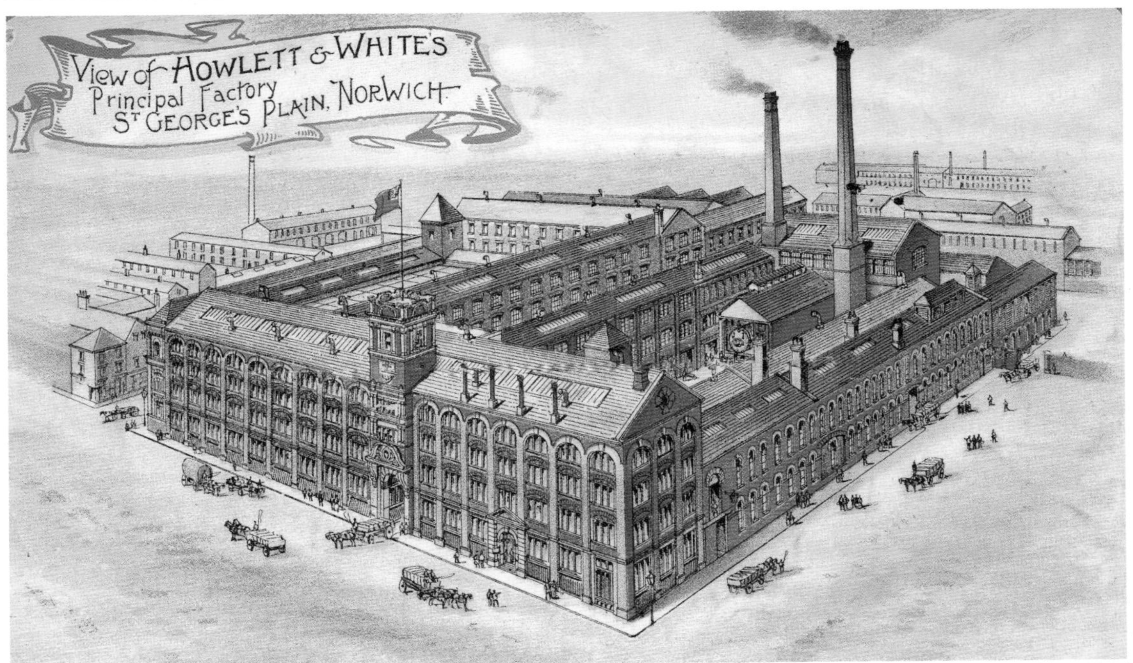

The Howlett & White factory, St George's Plain, as depicted on the cover of its 50th-anniversary booklet, 1896

In 1931 the Norwich boot and shoe trade employed over 10,000 people, a staggering 15% of Norwich's total workforce, making it the City's premier industry. Firms such as: P. Haldinstein & Sons, Sexton, Son & Everard, James Southall & Co., Edwards & Holmes and the Norvic Shoe Co. were major producers with national reputations.

Despite the devastation wreaked by WWII the shoe industry continued to flourish. In 1972 the Norwich shoe firms collectively produced a staggering 10.8 million pairs of shoes and fashion boots, which was heralded in the local press as an 'all-time record'. On the face of it this figure indicates a strong, buoyant sector, but in fact it masked reality. In the years that followed the industry was decimated by a combination of cheap imports, the vagaries of fashion and changes in distribution and marketing.

By the beginning of the 21st century the Norwich footwear industry was a shadow of its former self, but all was not lost. Old firms have survived, others have been formed. The City is still home to companies that are market leaders with worldwide reputations, who look to the future but are proud of their past.

Excavations around Whitefriars' Bridge revealed that as early as the 10th century simple turnshoes were being made in Norwich.

Early Days

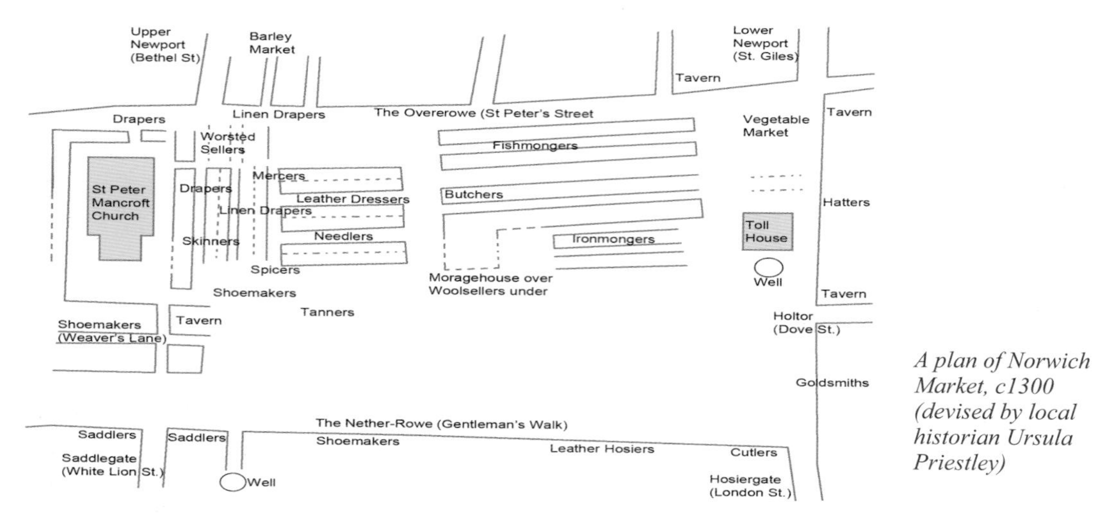

A plan of Norwich Market, c1300 (devised by local historian Ursula Priestley)

By the early 14th century Norwich was already a thriving commercial centre, and shoemaking was just one of 130 trades practised here. Around 7% of all workers were employed in producing leather, which could be fashioned into footwear by shoemakers and cordwainers (who made fine soft-leather shoes and other luxury footwear articles). The importance of leather production to the local economy was clearly reflected in the goods that were traded on and around Norwich market, where craftsmen including leather dressers, saddlers and shoemakers all plied their trade.

Because early leather workers tended to settle in the same neighbourhood, they often gave their names to streets and buildings in the areas where they worked. For example:

- White Lion Street was called Saddlegate, later changing its name to Saddlers' Row
- London Street was known as Hosiergate whilst Gentleman's Walk was called Cordwainers' Row
- St Peter Parmentergate Church (King Street) indicates the position of the street where leather sellers (parmenters) traded.

Typically, in these early years shoemakers operated on a small scale, sewing bespoke orders for the local community. By 1650 only London and Northampton manufactured shoes for an extended market. Large orders for relatively standard products, such as boots for the military, were a prerequisite for wholesale production. From the mid-17th century it was such orders, one of the earliest being from Cromwell's Parliamentary Army, that boosted the Northampton wholesale trade. In Norwich it began much later.

It was in 1792 that James Smith established a shop and factory providing ready-made shoes in the Upper Market (St Peter's Street), on the site of what is now City Hall. He had realised that since many people had the same size feet it was unnecessary for all footwear to be made to measure. Instead, he perfected a series of lasts of pre-determined dimensions from which standard footwear was made. Although it is sometimes claimed that Smith was the first manufacturer to produce ready-made shoes, sadly this is an inaccurate assertion. It is impossible to imagine that the Northampton bootmakers measured every soldier to whom they supplied footwear whilst mid-18th-century trade cards show that London makers already supplied ready-made shoes. Notwithstanding this, James Smith showed exceptional forward thinking. Yet it is unlikely that even he predicted that his family business would still be trading in the 21st century. It remains one of the City's best known firms and is now called Start-rite.

Despite the entrepreneurship shown by Smith it was not until the 1840s that the Norwich shoe trade significantly expanded. By then the City's textile industry was in serious decline, as the Norwich producers lost out to the industrial cities of the north with their superior transport systems and natural resources. As weaving waned the shoe industry became an attractive substitute. Not only did it require the same manual dexterity from its workers, but also production could be structured in a similar fashion and even on the same premises.

The name cordwainer derived from the fact that they worked with fine skins that originated from Cordoba in Spain.

Garret master transporting shoes, undated

Shoeworkers through the ages, various dates

Accordingly, just as master weavers had sent out spinning and weaving to be completed by workers in their homes, the so-called garret master organised shoe production as follows:

- Clicking and pressing (cutting out the uppers and soles) were carried out on the garret master's premises. These roles would have been undertaken by men
- The uppers were then distributed to women who closed, or sewed, the uppers in their homes
- The uppers were returned to the garret master to be fitted up (matched) with the bottom stuff (soles, heels, linings etc.) and the constituent parts were sent out to men to be lasted. This involved shaping the shoe and bringing together the outsoles, insoles and uppers
- When lasted the shoes were sent back to the garret master for final sewing
- The shoes were then sent out again to women to be finished; a process that involved trimming and tidying up the shoe.

Working in this way gave the garret master a number of advantages. In particular:

- Capital investment and overheads could be kept low because his premises needed only to be large enough to provide a storage facility and an area for clicking and cutting out soles with a press
- Because his workers were all self-employed, if he had no work he didn't need to employ them or, more importantly, pay them. This was particularly important in a trade which was cyclical, largely because it was built around two seasons.

Often entire families were employed in the different stages of production, working in their homes in the same way that weavers had before.

In 1831 only 829 people were employed in shoemaking. Subsequently in the following decade numbers more than doubled to 1740 before escalating to 5038 (14% of the Norwich workforce) by 1851.

An old custom amongst Norwich shoemakers was to enjoy every Monday, commonly known as Saint Monday, as a holiday. This died out when they started to work in factories.

Expansion: 1850 – 1900

Despite the expansion in the workforce, shoe production remained a slow process. Inevitably much time was wasted under the garret system delivering work between various workshops, and even the early factories relied heavily on homeworkers. Then in 1856 Charles Winter, James Smith's grandson and successor, became the first manufacturer in Norwich to use sewing machines for closing uppers. As one straight-sewing machine could produce 3,000 stitches a minute the incentive to mechanise, and hence base more workers in a factory, was enormous.

As the century progressed other procedures became automated. In particular:

- In the 1860s the Blake sole-sewer, which was strong enough to sew through the inner and outer sole, was introduced into Norwich. The machines were initially driven by steam power
- By the end of the 19th century the sole-cutting machine, the forerunner of the revolution press (a shaft driven press which was widely employed by the 1940s) was in use. Prior to its invention soles were punched out by hand, which was both slow and costly
- Around 1900 the firm of Edwards & Holmes installed a Consolidated lasting machine (Consol), which proved so successful in terms of the quality and quantity of work produced, that soon most of the other large shoe firms followed suit.

Initially there was little opposition by the workforce to technical innovations. This was mainly because new methods produced better shoes at lower prices leading to increased demand and hence higher employment. Already by 1861 the shoe industry was the City's leading sector employing over 6,000 workers.

Early Singer sewing machine

Although much of the industry still remained in the hands of small-scale operators and garret masters, the number of wholesale manufacturers (i.e. producing for the wholesale market but not necessarily based in a factory), rose steadily from 23 in 1867 to 77 by 1890. However, in the years that followed, factory production was further facilitated by the widespread introduction of electricity, initially using D.C. (direct current) motors, which was much more suited to the needs of light industry than steam power.

Although the larger firms did more work inside the factory than out, machining and finishing were still distributed to homeworkers, a tradition that continued into the second half of the 20th century. In fact one of the most important departments in the factory was the 'wicket receiving room', which was a gate or counter over which the boots and shoes in various stages of manufacture were handed in and out of the factory, to and from outworkers.

(L to r) Consolidated lasting machine, the Blake sole-sewer, revolution press, various dates

The shoe trade did not offer stable employment. The use of outworkers provided the manufacturers with a workforce which could be taken on or laid off at will. Even factory employees were often put on short time when demand was slack. In this environment employees had little power. Despite this in 1874 the National Union of Boot and Shoe Operatives was established. In 1897 their workers struck for a minimum wage, a 54-hour week and 'constraint' on the part of employers in the employment of boys (i.e. cheap labour). Despite 1500 workers striking for 34 weeks the workers gained little. In 1952, Henry J. Sexton (founder of Sexton, Son & Everard Ltd) could still recall this period: 'The great event of the nineties in the shoe trade was the nine-month strike in 1897, two years before I started my career in the trade...It was a very bitter fight indeed. I remember the yelling crowds outside St Edmund's Mills [Fishergate], where H. Sexton & Sons were then installed, and the hue and cry about a clicker named Harmer who refused to strike. More than once he got out of the factory in a packing case.' After the failure of the strike the union lost a lot of members, and it was only in 1908 that a minimum wage was finally agreed.

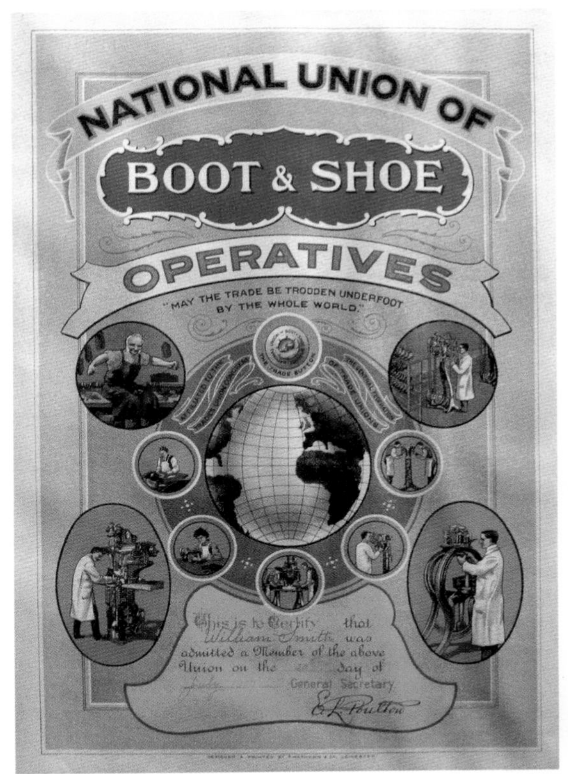

Union membership certificate, 1907

There are a number of explanations as to why Norwich emerged as an important centre for shoe production. Few would argue that the failure of the textile trade provided a catalyst for its growth. This was not only because it provided a ready-made workforce, but also because through it Norwich had established contacts and a reputation of being a centre of excellence in the manufacturing of quality goods. An additional fillip came from improved rail links (in 1845 the first train ran from Trowse station all the way to London), which meant that production could reach an extended market. Also, by 1901 Norwich's population had reached 111,700 (rising from 68,200 in 1851), which in turn provided more labour and a larger home market for footwear manufacturers. But all of this would have come to nothing if the industry hadn't been blessed with entrepreneurs. Men who were not only willing to embrace new methods of production but could also manage the vagaries of the market.

Just as Northampton specialised in the production of quality footwear for men, Norwich firms specialised in the production of high-quality shoes mainly for women and children. Additionally a wider range, which included sports shoes, was manufactured for foreign markets. In the 1850s shoe manufacturers were already exporting their products, successfully exploiting links built up by the textile traders, such that by 1913 exports accounted for around 35% of all production. By this time Norwich had established itself as the third-largest centre of shoemaking in Britain, behind Northampton and Leicester, the latter producing cheaper ranges for both men and women.

As we come to the end of the 19th century the foundations had already been laid for the rise of five firms who would dominate the industry for years to come: Edwards & Holmes, Howlett & White (later Norvic Shoe Co. Ltd), P Haldinstein & Sons (later Bally Shoe Factories (Norwich) Ltd), James Southall & Co. (later Start-rite Ltd), and H. Sexton & Sons (the forerunner of Sexton, Son & Everard Ltd).

Lasting Memories

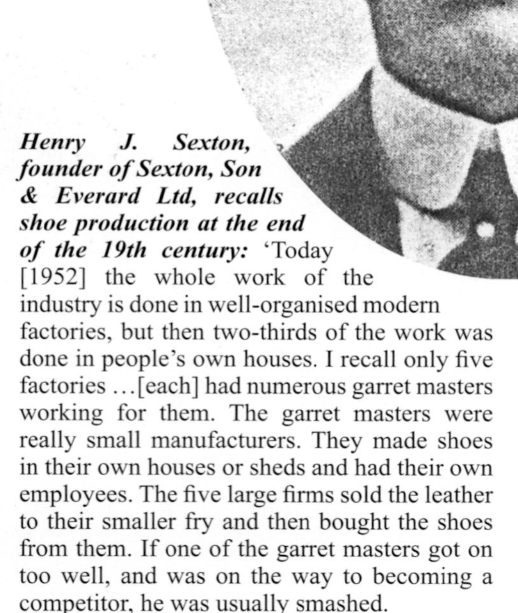

Henry J. Sexton, c1916

Henry J. Sexton, founder of Sexton, Son & Everard Ltd, recalls shoe production at the end of the 19th century: 'Today [1952] the whole work of the industry is done in well-organised modern factories, but then two-thirds of the work was done in people's own houses. I recall only five factories ...[each] had numerous garret masters working for them. The garret masters were really small manufacturers. They made shoes in their own houses or sheds and had their own employees. The five large firms sold the leather to their smaller fry and then bought the shoes from them. If one of the garret masters got on too well, and was on the way to becoming a competitor, he was usually smashed.

'The most important department in a shoe factory was the wicket, where the work was handed out to the homeworkers and taken in from them. It was a common sight in the Norwich streets to see men carrying their work on poles, tied up through holes in the backs of the shoes. Each pair was strung together, and they were usually covered with a blue-print wrapper. The "snobs" [garret masters] did not worry much about their personal appearance. Most of them wore white aprons, even when they were not working. Towards the end of the week they became... somewhat discoloured. The women carried their work in old perambulators.

'It was quite a common idea for a little group of lasters and finishers to hire a room in which they could work together...It was an economy to share candles and firing, and it was pleasant to be able to gossip while they worked.

'I spent a lot of time in my childhood watching the old gas engine which supplied the power for three or four straight-needle turnshoe sewers and old-fashioned presses cutting out bottom stuff. In the closing rooms they used treadle machines. This one small gas engine provided all the power necessary to run a factory of 500 operatives.'

Consolidation and Growth: 1900 – 1939

By 1900 approximately 7,500 people were employed making footwear in Norwich, of whom 66% were male. Around 15% of the City's labour force worked in the industry, which made it Norwich's largest employer.

In the early 20th century the number of factories operating in Norwich continued to increase. Writing in 1910, the sociologist C.B. Hawkins defined the shoe factory system as encompassing:

- The use of machinery
- A team system of organised labour
- An intricate process of manufacture involving six distinct stages (clicking, machining and upper closing, fitting, lasting, finishing, cleaning and boxing)
- More than 100 operations.

Despite these rather strict criteria, Hawkins estimated that 12 firms were working in this way in 1910, whilst another 20 firms had sufficient machinery to enable them to do so. Their output was supplemented by the work of at least 40 garret masters.

During this period factories were expanding at a rapid rate. For example, by 1904 P. Haldinstein & Sons had branches in London, Leicester, Kettering and Wymondham and in total employed 2,000 people. Additionally by 1914 Howlett & White were describing their factory on St George's Plain as being the largest 'under one roof' in the British Isles.

Images published in Howlett & White's 50th-anniversary booklet, 1896

Athletic and Tennis Lasting Room.

Upper Closing Room.

Machine Sewn Lasting Room.

Finishing Room.

Number 12 NORVIC WAY February, 1917

F. W. HULL, R.E. — H. ROBERTS, R.G.A. — H. J. CAMPLING, R.G.A. — W. HEBBLEWHITE, R.F.A.

Brothers in Arms.

Representatives of the Norvic Shoe Co. now in training or at the Front.

Interests of Maker & Retailer Identical.

CO-OPERATION.

MANUFACTURERS necessarily contest among themselves to divide a market, and retailers also of necessity contest among themselves in the division of a market. To be sure the result of this contest may be the development of the market so that there is an increased volume to divide, but nevertheless the contest between retailers is inevitably a contest for the division of the market, be it stationary or growing. *But between manufacturers and retailers no such contest is essential; for each handles in turn the same merchandise and each may secure the whole; that is, manufacturers' selling and retailers' selling are fundamentally not antagonistic, but are simply two steps in the same selling problem.* There may be some rivalry over the division of the profits, but over the market there should be no contest, for the interest of both demands that the market be held together.

The outbreak of WWI had an immediate effect on the shoe trade in that it lost most of its overseas market. This was devastating because at the time it accounted for more than 30% of total sales. Amongst those hit was Howlett & White, where large orders for German sports shoes immediately collapsed.

Being specialists in making high-class footwear for women and children, the shoemakers could not immediately turn to war work and early orders went to centres such as Northampton, who already made sturdy footwear for men.

However, the Norwich owners responded rapidly by installing new machinery and reorganising production, and soon began to make footwear for both the British Army and its allies. Their contribution to the war effort included: canvas fatigue shoes, heavy brogue shoes for Highland Regiments, cossack boots for the Russian Army and lambs wool-lined thigh boots for airmen in the Royal Flying Corps.

Number 12 — NORVIC WAY — February, 1917

Gaining the Whole Retail Market.

CO-OPERATION.

IN the contest among manufacturers those who adopt national advertising tend to gain the major portion of the market. In the contest among retailers those who unite their selling force to that of the manufacturers' advertising are the ones who in turn tend to win the major portion of the retail market. This is, in a line where national advertising is effectively used, the advertisers and those dealers who co-operate with the advertisers, secure the major portion of the market. Thus, *national advertising plus co-operation between manufacturers and dealers make at the same time strong manufacturers and strong dealers.*

(See page 5 for continuation)

ARMY BOOT and SHOE SHOWCARDS.

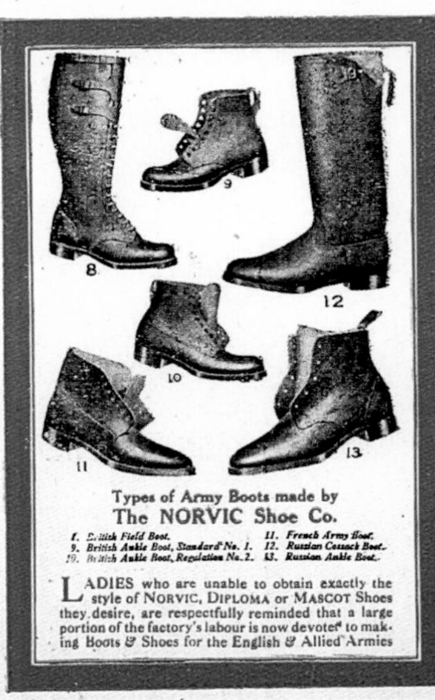

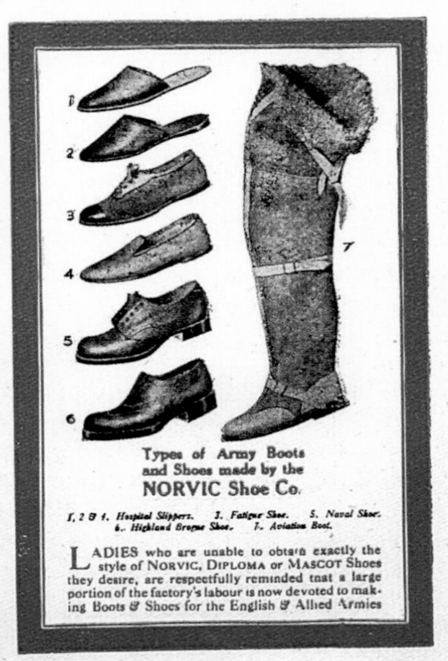

NOW READY.

ILLUSTRATIONS of Two Small Showcards illustrating Army Boots. The cards will interest your customers. One of each is enclosed with this copy of 'Norvic Way.' Kindly put them in your window as near the line of sight as possible.

During WWI patriotism and marketing went hand in hand. Both pages are from the 1917 copy of Norvic Way, Howlett & White's in-house magazine.

Clicking room, Walter Edwards, 1925

Although the majority of Norwich shoe manufacturing firms survived the war years, during the hostilities many of their overseas customers developed their own footwear industries, which after the war were protected by tariff barriers. In response it was essential that the Norwich producers extended their home markets. Immediately after the war this was not a problem, as the shoe industry benefitted from a UK post-war boom fuelled by a need to restock. However, once this was achieved trade proved difficult and in 1921 the shoe industry suffered a slump during which Henry J. Sexton estimates that 30 Norwich shoe manufacturers were forced into bankruptcy.

This was followed by a period of strong growth fuelled by a change in women's fashion coupled with the increasing popularity of dancing. As recalled by Henry J. Sexton: 'The war had created a most interesting revolution in women's shoe styles. Previously skirts had trailed along the ground, but now they were knee high, and shoes became one of the most important and attractive parts of a lady's apparel…High-legged boots and fancy, high, Louis-heeled shoes [a heel with graceful curves on the side and back where the front surface is covered by the downward extension of the sole] became the rage.'

Apart from London, no other centre in England could produce Louis-heeled turnshoes on which the fashions were based. This caused huge demand for turnshoe makers who took advantage of their position, frequently striking and forcing up their wages. Their actions were making Norwich shoes uncompetitive, a situation that the manufacturers were not prepared to accept. In response they started to experiment with alternative types of production. Eventually Sexton, Son & Everard perfected a means of producing light machine-sewn shoes not only out of leather but also in satins and crepes.

Brocade shoe with Louis heel, Howlett & White, c1925

Bar shoe with Louis heel, Sexton, Son & Everard, 1927

The Louis heel, which became very popular in the early 20th century, was originally designed for King Louis XIV of France (1643 – 1715) who, being only 5 feet 3 inches tall, needed them to boost his height. He often wore red heels, which resulted in them becoming a status symbol.

Closing room, Walter Edwards, 1925

This alternative manufacturing process led to the collapse of traditional turnshoe making. The popularity of the new shoes led to many manufacturers setting up plants to make them, and heralded a prosperous time for the Norwich industry. The growth was such that between 1921 and 1931 census returns recorded that the numbers employed in shoemaking in the City rose from 7,800 (13.8% of the workforce) to 10,700 (17.5%).

The figure hides a change in the structure of the workforce. In 1921, 36.5% of employees were women. By 1931 they made up 43.5% of the total. This change can be credited to the decline in turnshoe manufacturing, a process which employed proportionately more men.

Inevitably the shoemakers in Northampton and Leicester started copying the styles made by the Norwich manufacturers. Although the producers in the Midlands had higher productivity (and therefore lower costs) Norwich shoes were made to superior designs and, by constantly bringing out new and stylish shoes, the Norwich industry held its own.

The growth in the numbers employed in the trade must be put in the context that in 1929 the Norwich shoe industry was hit by the world trade depression, such that by December 1930 over 50% of the workforce was on short time. As in the 1920s, many smaller firms went bankrupt or ceased trading, but the larger firms were in a stronger position to review both production methods and marketing techniques. Since the end of WWI, the major Norwich shoe manufacturers had increasingly recognised the advantages of advertising and building strong, recognisable brands names, as exemplified by Howlett & White Ltd. In 1909 they had successfully used the brand name 'Norvic' to market a range of shoes. Subsequently in 1935, when they were the largest footwear manufacturing group in England, they renamed their entire business the Norvic Shoe Co. Ltd, and adopted a programme of national advertising.

In the meantime Sextons had extended their range and started to make American shoes under licence. New lines included Joyce 'Coolees' shoes, which were brought out in 1937 when they were described as a 'modern version of the platform shoe'. Haldinsteins (which merged with Bally of Switzerland in 1933) also successfully developed by supplying independent chains such as Dolcis, Saxone and Lilley & Skinner.

Despite such innovations 1,684 footwear workers were unemployed in January 1933. Subsequently, although there was a gradual recovery of the sector in terms of output (by 1935 the total quarterly production of all types of footwear in Norwich was over 1.5 million pairs) there was little improvement in employment. In fact through the rest of the decade between 1,000 and 1,500 shoeworkers remained unemployed each week. Paradoxically the switch from turnshoe making had significantly worsened the problem on two fronts. Firstly productivity had improved (i.e. more shoes could be produced with a smaller workforce), secondly men (often the major breadwinner) were worst affected because machine-sewn shoe production employed proportionately more women then turnshoe making.

Then, on 3 September 1939 war was declared, a war in which the City-based shoe manufacturers had to overcome both a disruption in trade and also the devastation wreaked by German bombers.

WWII and Beyond: 1939 – 1950

During the war years the Norwich footwear industry had to deal with a whole range of difficulties.

One firm which immediately faced problems was that of Bally & Haldinstein. At the end of 1933 Bally's of Switzerland and the Norwich firm of P. Haldinstein & Sons Ltd had made a partnership agreement. In the following year Paul Moll was sent over from Switzerland to work with George Haldinstein. The outbreak of war resulted in two major management changes. Firstly George Haldinstein, who was Jewish, was worried about a Nazi invasion and moved to South Africa, leaving Paul Moll to run the company. Subsequently, because he was a German-speaking Swiss subject, Paul Moll was deemed a potential danger to the country if an invasion occurred on the east coast. As a result he had to move from Norwich, but only as far as Thetford, from where he managed the business. Walter Moll, who later became a director of the company, recalls: 'My father used to meet up weekly with his management team outside the restricted zone. The extraordinary thing was that after a time people began to see that the factory was producing WAAF shoes, army shoes etc. all helping the war effort. At the same time they realised that my father was not dangerous, and so in April 1942 they let him move back. He just had time to settle into his house on Newmarket Road when the Baedeker Raids started.'

Although they were in competition with each other, the factory owners formed a close-knit group. During the 20th century there are repeated examples of them supporting each other, but never more so than during WWII. This attitude was exemplified by the actions of Arthur Howlett, a director at Batson & Webster, who stored machinery, equipment and materials in a barn at Panxworth. Some of his competitors thought that he was being ultra cautious, but the raids came and he was proved right. The store was used to help all those in trouble. Similarly firms whose factories were requisitioned under the government's rationalisation of production scheme, simply moved in with their supposed rivals. For example, after Shorten & Armes premises on Esdelle Street was commandeered they operated as a unit within Norvic's factory on St George's Plain until the end of the war.

With so many of the factories based in the City centre, it was inevitable that they would suffer bomb damage. One of the earliest to be hit was James Southall's factory on Crome Road, where in March 1941 an incendiary device did less damage than the sprinkler system! Others weren't so lucky.

W. H. H. Clarke & Co. Ltd suffered badly during the war, to the extent that it was described in an article in the *Eastern Evening News* as 'probably the worst-bombed firm in Norwich'. Their Northumberland Street factory was completely destroyed in April 1942 after which they relocated for a short time to Mansfields (Norwich) Ltd (box manufacturers) on St Saviours. Sadly a few months later Mansfields were also burnt out and so Clarkes threw in their lot with Sextons, that is until the August Bank Holiday (1942) when the same fate befell them again. They then

Bomb damage, Westwick Street, 1942

transferred to Dibden Street, where they were taken in by Chittock & Sons Ltd, where they safely remained until the end of the war.

Edwards & Holmes' factory on Drayton Road was totally destroyed in April 1942, when they lost everything, including fixtures, lasts and patterns. Undeterred they carried on their business by splitting it between two sites, one on Starling Road the other on Westwick Street opposite Bullards' Brewery. Then on the morning of 19 October 1942 a bomb made a direct hit on the Westwick Street factory demolishing half of it and leaving the rest unusable. Fortunately the majority of the staff had taken shelter when the crash warning sounded and there were only a few minor casualties. As a result the firm transferred all production across to the Starling Road site. They later managed to repair the damaged portion of Westwick Street and bring it back into use.

Sexton, Son & Everard didn't fare much better. Before the war the firm operated on three main sites: Oak Street, Westwick Street and St Mary's Plain, the latter being their main plant. In April 1942 both of the former buildings were destroyed, then later in the same year, over the August Bank Holiday, the main factory was hit. Henry J. Sexton recalls: 'My original total floor space of 150,000 feet was reduced to 30,000 feet. It was almost miraculous that I escaped losing everything, for a large explosive incendiary bomb penetrated the only remaining building, but it failed to explode, and was found the next day in three unexploded pieces in my leather stores.' Despite incurring such losses, which included most of their machinery, the directors were not cowed. Instead they obtained permission to build a temporary building and to replace some of its machinery and plant. Miraculously 11 weeks after the raid they were again in production. Necessity was clearly the mother of invention as, notwithstanding the devastation, the firm still managed to meet targeted production levels which included completion of contracts for the armed services. A fact noted by Mr Sexton who commented: 'We learnt, to our surprise, how much work can be concentrated in a small area by a change of methods.'

Subsequently, in September 1942, Batson & Webster's premises on Fishergate was damaged when a bomb landed in the courtyard. Graham Howlett remembers that his father, Arthur, had a lucky escape: 'He'd been working in his office but just before the bomb fell he went into the factory and left his jacket on the back of his chair. His office was blown up. I still remember him coming home that evening just in his short-sleeved shirt.' Others weren't so lucky. Joan Knights, who was only 15, and machine-room foreman George Smith, were both killed, whilst another 14 were injured in the attack.

Other firms which were bombed in 1942 included W. Hurrell Ltd whose premises on Magdalen Street were destroyed and Thomas Bowhill & Hubbard Ltd whose Heigham Street factory was gutted by fire.

All-in-all, between 1939 and 1945, it is estimated that as a combined result of enemy action and requisitioning, the industry lost 316,000 square feet of productive floor space, an overall reduction of 40%. Over the same period its workforce was reduced by 50%. Despite such adversity it says much for the tenacity and inventiveness of the directors and workers that on average throughout the conflict over

Edwards & Holmes' demolished Drayton Road factory, April 1942

five million pairs of boots and shoes were produced each year. This was particularly important as much of the industry's production capacity had been given over to making footwear for the armed forces. Innovations during this time included a prototype boot for nurses serving in the Burmese jungle. The rather splendid boot (pictured right), made by Norvic Shoe Co. Ltd, was designed to protect the wearer from snakes and leeches.

The immediate post-war years marked a period of reconstruction for the Norwich footwear industry. As happened during the war, the period was again exemplified by the comradeship shown by the firms as recorded in 1946 in the *Eastern Evening News*: 'One splendid feature to offset against the whole sorry mess of war damage has been the co-operation between the company directors, and the way that the luckier firms have helped those less fortunate.'

As factories were rebuilt directors took the opportunity to modernise their factories. For example, the new Esdelle Works built by Edwards & Holmes on Drayton Road was described by the directors as being one of the most up-to-date shoe factories in the world. Meanwhile W. H. H. Clarke Ltd, who had taken over the old A.R.P. (Air Raid Precaution) site on Sussex Street, claimed to own the first factory in Norwich in which every machine had an individual electric motor.

After the war recovery was fairly swift, such that by 1949 there were 25 footwear firms in Norwich, employing 10,000 workers turning out around seven million pairs of shoes each year.

Boot designed to protect nurses from snakes and leeches in the jungle, Norvic Shoe Co. Ltd, c1940

Edwards & Holmes rebuilt Drayton Road factory, c1950

Lasting Memories

Walter Moll, c1955

In 1934 Walter Moll moved from Switzerland to Norwich with his father, who was responsible for overseeing Ballys' partnership with Haldinsteins: 'By the time war broke out, I was at Gresham's school in Holt from where in 1940, together with my schoolmates, I was evacuated to Newquay in Cornwall. At the time, as a foreigner, I had a grey book in which I had to register every move I made, and even had to report to the police station once a week. The ironic thing was that I became a sergeant in the school's Officer Training Corps, where I was allowed to carry a gun whilst still reporting to the police weekly!'

Graham Howlett recalls a family story about his father Arthur, a director at Batson & Webster: 'During the war it is told that my father was very good at obtaining items that were difficult to find. The story goes that he realised that the Americans, who had a big presence in Norwich, had a very high demand for condoms. So he hit on the idea of supplying them. He finished up with three changing-room lockers full of them in his office. When the factory was bombed these lockers headed for the sky, and when they were high over Magdalen Street they opened and their contents rained down on the unsuspecting public below. My father was absolutely staggered at what had happened, but undeterred he put in for war damage for his lost "stock", describing it as "items for staff recreational use". It is said that he got all of his money back.'

Arthur Howlett, Oulton Broad, c1950

Betty Barnard (right), Great Yarmouth, c1950

Betty Barnard started work at Shorten & Armes in 1940 when she was a girl of 14: 'During the war when the government took over our factory we had to transfer everything into Howlett & White's [Norvic's] factory on St George's. I remember one day we were coming down the stairs when a bomb was dropped a few yards away, if it had landed on our building I hate to think how many would've been killed. We spent a lot of time in the shelters which were at the side of the factory. We never went down when the siren first went but only when it changed to the "crash warning tone", which meant that the planes were definitely coming our way. At that point we grabbed what we could and ran. The problem was that when we were in the shelters we couldn't work, which meant that we couldn't earn. I remember one week we spent so long in them my wage was just half-a-crown.'

An Industry on its Uppers: 1950 – 2000

The UK Footwear Trade

In 1957 sales of footwear in the UK amounted to some 150 million pairs subsequently rising to 225 million pairs in 1965. Annual sales then fluctuated between 225 and 260 million pairs until 1983, after which they increased to around 280 million pairs. Unfortunately these buoyant figures hid disturbing underlying trends.

Over these years the home industry was decimated by a massive increase in imports which rose from 20 million (13% market penetration) to 135 million (53% market penetration). Meanwhile UK firms' output rose from 170 million pairs a year in 1957 peaking in 1968 at around 210 million pairs, after which production began a downward trend. By 1983 output had fallen to around 120 million pairs a year. (See graph for full details.)

Imports were growing for a number of reasons:

Costs

Foreign competitors, who generally paid lower wage bills than the UK manufacturers, could make shoes significantly more cheaply than the UK producers. The position was further aggravated by inflationary pressures. Between 1968 and 1973 the UK average annual rate of inflation had been 7.5% per annum, then in 1973 the retail price index increased by a massive 16% and this remained the average annual rate of inflation through to 1980. As a result British industry in general became less competitive internationally and British goods increased in price relative to imports. By the late 1970s many British shoe manufacturers were complaining that shoes imported from the Far East were being sold at price less than they paid for the cost of materials alone. Across manufacturing as a whole, unions negotiated pay increases to maintain their members' standards of living. As a consequence the average male employed in manufacturing saw his weekly earnings rise from £7.83 in 1950 to £41.52 in 1973. At the same time the average number of hours worked per week fell from 47.5 to 44.7. In real terms, taking inflation into account, this represented a doubling of the average earnings per hour worked. In an industry such as footwear manufacture, which is very labour intensive, this growth in wages resulted in the industry becoming increasingly uncompetitive.

Fashion

In the 1960s consumers were becoming more fashion conscious and wanted frequent changes of style throughout the year. The large UK producers were geared to produce new ranges twice a year, in autumn and spring. In contrast overseas producers, in countries such as Italy and Spain, produced a small number of shoes in each design and constantly introduced new collections. The British manufacturers were slow to react which put them at a competitive disadvantage.

Distribution and marketing

In the 1950s the vast majority of shoe manufacturers sold their footwear either through their own shops, small independent retailers or specialist retailing chains. However, with the formation of the British Shoe Corporation (BSC) this all changed. The Corporation's roots can be traced back as far as 1891, when John and William Sears formed a small

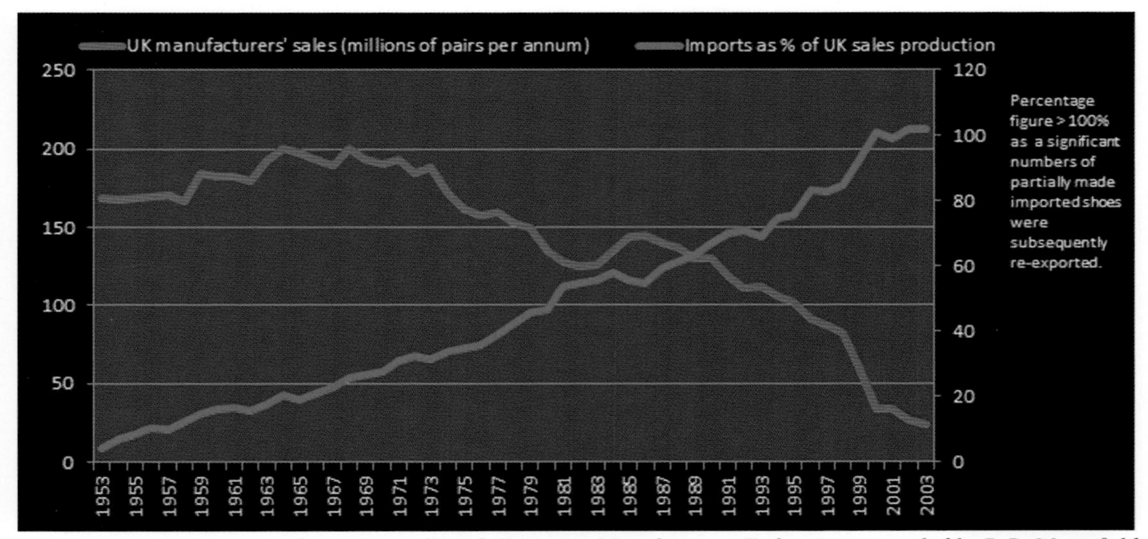

Data source: British Footwear Manufacturers Federation, compiled by P. R. Mountfield

bootmaking business under the name of True-Form. By 1929 they had taken over Freeman, Hardy & Willis, but it wasn't until 1953, when Charles Clore came to the helm, that the business really began to expand. By 1962 the group, which by now had been renamed BSC, had absorbed a number of shoe-shop chains including those previously belonging to Dolcis, Saxone and Lilley & Skinner. As the BSC expanded their size gave them huge buying power, allowing them to supply shoes much more cheaply than small independent retailers, many of whom were forced out of business. By 1975 their outlets handled over 20% of the country's footwear sales. As explained by Simon Goodman (chairman of the Florida Group): 'The BSC made the UK an easy market for overseas producers to access…Rather than deal with lots of smaller retailers they could deal with one which covered the entire country.' By 1986 other companies with a significant high-street presence included Marks & Spencer, C. & J. Clark Ltd (Clarks), Peter Lord and Storehouse. Footwear producers were very aware that imports were growing and that the government was doing very little to protect their industry. The position was summed up by David White (director and later chairman of Start-rite) in 1968: 'The Government makes trade agreements to help our major exporting industries, heavy goods in particular, and does not want to upset these agreements. It thinks, not without some justification, that the footwear industry – a disjointed trade full of small non-co-operating units – is expendable.'

As production fell, inevitably so did the labour force. Nationally between 1950 and 1981 there was an average yearly net loss of around 1,600 footwear-manufacturing jobs resulting in a drop from 107,000 in 1957 to 67,000 in 1980. The reduction was not only caused by falling sales but also by technological improvements (which improved productivity) and firms buying in pre-fabricated units, e.g. soles.

Between 1984 and 2000 the UK footwear market fluctuated at around 285 million pairs. Again this apparent stability masked the decline of this once great British industry such that according to the British Footwear Manufacturer's Federation (later Association), by 2001 import penetration had reached 99% and UK footwear manufacturers were producing as few as 34 million pairs a year (exports and re-exports amounted to some 32 million pairs). Not surprisingly the labour force also fell significantly and by the turn of the 21st century only 15,000 workers were employed in the industry.

Over this period a number of UK footwear companies totally changed their structure. Some adopted a strategy of: 'if you can't beat them join them' and started to work with overseas producers. Walter Moll, director at Bally, recalls: 'In 1984 I was invited to lead an international delegation of shoe manufacturers to India. We had been invited by the Indians who were aware that they had a lot to learn from Europeans about all aspects of shoe making.' As production methods improved in countries such as India, UK manufacturers stopped making shoes and re-invented themselves as design, development and marketing companies. One of the major companies to change in this way was Clarks. In the 1990s they decided that major changes in world trade meant the company could no longer stay competitive while manufacturing in the UK. Initially some production was moved to the continent but eventually they closed their UK factories and transferred their entire production overseas.

Dolcis, Manfield, and True-Form shoe shops, Gentleman's Walk, c1975

Lasting Memories

Martin Miller, a manager at the Norvic Shoe Company Ltd, recounts the challenges faced by footwear manufacturers: 'In 1969, when I left Norvic, the Norwich shoe trade was already contracting. At the time customers were increasingly being sold shoes from foreign manufacturers, at first from Italy and Spain, and subsequently from the Far East. British labour costs were significantly higher than foreign producers, which eventually led to us being priced out of the market. But we had another major problem…we couldn't get our ranges together quickly enough. The Italian and Spanish producers were very different to us because they produced small ranges very quickly. Norvic's ability to change its processes was severely hampered because of the huge investment made in the Vulcan Road plant. It was partly that we wouldn't change but also, largely because of the mistimed investment, that we couldn't change. We weren't the only ones, Clarks and K's and many others were in the same boat. At Norvic we had an autumn and spring range both of which had a lead in time of around six months. In contrast new shoe designs imported from our overseas competitors were coming in throughout the year. The trade's mode of production was in a rut.'

Barbara Miller, 1955

Barbara Miller observes how life has changed since the 1950s: 'The shoe trade in Norwich failed not because factories were producing inferior shoes, but because life changed. Take my aunt Belle, who lived in King Street. Every other year she had a new winter coat, with a hat to match together with new shoes, gloves and a handbag, and that was it for another two years. But no one lives like that now.'

Martin Miller, 1951

Classic Edwards & Holmes shoe from the 1960s

Christine Thorpe didn't always see eye-to-eye with her father, Harold Peace Johnson, a director at Edwards & Holmes: 'When I was at school and a teenager in the 1960s I really didn't want to wear Edwards & Holmes' shoes, even though they were really high quality and free! They were classic but I wanted to be trendy. I once bought a pair of lime green shoes, I loved them but dad was horrified.'

The Norwich Footwear Trade

The situation in Norwich largely mirrored the pattern exhibited throughout the UK. From the 1950s to the end of the 1960s output remained fairly steady with between seven and eight-and-a-half million pairs of shoes being produced per annum. This was followed by an 'all-time record' in 1972, when the Norwich shoe firms produced around 10.8 million pairs of shoes and fashion boots.

Between 1954 and 1971 the numbers employed in the Norwich footwear industry fell from 9,350 to 5,800. This was mainly accounted for by technological innovations which resulted in improved productivity. Major advancements included: heat setting of uppers, use of strong adhesives, which enabled soles to be cemented on instead of being stitched, and the introduction of rubber and plastic components which could be used to mould the whole sole and heel on to the upper. Although the numbers employed in shoe manufacturing were falling, the growth of other sectors in Norwich, in particular the service sector, enabled unemployed shoeworkers to find jobs outside shoe production. Paradoxically, despite the decline in overall demand for skilled shoeworkers, at peak times there was often a shortage of female machinists in the City. As a consequence many of the major firms owned factories where uppers were stitched (i.e. closed) outside Norwich, e.g. Norvic operated in Gressenhall and Edwards & Holmes in Sheringham. For those who worked in the industry at the time there were generally few problems getting a new job, and the workforce moved fairly freely between the factories.

As with the rest of the UK, this seemingly stable position hid underlying problems which were not addressed and eventually led to the decline of the Norwich footwear industry:

Fashion

As with other UK centres, the Norwich shoe making industry faced a huge challenge in the 1960s because fashion was starting to drive shoe design. This was particular pertinent for the large number of Norwich manufacturers who specialised in making high-quality shoes for ladies. Consumers were becoming more fashion conscious and wanted frequent changes of style through the year. The Norwich firms were geared up to introduce new designs twice a year, in autumn and spring. Their production methods meant that there was a significant time between the creation of an idea and it appearing in the shops. Not so with the Italian producers, who were producing similar quality shoes to the Norwich manufacturers and could be much more flexible. In the first half of 1966, 10.7 million pairs of leather shoes were imported into the UK, a 30% increase compared with the previous year. Two million of these were women's shoes from Italy. In the 1970s as inflation rose the position became worse. Walter Moll recalls: 'In the early 1970s Portugal and Italy were beginning to make fashion shoes better than us in terms of using better materials, having better styling and charging less. This was largely because many of these factories were non-unionised and paid less than us, and we basically became uncompetitive.'

Distribution and marketing

With the growth of the BSC and other large retailers many Norwich manufacturers found trading conditions much more challenging. Walter Moll recalls: '...where we had previously been dealing with a number of retailers, we were now dealing with just one – who had huge buying power. Even Bally, with our name, found the new trading conditions tough. Many smaller factories just went out of business.' Particular problems included:

- Over dependence on relatively few firms who could dictate terms. Sexton's was a volume business with a tendency to chase sales. As competition grew from abroad they were constantly under pressure to reduce prices from big organisations such as Marks & Spencer and the BSC, both of which could dictate terms. They never quite recovered from losing their Marks & Spencer contract in the mid-1960s
- As many retailers amalgamated, manufacturers suddenly found that where they were previously supplying a number of firms, they were dealing with only one. For example, in 1962 W. H. H. Clarke's largest customers were bought by the BSC, who imposed a complete ban on buying while stocks were sorted. Luckily in 1961 Clarke's had become a subsidiary of K Shoes and production in both Clarkes' factories could be switched to the manufacture of K-branded footwear.

Between 1970 and 1990 the Norwich footwear industry imploded. During these years firms that went out of production included: Sexton, Son & Everard Ltd, the Norvic Shoe Co. Ltd, Edwards & Holmes Ltd and Shorten & Armes Ltd. Over the same period the numbers employed in the industry reduced by over 60% to 2,000. Contraction continued over the next decade when casualties included: W. H. H. Clarke Ltd, Bally Shoe Factories (Norwich) Ltd and Shingler & Thetford Ltd.

Until the mid-1970s a number of local firms had been buffeted from adverse conditions because of their association with Start-rite, which from 1952 only manufactured children's shoes. Over this period Start-rite was often unable to meet orders from their own factories, and so they contracted them out to other Norwich firms. Unlike companies who made ladies' fashion shoes Start-rite's sales had been buoyed up by two main factors, as summed up by David White: 'The birth rate was going up and fashion didn't really play a part in the trade. We only made black and brown shoes and if they didn't sell one year you'd put them back into stock, increase the price and sell them the following year.' In the 1970s not only did the birth rate fall but children became more fashion conscious. As a result demand for Start-rite shoes fell. In response, in the mid-1970s Start-rite introduced short-time working in preference to making the workforce redundant. But soon they too had to lay workers off, close down their own smaller factories and stop contracting out to other factories. As a result firms that had become over dependent on Start-rite, such as Trimfoot Ltd, simply went out of business.

Firms that survived knew that they had to introduce change. Simon Goodman (chairman of the Florida Group) recalls: 'We first had a flirtation with making shoes abroad in the late 1970s when we brought in a few machined uppers from Cyprus.' A little later Start-rite started to import uppers from India. Nigel Brown, who was working in their making room, recalls early problems: 'We had to wrap them in wet rags because they were so hard. At the time those of us in the factory were quite pleased it wasn't working too well, because we thought our jobs would be safer, but obviously processes got better.'

Meanwhile factory managers started to review long-established production methods. In 1992 Florida introduced a new staff payment system which replaced piecework. Subsequently, in a bid to increase efficiency, traditional methods of shoe production were ousted in favour of modern techniques. Janet Metcalf, supervisor at Florida, recalls: 'In many ways the factory was becoming a lot more professional. When I started (in 1959) you just did what you thought was right, but then management started to introduce procedures that we all had to follow. We had to do things by the book, which improved productivity.'

And so, as the century came to an end, footwear production was no longer Norwich's major industry. Shoe manufacturers that survived did so because they made difficult decisions and adapted their businesses to changing market conditions. Strong leadership and management inevitably contributed to their survival.

Former Norvic Kiltie factory, c1982

Former CWS factory, 1987

Former Edwards & Holmes factory, 2002

Former Sexton, Son & Everard factory, 2012

The 21st Century

The Footwear Trade in the UK

In 2012 around five million pairs of footwear were being produced annually in the UK by 4,500 people. As such, although the trade is very much a shadow of its former self, reports of its demise have been greatly exaggerated.

In the 1950s over 200 factories were based in Northamptonshire. In 2012, although there were only 19, it remained the largest footwear manufacturing centre in the UK. The majority of firms based there specialise in the production of high-quality shoes for men. Their main focus is on footwear that has been produced using the Goodyear Welted Process (a method of production that allows soles to be removed for repair without affecting the uppers). Firms founded in the 19th century, such as Edward Green, Crockett & Jones and Church's (the largest in the county with 180 employees), make hand-crafted shoes using traditional methods which they sell at a premium. They trade on quality not quantity. For example, Edward Green has 65 craftsmen who make around 60 pairs of shoes a week. These firms not only promote the fact that their shoes are 'Made in Britain' but specifically are 'Made in Northampton'. There is a high international demand for their footwear, and about 70% of their production is exported.

Beaconsfield Footwear Ltd (who make the Hotter Brand) and New Balance Athletic Shoe Inc. are the two biggest manufacturers of shoes in Britain; together they account for around half of all footwear made in the UK. With factories based in Lancashire and Cumbria respectively, both companies are directly competing with low-cost countries and succeeding, which is mainly attributed to the considerable investment both have made in equipment and staff.

Many firms have stopped manufacturing in the UK, and re-invented themselves as design and marketing businesses who work very closely with overseas manufacturers, often on a partnership basis. Using this approach Clarks has emerged as the number-one shoe brand in the UK and the fourth largest footwear company in the world.

Despite this move, recently demand has been driven by the increasing popularity of the concept of 'Made in Britain'. This initiative is being promoted by the British Footwear Association (BFA); a group that represents British footwear manufacturers, British shoemakers and British footwear brands. The importance of the 'Made in Britain' label is clearly illustrated by the experiences of R. Griggs and Co. Ltd, better known as the manufacturers of 'Doc Martens'. The firm was established in Northampton in 1901, but it wasn't until April 1960 that they first produced their iconic boot. Subsequently in 2003, after the firm generated huge trading losses, they made the decision to transfer their manufacturing operation to China, which offered the company labour costs amounting to one-tenth of those in the UK. Following the move they retained a small staff in Wollaston (Northampton), to handle marketing, sales and design. However, it soon became clear that there was a market for English-made shoes. In response, as early as 2004, the firm made the decision to start producing some footwear at Wollaston. Although most of the company's shoes are still made in the Far East, the demand for their English-made shoes remains strong.

To summarise, four basic models have been adopted by UK footwear companies:

- To manufacture footwear using traditional hand-crafted methods in UK factories
- To manufacture footwear using automated methods in their own UK factories
- To design and market footwear which is manufactured by companies who are based overseas
- A combination of the above.

But what about the future ? If the demand for 'Made in Britain' products stays buoyant the BFA believes that footwear manufacturing will grow steadily, but will always remain small. But as has been proved in the past only those that evolve to meet changing market conditions will survive.

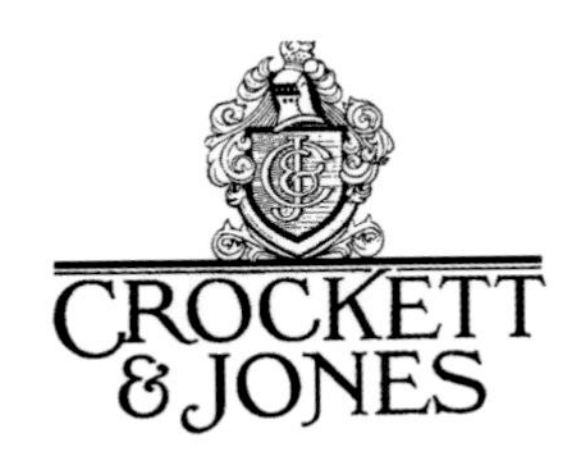

(L to r) Church's, Crockett & Jones, Edward Green, Northampton shoe manufacturers, 2013

The Footwear Trade in Norwich

As the new century began the once-powerful Norwich footwear industry had all but disappeared. Of the major companies trading in 1950 the only ones to survive in some form were: Start-rite, Florida, Shorten & Armes (which had been bought out of receivership by John Barrett and launched as Meadows Bridal Shoes Ltd) and Osoeasie Slippers (which had been bought by Bowhill & Elliott Ltd). They developed along different lines.

Following the takeover of Osoeasie Slippers Ltd, Bowhill & Elliott Ltd continue to make slippers in their small factory on London Street using traditional hand-crafted methods.

At the other end of the scale, from the 1980s Start-rite gradually transferred all manufacturing overseas. They stopped making footwear and closed Crome Road in 2003. Today, similar to Clarks, they are a design, marketing and distribution company. They still employ around 100 people in Norwich including: warehouse operatives, fitting specialists, sales and telesales staff, designers, and marketing specialists. Despite the change in business model, the firm remains focussed on supplying high-quality shoes specifically designed for the developing foot of a child. In a similar manner, Meadows Bridal Shoes continued to make shoes in Norwich until around 2000 after which they too began to design and market shoes in the UK which were manufactured abroad.

Florida have also transferred the majority of their production overseas, but they still make between 12% and 15% of their footwear at their Dibden Road factory and are proud to be the second biggest manufacturers of ladies' shoes in Britain. Of necessity they have to take a pragmatic approach to production. As explained by Jason Larke, Head of Marketing: 'Over the years the supply chain to the UK shoe industry has been devastated, and so we need to import many of our materials and components. If we are importing a hide from a country that has the capability of cutting the upper it sometimes makes economic sense to import the upper, rather than the entire skin, we will then last and make the shoe in Norwich.' Using a highly- skilled workforce they now manufacture over 1,000 pairs of ladies' shoes a week. Production has been given a boost by a growth in demand for 'Made in England' products. As these retail for around £10 more a pair than if they'd been made in India it is essential that the public buy into the ideology and accept that they carry a premium.

Alongside these firms, new footwear manufacturers have been established in Norwich. These include: Broadland Slippers who, similar to Bowhill & Elliott, manufacture hand-crafted slippers, and Freed of London, who make dance shoes. Both capitalise on the fact that they make footwear in Britain using traditional techniques.

Unsurprisingly, Norwich has lost its pool of skilled shoeworkers whilst the extensive infrastructure that supported the shoe industry has long since gone. However, all is not lost. Although the firms retain a number of employees past retirement age they also train staff who are new to the trade. Also a few firms making ancillary products still operate around Norwich. These include Bobcol, who manufacture heels, lasts and platforms, all out of wood.

Thus, although the Norwich footwear industry has declined since its golden years, it still contributes to the local economy. Looking to the future, the position is possibly best summed up by Ian Gibson, MP for Norwich North from 1997 to 2009: 'It is impractical to think that the Norwich boot and shoe trade will ever employ thousands of workers again. However, I do think that with good marketing coupled with local-design skills, shoemaking firms could once again flourish in the area. Shoes are a commodity, everyone needs them for a whole range of activities. Let's think of how we can find a niche market and bring the industry back. Because deep, deep down there is a political challenge to bring back community pride. We need to rise to the challenge. In Norwich we were once proud of what we made...we can be proud again.'

Florida factory, Dibden Road, 2012

Start-rite offices and distribution centre, Peachman Way, 2012

Lasting Memories

Start-rite's 'Union flag' shoe, 2012

Peter Lamble, Chairman and Managing Director at Start-rite, explains: 'We've survived because we've adapted. Since 1952, when we took the decision to only make children's footwear, our aim has been to make shoes that are essentially good for children's feet in a style which is attractive to them. Within this parameter we've changed our business model more than once. The businesses that weren't prepared to adapt have failed. Both Florida and ourselves still service the same customers that we did when the Norwich shoe trade was at its peak, but we both do so in a different way.'

Peter Metcalf, manager, was responsible for reviewing work methods at Florida in the 1990s: 'In retrospect too many of us who managed and owned the factories were too staid and stuck in our ways. Most of us had worked in the industry for years and we had the attitude: "This is how it's always been done so this is how it'll always be done." The world moved on and we didn't. By the time we realised that we needed to change for many it was too late. That said, although I fought to keep production in Norwich, in today's climate you need to be doing at least part of your production abroad. In the UK not only do we have higher labour costs but factory owners are subject to much tighter legislation which has had an adverse effect on the cost of production. By the 1990s I knew we couldn't compete with India and China.'

Peter Metcalf, 2002

Audrey and Arthur Holmes, c1960

Arthur Holmes, cost accountant at Start-rite, recalls how local firms became dependent on Start-rite: 'Norwich firms, such as Trimfoot, made shoes for us. The problem was that after small firms got contracts from us they put all of their effort into the Start-rite business and they took it easy. They let their sales reps go and they just relied on Start-rite keeping them.'

Ian Gibson, MP for Norwich North from 1997 to 2009, took an active role in supporting the Norwich footwear trade: 'In 2001 I led a debate in Parliament on the decline of the Norwich shoe industry. I thought that it should never have disappeared from Norwich. I believed at the time, and still do, that faced with cheap imports the directors of local firms failed to take the initiative. In Norwich we had, and still have, a great entrepreneurial spirit. I felt that if this had been harnessed and the firms had been given governmental support, that the industry may have had a future. At the time of the debate government had made the decision that it would not support local industry. They believed that it should support itself. That's one way of looking at it. Another would have been for the government to inject money into it, that would be repaid if businesses produced something that was needed – and everyone needs shoes. There was also an argument that import control could've helped the shoe industry, but this was never enacted. I believe that the Norwich shoe industry didn't receive governmental support because our workforce was not militant and local businesses didn't have enough political clout.'

2. The Structure of a Traditional Shoe Factory

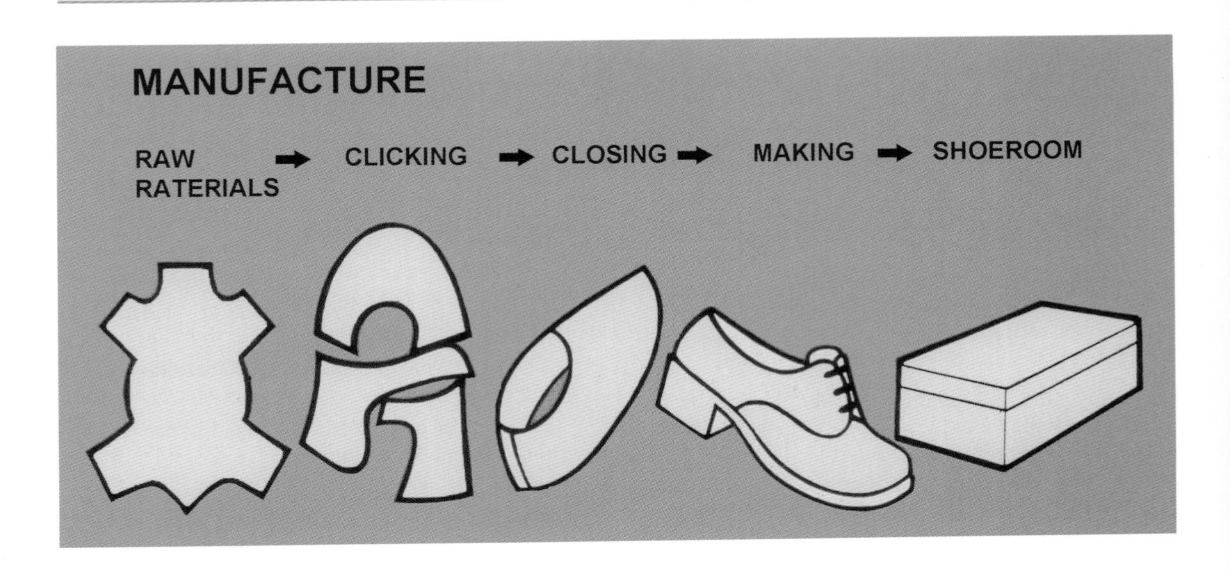

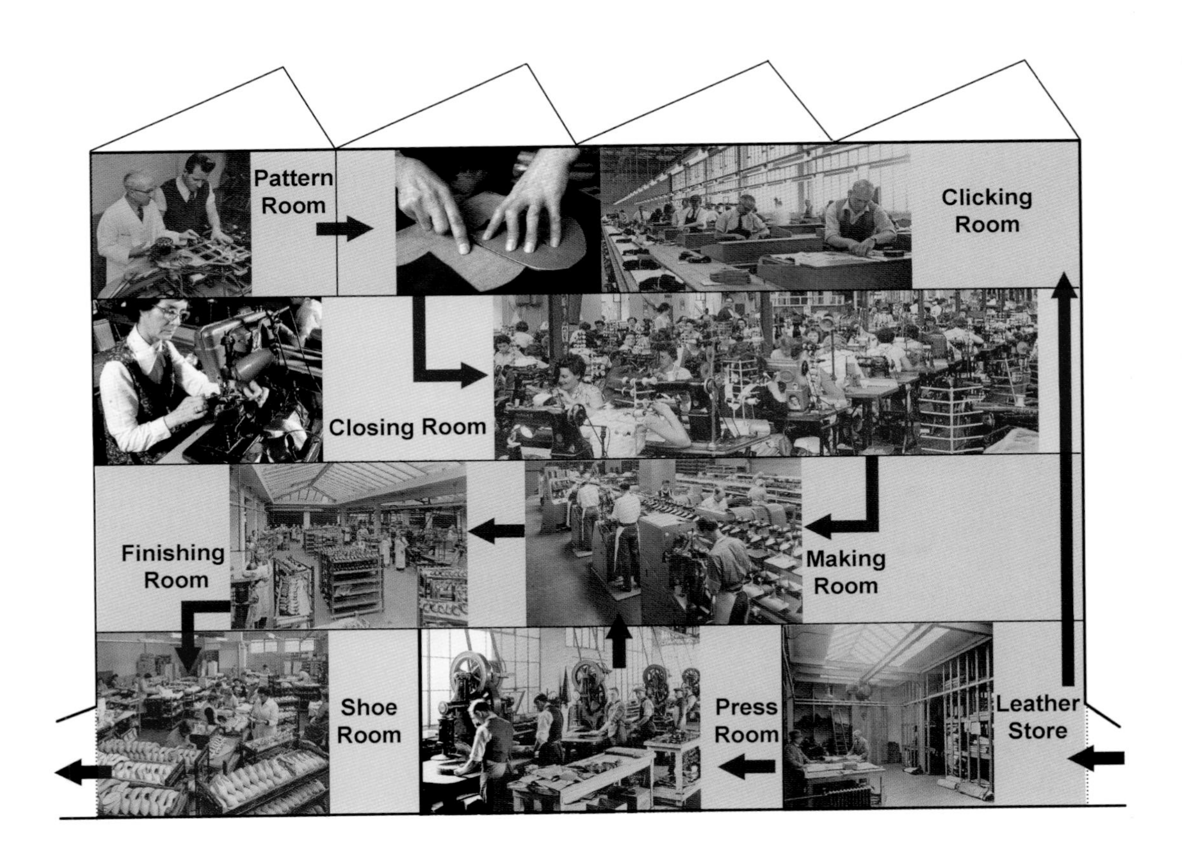

Introduction

The structure of the shoe factories evolved over time. However, for the majority of the 20th century the major factories were sub-divided into rooms (departments) where specific tasks were undertaken. Work in progress would generally be transported between the rooms on racks (trolleys) although by the 1930s conveyor belts were also used.

The rooms were very gender specific which gave each their own character. Audrey Holmes recalls: 'In Start-rite's clicking room, which was all men, there was little talking and even the foreman hardly said a word. It was different in the all-female closing room where there was lots of chattering and gossip.'

Inevitably, the segregation of the sexes led to behaviours which would now be stigmatised as being politically incorrect, as recounted by Derek Rye: 'In the machine room some of the women had strong personalities so when us men went into their domain you had to be ready for the banter, which could be somewhat ribald. But you got used to it. That said when they came into the men's room they got the same treatment, because we felt that if they dished it out so could we. But it was all done in fun and was part of factory life.'

In each room a variety of tasks was undertaken, each having a descriptive name, many of which have very different meanings today. For example, you could have been a skiver, a boxer, a passer, a feeder or even a slasher! Unlike now, when job descriptions often verge on the grandiose, in the shoe factories they tended to be literal. Thus, a passer used to 'pass' the shoes, a similar job today would be in quality control.

Historically shoes were worked on in batches of twelve pairs, although this would be reduced to six for less popular sizes and designs. Each batch was sent around a factory accompanied by a work ticket which gave information such as what the shoe looked like together with a perforated list of the operations which were needed to make the shoe. Each perforated section was known as a coupon.

Upon completing a specified task the operator in each room took the appropriate coupon. The coupons were collected daily and used to work out how much each person should be paid. The workers also kept their own books where they recorded how much they were owed.

Although each factory would have had its own idiosyncrasies the main rooms were:

- The pattern room: which housed the designers, pattern cutters and pattern makers
- The clicking room: where uppers were cut out
- The closing, or machine, room: where the uppers were sewn together
- The press, or bottom-stock, room and preparation room: where soles and heels were cut out and made ready for joining to the uppers
- Making, or lasting, room: where the uppers and bottoms (sole and heels) were assembled to make a shoe
- Finishing room: where the bottoms were trimmed, made weatherproof and polished
- The shoe, or trimming, room: where the uppers were cleaned, polished, trimmed and boxed.

The following pages describe the various rooms in the period between the 1940s through to the 1970s.

Florence Durrant, Edwards & Holmes, c1965

The Pattern Room

The three main roles undertaken in the pattern room were: designing, pattern cutting and pattern making. All were typically undertaken by men.

Similar to today, the designers were responsible for producing styles which would both sell and be profitable. One of the biggest factors they had to take into account then, and still do today, was the cost of lasts. This is because each shoe is moulded around a last, and replacing them is an expensive business. As such the aim has always been to use the same last for as many designs as possible.

In their heyday the factories made two ranges of shoes one for the spring and the other for the autumn. They all followed similar procedures, as recalled by shoe-designer John St Quintin who worked in the trade from 1948 – 1981: 'We'd start by making what we called a pullover, which was a roughly made shoe without a sole but with an insole and heel. They were always made in a size four and finished to the extent that they could be modelled for me and the governors such that we could judge what alterations needed to be made. If we decided that we liked the designs the next step was to make a sample shoe. We'd then give them to salesmen to take around our customers who included such firms as Harvey Nicholls, Russell & Bromley and Harrods. Their job was to drum up sales.'

The French and Italians have long been reputed to be amongst the best shoe designers in the world and many of the Norwich companies sent their design and sales teams abroad to view their work. In particular, many companies sent representatives to the Milan Exhibition where they could view thousands of designs made by small-scale Italian designers. Peter Holmes recalls attending the show in the 1960s: 'In order to go in you had to buy one design, just to show that you meant business, but once you were in you could look at all of the work on display. Many of the local firms visited the show, and subsequently a number of shoes made in Norwich were influenced by the designs they saw there.'

In those days once the firms had created their collections a sales team from each company, including designers, managers and owners travelled to London for the spring and autumn fairs, where they would display their shoes for the coming season. Despite the fact that they were theoretically in competition, they would all catch the same train and after a day of showing off their designs they would go out to celebrate together in the evening.

Designers often entered shoe-design competitions, which they saw as a good way to enhance their reputation. To prevent favouritism by the judges competitors could not put their own name on the shoes, instead they used a pseudonym. John St Quintin first won an award in 1950 and subsequently won many competitions and diplomas. He recalls that he used to make his competition shoes on a special last, which was slightly smaller than normal, to enhance their elegance, a strategy which was obviously successful.

John St Quintin, Shorten & Armes, c1965

Once a design had been selected the designer produced a drawing or a model shoe, which was passed on to a pattern cutter. In pre-computer days the pattern cutter was responsible for cutting a paper pattern. Once satisfied that the pattern was accurate, a master pattern was created out of thin sheet metal. A pattern maker then used a grading machine, similar to a pantograph, to produce a set of working patterns for every size and fitting that was going to be made in the design. The patterns were made out of stout cardboard and bound by brass to make them more durable. Once presses were used to cut leather uppers (from the mid-1960s), patterns were replaced by appropriately shaped press knives.

It was in 1945, at the age of 14, that Bruce Rampley started work as a trainee pattern cutter at Edward & Holmes' temporary factory on Starling Road. Bruce recalls the first thing that a trained pattern cutter did after being presented with a design was to determine the shape of the last, they would then devise a pattern to fit around it. He explains: 'Although each factory had slightly different methods, wherever possible all re-used existing lasts, which you could do if the shape of the toe and height of the heel were unchanged.' Once the pattern was designed sample shoes were made. At Edwards & Holmes these were always in size four and for the left foot. This was done to both check that the patterns were accurate and also that the shoes looked attractive. Bruce recalls: 'They used to make the sample shoes at Westwick Street and when they were ready I was sent across from Starling Road to pick them up, which I duly did on my racing bike. I used to have four boxes tied up with string attached to each side of the dropped handle bars. It was quite dangerous but at 14 you don't worry about things like that.' Once everyone was satisfied the shoe could go into production.

In 1966, a young John Thain started his career in the shoe industry as a trainee pattern maker at the Norvic factory on St George's Street. He remembers: 'The pattern room was on the top floor. The six pattern cutters sat on tall benches. They wore white coats, as a sign that they were high up in the factory, above us pattern makers.' Although by then clickers had begun to use presses, they still did a lot of hand cutting. John recalls that: '…a little old chap there called Tommy Minns spent all week putting brass binding around the patterns, then on Saturdays he had a stall on the market where he sold budgies!' John's first job was to solder the ends of the brass binding, file them up and then stamp each piece with the size, name or number given to the style.

John still works in the shoe trade today and, almost 50 years on from his early years at Norvic, is now head of fitting at Start-rite. He observes: 'Technology moved on. By the early 1990s patterns were being designed and made on the computer in the CAD room – which was a far cry from my first job in the pattern room at St George's.'

Traditional brass-bound patterns, Norvic, undated

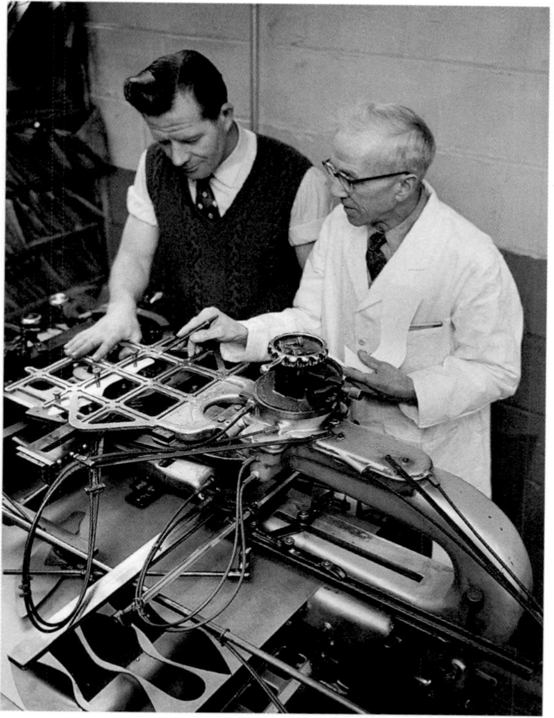

Grading machine, Shorten & Armes, c1950

Lasting Memories

John St Quintin recalls going to the London shoes fairs in the 1960s: 'All of the local firms used to go to London for the spring and autumn fairs where they would display their shoes for the coming season. The hotel rooms at the Washington Hotel in London [on Mayfair] were taken over by the shoe companies who displayed their ranges to potential buyers. We filled the hotel. A plan was made of the hotel so that visitors would know which room to visit to see the various ranges. The Norwich firms took up a fair bit of the hotel. Shows were also held at the Mount Royal Hotel.

'I remember travelling on the train with some of the celebrities from the Norwich shoe trade including: Arthur Howlett, Reggie Batson, John Kirby and salesman Harry Barter. In particular Arthur Howlett used to be a real comedian who had the train rocking with laughter. We used to show shoes all day then go out for a meal in the evening…they were lovely days.'

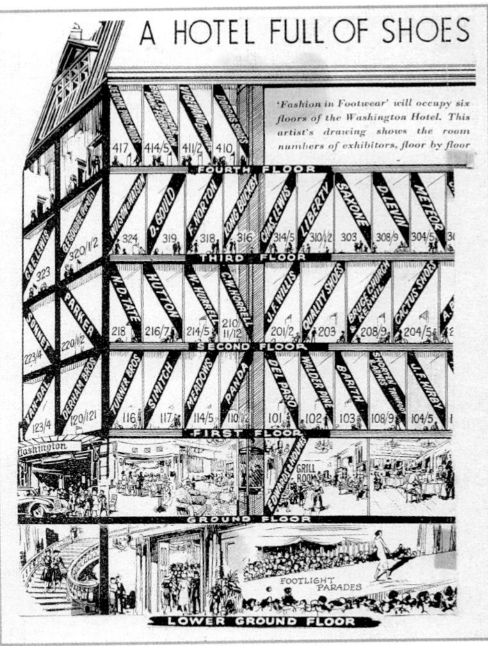

The Washington Hotel hosted shoe fairs in the 1960s

Arthur Howlett (2nd from right), c1960

John Thain explains how patterns were stored: 'Everywhere I've worked you used to lock the patterns away in safes or in a little room tucked out of the way. This wasn't to prevent them being stolen but to make sure they weren't lost. You see if you had a really good pattern which was used to make a popular pair of shoes you may use it, or a variation of it, for a number of seasons. Nowadays you wouldn't because patterns are made and stored on a computer.'

Arthur Holmes was responsible for keeping expenditure as low as possible: 'Pricing was always a juggling act. As Start-rite's cost accountant I was under pressure from the sales reps who'd say: "Clarks can do it at this price, why can't we?" Lasts were a big expense which had to be brought into costing a pair of shoes. The more you could use the same last, the less it cost. You didn't only have to cost in the price of buying a last, but if we used a new last we also needed to buy other equipment such as new knives. Put simplistically if the last and other equipment cost £100, and it was used to make 100 shoes, it added £1 onto the cost of every shoe we made. Alternatively if you made 1000 shoes it would account for 10p. We had one London customer who wanted a small number of specially designed shoes. I became involved because the cost of the lasts wasn't being included in the production costs. Once they were, the customer couldn't sell the shoe profitably.'

The Clicking Room

Trained clickers were responsible for cutting the uppers. Historically clickers cut leather on boards made of blocks of wood. When they came to the end of a cut they withdrew their knife and a 'clicking' sound was heard – hence their name. The job of a trained clicker was considered to be one of the most skilled and responsible, and so highest paid, in the factory. Their skill lay in their ability take a skin and recognise how to cut uppers from it in a way that maximised its value. For example, as the best leather was down the animal's back, they used it to make the vamp (the upper front part of the shoe). The area where the animal's legs joined the body was always flabby and so this was placed at the back of the shoe where it was strengthened by a stiffener. Mike Batson recalls that even into the 1960s: 'The clickers were considered as the elite of the workforce and they were expected to dress accordingly. When they travelled to work they always wore a bowler hat rather than a cap, and always wore a tie in the workplace. As a result they were often called the "gentlemen" or "snobs" of the shoe trade.'

The clickers needed as much light as possible. It was essential that they could see all of the details in the skin because, for example, they had to ensure pairs of shoes were made from leather of the same shade. This was why the clicking department at the Norvic factory on St George's was located on the top floor where extra windows had been cut into the roof.

Ray Newman recalls the day he started in Kirbys' clicking room in 1953: 'I can still see the men all working in rows, all stood next to their wooden boards.' As the 'boy', Ray started by doing jobs where he could do minimum damage. His first task was to cut fittings, such as the cardboard stiffener that went between the linings and upper. His next step was to work on linings. Only skilled clickers were allowed to work on more expensive skins. Derek Rye who started training as a clicker at Clarkes in 1964 took around four years to progress from cutting linings to uppers. You had to be really skilled before you were let loose on really exclusive skins such as lizards and snakes. Making shoes out of lizard skins was particularly testing as you could only produce one shoe out of each animal, so making a matching pair could prove difficult!

Although clicking was a relatively safe job Derek can still recall his first injury: 'I was being trained at the time and my instructor just looked at the blood and said: "Well now you've earned your apprenticeship." That was all of the sympathy I got.'

Clicking room, Howlett & White, 1925

Machine presses were initially used to cut linings and cheaper materials. However, by the 1960s they were being used to cut leather uppers. Derek recalls: 'Around 1969, the first clicking press was introduced at Clarkes. It was an old machine that was belt driven. It was viewed with some suspicion by the clickers who thought that it might lead to redundancies, because press cutting was quicker than hand cutting. But it didn't really.' Derek noted that unlike the presses which were used to cut the bottom stuff, which were operated by a foot treadle, the presses used in the clicking room needed two hands to work them. This meant that a hand could not be under the knife when the press came down, and so they were much safer. Eventually the vast majority of clicking in the Norwich factories was being done with presses, and uppers were only cut by hand if they were one-offs, such as samples. This was because if you were just making one shoe, it was both quicker and cheaper to cut around a pattern with a clicker's knife rather than to make a set of press knives.

Until the 1980s it was almost unheard of for a woman to work in the clicking room, but in the latter part of that decade Glenda Bradford started work as a clicker at the Florida factory. She'd previously worked in the machine room and immediately noticed how different it was to work in a 'men's room': 'There was a lot more swearing and the men would get onto you a bit, but not in a horrible way. I was treated like one of the boys but being the only women I felt special. I got on well with them all, and in fact I met my husband in the clicking room. I sometimes couldn't lift the heavier materials, but if that happened someone would help me. A lot of the men had years of experience and knew the tricks of the trade, and they were more than happy to share their knowledge with me. In fact all of my training was in-house. When I first went in there the attitude from the men was that the job was hard work and that I probably wouldn't survive. You weren't a proper machinist until you got a needle in your finger, and you weren't a proper clicker until you'd cut yourself with your knife. I don't know why women hadn't had the opportunity to do clicking before. Some of the materials were heavy, but I could just pick up foams and lining materials and sling them over my shoulder. There was no discrimination. In all my years at Florida I can honestly say that I enjoyed being a clicker more than anything else. If I could do that now I would.'

As with so many aspects of the shoe trade, IT has revolutionised the process of cutting uppers. You still need the human eye to highlight flaws in a skin, but now a computer works out how to maximise the number of uppers per skin, thus removing the aspect of the job that made the clickers so important in the shoemaking process.

Clicking room, Bally, 1959

Clicking room, Norvic, 1952

A Clicker's Story

Keith Richardson worked as a clicker at Start-rite from 1982 until 1997. Today he still works for the company. Here he tells the story of his time in the Crome Road factory.

'In 1982, when I was 16, I left school. My uncle was a foreman in the making room at Start-rite and had known there was a job coming up in the clicking room. At the time at least 14 members of my family worked for the company, so I think that you can safely say that the family connection got me an interview! After school broke-up I had a week's holiday and then immediately began as a trainee-cum-boy in the clicking room.

'When I joined the factory I found it nerve-racking, not only because it was a big place and I was in an adult community, but also because of the stories I was told about things like initiation ceremonies – but none of it came to fruition. When I was a boy, if I had to go to the closing rooms at Christmas time, they used to say that the ladies would get me in the cupboards. Well as a 16-year-old the thought of walking into a room that contained 100 women petrified me, but nothing ever happened. It was mainly talk. It might have been worse before then.

'One of my first tasks was to send materials out to our satellite factories at King's Lynn and Lowestoft. At the time we used to send out part components to them and they'd come back as complete uppers. After that I moved on to cutting the fabric parts of the shoe, such as linings, where I worked with materials that were less valuable than leather. When I was deemed good enough I went on to cut leather uppers.

'I was trained in-house mainly by the foreman and under-foreman. By then the bulk of cutting was done with press knives and we only used hand-cutting patterns and a clicking knife when we were making samples.

'For each job, clickers were given a bundle of leather and a work ticket, which was basically an A4 size sheet of paper, which told us exactly what we had to produce. The ticket would tell us things like the sizes and which patterns to use. It was then up to us to check that the standard of leather was up to scratch. Once that was sorted we had to go to the lockers where they held the metal press knives and select the correct ones so that we could cut the leather into the correct shapes. We'd stack those onto a tray and take them back to our workbench. It was our responsibility to get a given number of shoes out of the piece of leather we'd been allocated, because leather was expensive and we couldn't afford to waste it. If you used less leather than you'd been allocated you'd earn a bonus based on the amount you'd saved. As we were on piecework some clickers aimed to work on speed whilst others concentrated on using less leather, and so for them the bonus could be a high part of their wages. However we worked the aim was to cut the leather to a high standard.

'At Start-rite we had a leather room which contained stock valued at around £1 million. We bought it from a variety of countries including the UK, Italy, France and South America. When the leather arrived it was checked on a measuring machine before it was handed out to us. At the time we always said that the best hides came from England or the Northern European countries. This was largely because of the damp climate and the fact the animals weren't bitten as much by insects. If any of the clickers felt they'd been allocated leather which wasn't up to standard, before going to management, they'd speak to the room's "leather representative", a clicker who was responsible for deciding if they had a case.

'The average size of a skin is between 18 and 22 square feet. We'd work with sides, which were basically half a hide which had been cut down the line of the spine. We used to roll the skin of leather up and slip it onto an arm, a bit like a toilet-roll holder. You could then pull out a piece at a time to work on. We worked on big boards which were around three-feet long. Hand cutting was done on wooden boards but press cutting was done on boards made out of nylon fibre.

'A piece of leather isn't of uniform quality, so something like the vamp [the front of the shoe] would always be cut out of the best part of the skin, which was the butt [rump] along the backbone. The skins would also have imperfections, such as tick marks and scratches. These flaws had to be avoided, but you couldn't afford to waste big pieces of leather, and so you had to carefully position the knives to make sure that you got the best out of each skin. Also different skins were allocated for different types of shoes. Roughly speaking an older animal not only has a larger skin, it also has a thicker skin, and this determined which type of shoes we'd make out of it. We used to make bigger-boys shoes, which would get more wear, out of heavier-weight older skins.

'To cut the upper you'd place the press knife, which was made out of steel, onto the leather and then push it through the skin using the pressure generated by a press. By then the presses were operated by two hands, which meant that one couldn't accidentally get caught under the knife. We cut a number of pieces of leather which were subsequently sewn together to make an upper. We only cut one piece at a time.

'The work was hard because you were paid for what you did, and at the end of an eight-hour shift you knew that you'd done it. It was quite a physical job, but it was mental as well because we also had to think two-or-three cuts ahead. The time it took to cut an upper was determined by its style and size, but I generally cut between 180 and 360 pairs of uppers a day.

'The amount of work we had on varied during the year. So from March to August we'd be busy and have overtime, but from September to the end of February we didn't have so much to do. During this period we'd all be allocated a reduced amount of work and could only earn about three-quarters of our normal money. It was great when I was single and finishing on a Wednesday evening…but not so good when I had a mortgage and a family.

'About 1997 I transferred from being a clicker to working on the resourcing side. At the time I could see that the factory was likely to close, and indeed my first job related to us buying in materials from India. Originally we bought in the cut uppers, and then it progressed till we got to the point that we provided the pattern and instructions, and the entire shoe was made overseas. At our peak, in busy weeks we'd probably be cutting around 30,000 pairs of shoes, but when I left the clicking room we were down to producing between 6,000 and 7,000 pairs a week. This was because more and more uppers were being brought in from India. Eventually the decision was made to move all production overseas, and in 2003 Start-rite's Crome Road factory closed.

'The camaraderie in the factory was great. There were 40 to 50 working in the clicking room alone. After work we often went out together for anything from a drink to a trip to the races. On top of that we all went to the social club where we played sport, had monthly discos and at Christmas we had great parties there. It's unbelievable today but we had a snooker club, table tennis tables and even had two tennis courts on site. In 1992 to celebrate our 200-year anniversary we had a huge dinner dance for staff, past and present, at the Norwich Sport Village. There were about 1,000 of us there, we really felt part of a big family. It was a really great evening, and they're the things I really remember about working in the factory – the good parts.'

Keith Richardson, 2012

Picture Gallery - Closing rooms

Walter Edwards, 1925

Norvic, 1952

Sexton, Son & Everard, 1959

The Closing Room

The closing room, often called the machine room, was where the parts of the uppers were first prepared for joining up and then stitched together. Almost all of the workers were female and it was said that young lads entered there at their peril.

According to John Thain: 'The women were a different breed altogether. As a lad you knew not to go into the closing room at Christmas time or you'd have been ambushed. It was said that if you went in there you'd be in great danger of losing your trousers and having glue put in places you'd prefer not to have it. It may have been just rumours because I never saw it happen…but I never put it to the test. That said they were lovely people.'

Young girls would start in the machine room as trainees and the first thing they needed were their tools, which they were expected to supply themselves. Betty Barnard remembers that in 1940, before she could start at Shorten & Armes, she had to own a pair of scissors as these were used in many of the jobs. Subsequently when she went on to become a folder she had to buy her own little hammer and folding knife, 70 years later she still has them!

As in other parts of the factory, trainees would start by doing jobs where they could cause the least damage. Additionally they were often overseen by women who knew how to instil discipline. Jean Smith recalls starting work at Edwards & Holmes in 1948:

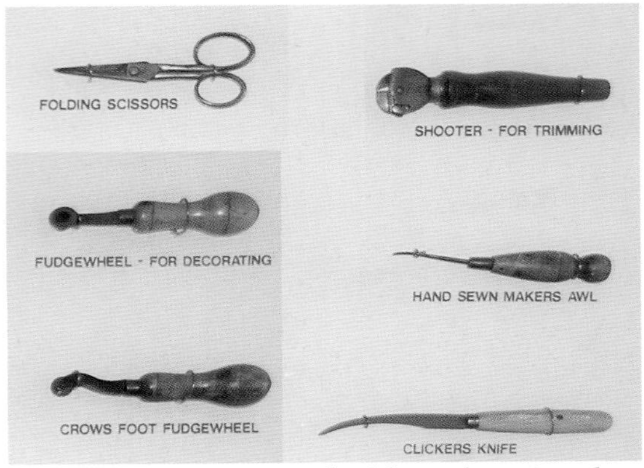

Tools of the trade, various dates

'My supervisor was called Miss Beck, we didn't use Christian names in those days. I also remember our forewoman who was called Miss Bristow, she was very strict and we weren't even allowed to talk. At the beginning we were each given a machine and pieces of leather to practice on. Gradually as we learnt our trade we were placed with the older women. When you were considered good enough, normally after a couple of months, you were put on linings. You started here because any mistakes that you made wouldn't be too costly. As you progressed, probably after another couple of months, you moved on to stitch the leather uppers.'

Closing room training, Sexton, Son & Everard, 1959

Closing room, John F. Kirby, 1960

By the 1950s many operations that had previously been completed by hand had been automated. By then, machines in the closing room included:

- The skiver: which thinned the edges of the pieces of upper (where a fold or joint was to be made) by guiding them over a sharp-edged disc
- The cementer: which ran the skived edge under a wheel which coated it with adhesives
- The folder: a machine with a little arm and hammer which pushed the edge over and stuck it down
- The perforator: which made decorative holes in the upper
- Closing machines: which were similar to a domestic sewing machine which were used to stitch flat pieces.

The list goes on to include machines that rubbed seams flat between two wheels, attached buttons, made eyelets, made buttonholes, and so on. Many of the jobs demanded huge levels of skills as described by Jean Woods, who in 1956 was trained how to be a folder: 'Folding is where you fold over the outside raw edges of leather uppers and stick them down to give a smooth, tidy finish. Before I received the uppers they'd been put through a machine which skived, or thinned, their edges. I ran an adhesive around the raw edge, then folded it over and passed it through a machine that pressed the edges down. Because of the skiving after I finished, the upper would be the same thickness all of the way across. I learnt how to hand fold first, because if you made a mistake on the machine, which you could easily do, you could lift the upper and cement it and then refold it by hand. The machine hammered it down. You had two treadles. My right foot made the machine go. I pressed down the toe of my left foot to pleat the upper which allowed me to go around a tight corner whilst the heel on my left foot operated a snipper which made little cuttings on outward curves. In the meantime I'd be using my fingers to operate the guide at the foot of the machine. Not only that, if the upper got stuck you used your knee to hit the machine foot, which held the upper down, and push it up... I got a good workout... it was better than going to the gym. I loved doing it.'

When the industry was at its peak there was a great shortage of closing skills, especially at busy times when the factories were all stocking up for the new season. This was partially overcome by using outworkers who stitched uppers in their own homes. At Norvic they even had one employee who was entirely responsible for organising the outwork. However, the main way the larger factories coped with the problem was to open closing rooms in the areas around Norwich. So, for example: Florida went to Gorleston, Sheringham and Holt; Edwards & Holmes were at Sheringham and Holt; Norvic at Gressenhall; Start-rite at Wymondham and King's Lynn; and Sextons at Fakenham. Simon Goodman notes: 'Not only did we teach the workforce a skill, they earned more money than they could earn from other jobs in the area. When we started pulling back it affected the outlying areas more than it affected Norwich, because these were the outlets we closed first.'

Although most towns and villages welcomed the shoe companies, some did not. It was in 1949 that Edwards & Holmes opened their closing room in the Oddfellows' Hall, a former lifeboat house overlooking the sea at Sheringham. The company employed a staff of 32 girls drawn from Cromer, Holt and Aylsham. It was reported in the local press of the time: 'This small factory is the first of its kind to open in the town. The building has been renovated, painted in cream and is well lighted. Canteen facilities have been provided.' So far so good, but then in February the Sheringham Chamber of Trade expressed their views, and it would be fair to say that they weren't best pleased: 'This chamber is not in favour of industries in general being introduced into Sheringam which would adversely affect its position as a seaside resort...We do not think the class of visitor who comes into Sheringham is going to be pleased with the sight of a lot of factory girls on the front between one and two o'clock.'

These remarks generated much comment in both the local, and national, press, best summarised as follows:

District Council: 'We dissociate ourselves from these views.'

Edwards & Holmes' directors: 'Most factory girls are as smart as anyone else.'

Chamber: 'Visitors come to Sheringham for its beauty. Where will this factory lead?'

Edwards & Holmes' directors: 'The decrepit building we took over looks much better after being repaired.'

Chamber: 'Sheringham does not need industry.'

Edwards & Holmes' directors: 'Nearly all the girls had been unemployed.'

Despite the furore the closing room operated in Sheringham for many years...maybe the chamber were swayed (shamed) by the arguments printed in the *Daily Mirror*: 'Perhaps Sheringham should adopt a by-law compelling fishermen to appear in pure white coats and straw hats and allow them on the front only after sunset. One wonders if the Sheringham traders are really concerned about the appearance of the factory girls or whether they may be deprived of cheap labour in the summer season.'

Closing room, Edwards & Holmes, Sheringham, c1950

Lasting Memories

Jean Woods, 2013

In 1978 Jean Woods started work at Start-rite's closing room in Wymondham where she did perforating: 'As the name suggests, I made holes. But you couldn't just make holes anywhere. Take for example the upper for a brogue. Before I received it a tracer would have marked out a pattern. It was a nice job, but not as well paid as folding. You put in one hole at a time using a die. You could get up quite a lot of speed, it went rat-a-tat-tat…sounding a bit like a machine gun.'

Martin Miller explains why it could be dangerous for a man to visit the Norvic closing room: 'On the first floor of the Norvic factory was the closing room which was staffed by 200 women machining uppers. In the room were very big baskets on wheels which were used to transport the sewn uppers to the making room. On odd occasions if the forewoman, who was an absolute disciplinarian, wasn't looking, some of the women would pounce from behind on any young chap who had gone into their domain and bundle him into a basket.'

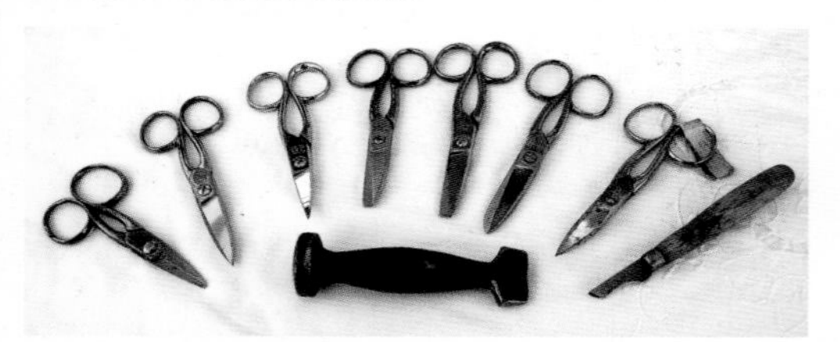

Barabara Miller, c2011

Barbara Miller recounts a trick played on boys newly arrived in the shoe factories: 'A long weight was used to hold items, such as patterns, in place. When a young lad joined the factory he'd be sent to the closing room to ask the charge hand for a long weight. He'd be given a knowing smile and told: "Just wait *[sic]* over there." Ten minutes later he suddenly twigged!'

Betty Barnard started work in the Shorten & Armes' machine room in 1940, when many jobs were still completed by hand: 'Scissors were used in many of the jobs in the closing room and you had to have your own pair if you wanted to work there.

Betty Barnard, c1954

'Tools like that weren't supplied by the factory. Eventually I was given a job as a folder so had to buy my own little hammer and folding knife. As a folder I had to take the leather uppers that had been cut into shape by the clickers, and put an adhesive around the raw edges with a little brush which I then turned over using the folding knife before hammering down. When I started we did hand folding although we eventually moved on to folding machines. But the girls who sewed the uppers after us always said that hand folding was the best…I still have my little hammer and knife.'

The Press Room

The press room, or bottom-stock room, was where the soles and heels were cut. When the operatives, who were invariably male, were working with leather they had to know how to utilise the skin to ensure they could cut as many parts as possible from one hide.

Press rooms contained heavy machinery, and so traditionally they were located on the ground floor. They were the noisiest and most dangerous areas in the factories, as explained by Peter Metcalf: 'At Edwards & Holmes' purpose-built factory, the press room was in the basement. But because in those early days [the factory opened in 1948] the soles were cut out of leather, skylights were built into the pavement to give the workers as much natural light as possible. We used around ten huge revolutionary presses which were about ten-feet across. They were shaft driven with one motor driving a number of machines. To do this each press had a whopping great turning wheel on the side which had a big belt running around it to the shaft. The press was operated by a foot treadle which ran along the length of the machine. The press knives, which operated on the same principle as pastry cutters, were made from forged steel and were about six-inches deep. When the press came down they were pushed through the material below. The quickest way to cut the soles would be to cut one, then the next etc. and allow them to build up inside the press knife. When it was full they would be pushed out. The number of men who had lost fingers and thumbs in that room was incredible. This was because they were trying to get the work out as quickly as possible and they'd press the treadle when their fingers were still under the knives. It all relied on foot – hand coordination. They were also incredibly noisy places.'

Heel building, which basically involved making up heels from graduated pieces of leather and then tacking them together on a machine which punched nails right through them, was also normally undertaken in the press room.

From the 1960s press rooms became either obsolete or shrank considerably in size. By then companies were starting to use prefabricated bottom stock, which was normally brought in by the smaller companies. Even where companies continued to make soles out of leather, e.g. at Edwards & Holmes, technological improvements resulted in a reduction in the number of presses needed to complete a job.

Press room, S. L. Witton, c1925

Lasting Memories

John Thain, recalls his early impressions of a shoe factory: 'The first thing I noticed when I started at the Norvic factory on St George's [in 1966] was the noise and the dirt. In the basement they were still making the bottom stock. At the time the soles were all made in-house out of leather and the heels were made separately. The basement had a low ceiling and it was crammed with machinery. Lots of the men wore brown smock coats. The sound of the presses crashing down made it a really noisy place to work. The room smelt like burning leather.'

John Thain, c1985

Ron Green explains why making heels could be a dangerous business: 'At Bally in the early 1950s we made many of our own heels out of layers of leather of increasing size. The leather was cut to shape and put in a mould, the smallest first. You needed two hands to operate the machine that held the pieces together and then fixed them with five nails that came up from below. You had one hand on the lever above and one on a side lever. Despite this a bad accident did occur when the operator's mate pressed one lever whilst the operator was adjusting the leather.

'A "top piece" was attached to the top of the heel with two nails. The machine that did this job left an indentation in the heel even if a nail hadn't been inserted. I had a job paring off the edges that stuck out with a cutting machine. It had no guard and whizzed around really fast. Although as the operator I should have checked that the nail was in place, I was on piecework so didn't always get around to it. I found to my cost if there was only one nail in the heel and you tried to pare it, the top piece spun around at great speed and flew off, which resulted in me suffering a badly cut finger.'

Press room, Walter Edwards, 1925

The Making Room

The making (or lasting) room, was where the shoe was built. In the early 1950s, three teams typically operated in a making room:

- The lasting team joined the upper to the insole which first involved roughly tacking each upper with its correct bottom-stock parts on a last. A puller-over would then use his machine to pull the upper down tightly over the last to give the shoe its shape and apply half a dozen tacks to hold the upper to the insole. The Consol operator completed the tacking around the insole. The shoe would then be passed along to the seat laster, who pleated the upper in and tacked it around the seat (the part of the shoe that the heel sits on).
- The bottoming team then attached a shank (strengthening piece) in the waist (narrowest part) of the shoes, and filled in the hollow space which ran down the centre of the bottom of the shoe. They then attached the sole.
- Finally the heeling team attached the heel.

As noted previously, many technological advances were made to the machinery employed in the making room, which both simplified the above process and reduced the number of operatives employed. The rate of change varied between the factories. In fact at Edwards & Holmes they were still hand lasting in 1960. However, as observed by Lenford Laband, one aspect of the work was uniform: 'It didn't matter what machinery we introduced to automate tacking, the chaps always put tacks in their mouths so that they were ready to tap in a tack manually if the machine missed. We [F. H. & H. S. Pochin] started to supply waxed tacks, which were more suited to the machines but the men complained because they didn't like the taste!'

(Above and below) All images are of making-room equipment. They were used by Norvic for staff training, c1970

Lasting Memories

Peter Metcalf describes how the lasting process became mechanised: 'When I started at Edwards & Holmes, in 1960, lasting was done by hand in the lasting department. They were the days when you used to see the guys stand there with the tacks in their mouths. They all had blood blisters on their lips and a worn, black tooth because the tacks were all smothered in graphite. Despite this they just used to throw a handful of tacks into their mouth, get them on their tongue and spit them out one-by-one, it really was an art. They were all craftsmen. As time progressed the process became more mechanised. So, for example, in the early 1970s we brought in four-part lasters which would pull the upper over and cement all of the front in one go. So basically, one guy with one machine replaced four hand lasters.'

Peter Metcalf, 2002

Mike Copland recalls that hand lasting could be anti-social: 'In the past hand lasters all held the tacks in their mouths which destroyed their teeth. They'd also swallow them and you'd hear someone gagging and turned around to see them taking out their false teeth and shake out the tacks…it was disgusting. Rather than use hammers to tap the uppers and tacks in they'd use a tool call a driver which was an old metal file that had been smoothed down.'

Mike Copeland, 2012

Martin Miller, 1951

Martin Miller admires the skill of the hand lasters: 'When I was there in the 1950s, the making room at Norvic was on the ground floor. If a shoe had an awkward toe shape, particularly a pointy one, you couldn't rely on the lasting machines to do the job properly, and so instead it was completed manually. The men held the heads of the tacks in their mouths, pointy side sticking out, then took the upper pulled it over the sole and took the tack out of their mouth and using shoemakers' pincers tapped the tack through the materials. They perfected the skill of being able to talk whilst having a mouth full of tacks. It was amazing to see. They seldom swallowed a tack and I never heard of anyone suffering a serious injury.'

The Finishing Room

By the time the shoes reached the finishing room they were complete, but the leather soles were rough, and not completely waterproof. It was here that men made the shoes fit to wear. In the 1950s the main roles undertaken were:

- Edge and heel trimmers: who respectively cut the edges of the sole and heel to shape
- Bottom scourers: who used an emery wheel to smooth the sole of the shoe
- Edge setters: who pressed the edge of the sole solid and then gave it a high polish
- The soles were then painted with a special ink containing wax, before burnishers polished them by pressing them on a heated metal plate.

In the 1960s with the introduction of prefabricated soles and plastic heels the finishing room became obsolete.

Finishing room, Walter Edwards, 1925

Finishing room, CWS, c1935

The Shoe Room

The shoe room, also known as the trimming room, was where the shoes were made spick and span and then boxed. Jobs included: cleaning the uppers; ironing out any wrinkles in the upper; stitching on ornaments such as buckles and bows; stamping the soles with the firm's name; sticking socks (a piece of material that was stuck inside the shoe to cover the insole) into the shoe; printing and sticking labels onto the boxes; and finally packing the completed shoe into the appropriate box.

Jean Rye remembers that, when she started in the shoe room at Sextons in the 1960s, there used to be a row of little old ladies sitting at desks who sewed accessories onto the shoes. As in other parts of the factory, she recalls that the jobs undertaken by the girls in the shoe room had somewhat unusual names: 'I did lots of different jobs such as: socking, which meant that I put the socks in the shoes; cleaning the shoes; boxing, which literally meant that I put the shoes in boxes; stuffing, where we used to push tissue paper into the toe of the shoe, to help it keep its shape in the box; and also faking, where we used to correct little faults. In the end I became a passer, which meant that I did the final check on the shoe. If they weren't up to scratch I should have returned them to the person who made the mistake, but I didn't like to do that so I tended to do the corrections myself – which meant that I worked slower than I should have done.'

Shoe room, Walter Edwards, 1925

The Norwich firms prided themselves on the quality of shoes that they produced, a quality that couldn't be delivered without the skills of the ladies in the shoe room. Avis Brown recalls working at Edwards & Holmes in the late 1950s: 'I started in the shoe room where I learnt how to clean the shoes, which we did before they were boxed. We had a special wash and then used a piece of crepe and went around the edges of the sole and upper to make sure as much solution as possible had been removed. Then someone would apply paint, which was the same colour as the leather, over any white solution which you couldn't wash off. From there I graduated to bigger things, and put bows on shoes and sewed diamantés onto the vamp. The diamantés were tiny, just like diamonds in a ring, but they had a piece of mesh behind them that matched the shoe and it was the mesh you sewed on. When we did that sort of work we were on a flat rate. You couldn't sew on the diamantés until you'd graded right up and proved your worth doing less skilled trimming jobs. It was a fiddly job and if we had an order for 12 pairs of diamanté-decorated shoes it would take forever for one person to do it, so we were asked if we wanted to take a pair home to work on overnight. You'd be lucky to do one pair in the evening as it took a good half-a-day to do a pair. We did a lot of fancy work like this because at Edwards & Holmes we made really high-class shoes for ladies.'

As the UK market became flooded with cheap imports many of the labour-intensive tasks completed in the shoe room could no longer be justified. Where possible they were simplified, e.g. accessories would be stapled onto the upper rather than be sewn.

Although much of the work in the finishing room, such as the intricate sewing completed by Avis, would not be cost-effective today, without doubt it gave the footwear the quality finish which epitomised a Norwich-made shoe.

Shoe room, Shorten & Armes, 1972

Shoe room, John F. Kirby, 1966

Daphne Nichols, shoe room, Bally, 1991

Lasting Memories

Janet Metcalf recalls her early career at the Florida factory: 'In 1959 I joined Florida where I worked in the shoe room. It was here that we did jobs such as socking, cleaning, ornament attaching and boxing-up. I immediately had a stroke of luck. The girl who printed the labels for the boxes was off sick and no one else could do the job, so loads of boxes had been piled up and they couldn't be sent out. When I found out what the problem was I said: "I know how to use the machine, I was taught at Start-rite." So I was immediately put on it and, what was more, I was put on piecework. At the end of the week I earned £10, which was a man's wage. I was called into the office because they thought that I'd made a mistake – but I hadn't, I was just very quick. I continued to do the job until 1968 when I left to start a family. It was great because even when I was ill I never lost any money as they just delivered the machine to my home and I worked from there. In fact I was a bit worried that I'd be expected to take it with me when I went on honeymoon…but I wasn't. Whilst working on the labeller I learnt all of the other procedures in the shoe room, but it was always a disappointment that shoe room workers weren't given day release to enable us to go to college. The machinists all went, but it was thought that our jobs weren't skilled enough – something I really disagreed with.'

Peter Metcalf explains why all of the shoe manufacturers employed repairers: 'In the shoe room at Edwards & Holmes we employed an army of shoe repairers. These were people who expertly masked any mistakes we had made. Because of all of the processes involved in making a shoe there were always going to be scratches.'

Peter and Janet Metcalf, c2000

3. Working in the Shoe Factories

Clicking room, Shorten & Armes, c1960

Mrs. Cullum (white coat) overseas the machine room, Shorten & Armes, c1960

Applying For A Job

'My mother, Annie Vines (née Smith), went to Wensum View School where the teachers wanted her to be a trainee teacher. This would have involved her father having to buy all of her books, and as she was one of five children her father couldn't afford the expenditure. Then one day in 1918, when she was still 14, she saw a job advert for clickers [who cut out the leather uppers] outside the Haldinsteins factory on Queen Street. When she saw what they were earning she went straight in to apply, but of course she was told that clickers were always men. Instead she was offered a job as a secretary, but when she found out that machinists were on piecework and could earn a lot of money, that's what she decided to do.' (Kris Hunt)

This one recollection tells us much about the shoe trade and also about society and the accepted norms of the time. In fact Annie's experiences were shared by many new entrants to the shoe trade right the way through to the 1970s.

The first thing to note is that Annie was only a girl of 14 when she started work. She left school in the same year that the Fisher Education Act was passed, which raised the school leaving age to this level. Subsequently, it was lifted to 15 in 1947 and reached 16 in 1973. Like Annie the vast majority of entrants into the shoe factories left school as soon as possible. Additionally they would be in school one day and on the shop floor the next.

The next point is that Annie was undoubtedly bright, yet because of circumstances she was forced to leave school and undertake a manual job that paid a good wage. This again is a recurrent theme in the history of the trade, and as a result many very intelligent people did manual work. Largely because of this, when shoe manufacturing declined many members of the workforce were easily able to take jobs in other sectors, such as financial services and retail.

Unlike today, Annie didn't need to scour newspapers, the internet, or go to a Job Centre to seek out work, she merely walked by the factory. This system still worked well in the 1960s when firms, such as Norvic, had boards listing vacancies outside. But this was not the main way to get a job – the emphasis being a lot more on 'who you knew'. Arthur Holmes (cost accountant at Start-rite 1950 – 86) recalls: 'If there was a job vacancy someone always recommended a relative to fill the position, which was a system that generally worked very well.' This often resulted in large family groups working in one factory, a situation which continued into the 1980s. In fact in 1982, when Keith Richardson began at Start-rite, he joined 14 members of his family. Of course, once you had started to work in the industry you built up your own network of contacts often through attending courses at Norwich City College and Art School. Here many friendships were made that lasted a lifetime.

Keith Richardson (back row, third from left) and other family members who work at Start-rite, c1983

Another point to consider is that Annie could not apply for what was one of the best paid jobs in the factory (clicking) because she was not a man. Through to the 1980s, jobs in the shoe trade and in many other manufacturing industries, were gender specific. As a result the press room, the making room, and the clicking room were often collectively referred to as the 'men's rooms'. Similarly, the closing room and the shoe room were often referred to as the 'women's rooms'. There were of course exceptions as recalled by Avis Brown: 'At Sextons [in the early 1960s] the main downstairs' finishing room was run by two gay gentlemen. We all knew that they lived together and, although at the time homosexuality was illegal, we all just accepted it and didn't bother about it.'

Finally Annie wanted to do piecework, i.e. be paid according to the amount of work she produced. This was the most common way that shoe-factory workers were paid through to the 1990s – a system not without its faults.

Annie was given the job without doing any formal tests, which was very much the norm. However, some factories required new entrants to prove their worth, as recalled by Jean Rye who, in 1964 at the age of 15, went for an interview at Sexton, Son & Everard: 'I had to do a simple little test where I had to put shapes into the right holes in a box, while they timed me. They were trying to see how quick we all were. I don't know how good I was…but I passed.'

Others had very different experiences to Annie. In 1951 Mike Quinton graduated from Cambridge University. In the same year he became the first arts graduate to be employed in the Norwich shoe industry when he joined Norvic. Norvic took this step when they found that their major rivals (Ks, Clarks and Lotus) were taking on arts graduates, and so decided that 'there must be something in it'. Additionally there are numerous examples of factory owners and directors being joined by their children and other family members in the firm. These include John Barrett whose father Geoffrey owned Shorten & Armes: 'I became involved in the family business in the 1960s. When I left school I didn't really know what I wanted to do but my father said: "Why don't you try the shoe trade and see if you like it?" I did, and 50 years on I find that I still like it.'

Annie Vines (back row, right) holds a reunion with former Haldinstein workmates, 1962

Lasting Memories

John Thain, who still works at Start-rite observes: 'In the 1960s it was very different to now. In those days if you got fed up with one factory, you just went up to another one where a mate worked and you'd get a new job just like that. So, after I'd been at Norvic for around a year [1967] and wanted to work in a smaller factory, I spoke to a pal at college who knew there was a job going at Shingler & Thetford in Pottergate. I called in and got the job. At Shinglers there was only me and another chap doing the pattern making so it was much more of an individual thing.'

John Thain, 2012

Mike Quinton, undated

Mike Quinton recollects joining Norvic: 'In 1951 I became the first arts graduate to be employed in the Norwich shoe industry. I was put on a special training programme. At the time Norvic had six factories, their own shops, reps on the road, plus a whole range of head office functions. In my first year I spent three months in London with the advertising department, I also had time in the shops and factories. It was a really great way to see how the company operated. At the end I was appointed PA to Ralph Colman, the managing director.'

Brian Lambert, worked in the shoe industry 1953–1990s: 'It always seemed strange to me that the most skilled jobs in the factory weren't necessarily the best paid. On piecework, if an operative was accurate and quick, they could earn a lot of money because of the amount of work they shifted. I remember that we had a lady [at Bally] who worked as a skiver in the closing room who was so good that she earned around twice as much as her workmates doing a similar job.'

Brian Lambert, c1960

Sockers wanted, Haldinsteins, 1935

Starting Work

'On my first day I arrived at the front door and was led through the factory. I'd never experienced anything like it. The noise was horrendous...the clanking, the banging, and the shouting. On top of that was the awful smell of acetone, glue and leather all mixed in together. It seemed like a madhouse to me.' (Bob Drake)

These are Bob Drake's first impressions of Sexton, Son & Everard Ltd, where he worked in the 1960s. As he and other new workers in the trade soon found out, the sounds and smells of a factory were just two aspects of the workplace that they had to come to terms with.

As was typical of their time the factories were very hierarchical. John Thain remembers joining Norvic as a young lad in 1966: 'We had to go to the canteen for the other men in the department. It used to open at a certain time in the morning and we used to go around all the blokes and take their orders. I used to bring up big glass bottles of tea and wander around pouring it into their mugs. It was a bit of a chore...but part of being "the boy".' It was the same for girls. Janet Metcalf recalls when she started at Start-rite in 1959: 'I was employed as a "run-around" in the shoe room, which meant that I cleared up everyone else's mess.'

Reg Kilbourn can still vividly remember his first day at work. It was in 1949 and he was 15 years old when he started in the clicking room at Barfield & Richardson. His foreman was Mr Frederick Waspe who he still remembers today as being a 'very strict gentleman who came to work wearing a bowler hat and carrying a briefcase and umbrella.' Being only 5ft 2in tall Reg found that he couldn't reach the cutting board, but this problem was soon overcome by the simple expedient of standing on a box. In the afternoon his mentor, a Mr Robinson, was sorting leather from the racks when Reg recalls: 'Suddenly little mice were running everywhere. I was given a dustpan and told to join in the hunt, it was a very dusty ten minutes. I don't think I had ever killed anything before.' When Reg arrived home his best white shirt, which he had worn for his first day at work, was filthy. The next day he wasn't so well dressed which led to him learning two lessons which stuck with him for the rest of his career, namely the importance of both discipline and dress code. You see when Mr Waspe saw Reg in his old clothes he beckoned him over instilling great fear into the lad. He then told Reg to cycle home, all the way to the Larkman Estate, and put on a necktie – thenceforth Reg always wore a tie to work!

The factories had a defined dress code. The clickers always considered themselves to be the elite of the workforce, hence Frederick Waspe's insistence that young Reg dressed the part. Additionally clerical staff, who worked in the offices, often saw themselves as being superior to their colleagues who worked on the factory floor and dressed accordingly. As such

Finishing room, CWS, c1935

when Vic Hopes worked at Sexton, Son & Everard in the late 1950s as an assistant production office manager, he was given a white starched coat to wear. As he wryly recalls: 'We had a clean one every week which they laundered…and charged us for! Although the directors also wore coats, theirs were of a different colour. So, for example; Reggie Wilch, the production director, wore a biscuit-coloured coat; Clem Martin, in charge of design, wore grey; whilst Eric Sexton sported cream.' Meanwhile, in 1956, at the age of 15, Jean Woods started her working life as a machinist at the Norvic closing room based at Gressenhall. Luckily, her supervisor didn't have the same sartorial leanings as Mr Waspe. She recalls: 'We used to go into work wearing a headscarf, and during the lunchtime we'd wash each other's hair and put in rollers. We found that if you kept your headscarf on the supervisor didn't notice!'

New entrants soon found that the factory hierarchy extended to how you addressed both managers and directors. John Thain recalls that in his early years in the industry (he started in 1966) you would always call your superiors 'sir' or 'Mr'. This was most people's experience although Jean Smith found that when she worked at Meadows in the 1950s, which was one of the smaller factories, the workforce called John and Paul Meadows by their Christian names.

Despite the formality, which is alien to many modern workplaces, there was obviously a lot of shared respect and affection between the directors (who were often also owners of the factory) and the workforce. Start-rite's director James Hanly was widely known as Mr Jim, whilst at Edwards & Holmes, Peter Holmes recalls: 'In our business my grandfather was always called Sir Henry, my father was Mr Geoffrey and I was Mr Peter.'

Obviously as time moved on attitudes changed, as neatly summed up by Ray Carpenter who started in the industry in the 1960s and now works at Florida: 'I can have a laugh and a joke with Simon [Goodman]. I'd never have spoken to the factory owners like that when I started; you really had to know your place then. It's one of the biggest changes I've noticed. At Norvic I didn't even know who the boss was…but I did know his chauffeur.'

J. Henry Sexton with his Rolls Royce, c1930

Lasting Memories

John St Quintin (designer) recalls the formality of the shoe trade: 'In the industry we would always refer to our senior work colleagues as "Mr". So, for example, at Kirbys I always called Harry Barter, the sales rep for both Kirbys and Shorten & Armes "Mr Barter", but John Kirby was always called "Mr Jack".'

John St Quintin, c1956

Nigel Brown started at Start-rite in 1974: 'James Hanly (director and chairman) was always known as Mr Jim. He always used to walk through the making room and talk to us. When he retired David White took over. He was always involved in the social club and was the goalkeeper for the Start-rite football team. He always insisted on being called David unless I saw him about union matters when he was always Mr White.'

Nigel Brown, 2013

John Barrett recalls joining his father Geoffrey, who owned Shorten & Armes, in the shoe trade: 'My father thought that it was important that I learnt the trade outside his own factory. He didn't want his employees to say that they had taught the boss's son. So my training included attendance at a college in the south of France that was in a shoemaking area. I arrived with my schoolboy French to find that no one else spoke English. I was there nine months and am proud to say that I did my final exams in French. I then went to Milan where I took a course of about the same length in shoe design at the Ars Sutoria School, which is still an international technical institute of art, footwear and leather goods. I then worked at K Shoes in Kendal in their design department and from there moved to a retail store called Bentalls, at Kingston upon Thames, where I worked in a shoe department. I then returned to Norwich and did an evening course at Norwich City College and Art School on St George's, where they ran shoe-making courses. In the meantime I had joined my father at Shorten & Armes where I specialised in sales.'

John Barrett, c1958

Peter Metcalf, recalls the 1960s: 'There was a strong hierarchy in the factory. The foremen and managers really were in positions of authority and when a director appeared, we almost saluted them!'

Peter Metcalf, c2000

Piecework

'We were on piecework so you were only paid for what you did, but you could earn a good income if you worked hard. So believe you me we worked as hard as we could.' (Betty Barnard)

Until the 1990s the majority of manual workers in a shoe factory were paid on a piecework basis i.e. their pay was determined according to the amount they produced. Vic Hopes explains how the system operated at Sexton, Son & Everard in the 1960s: 'Shoes were generally made in blocks of 12 and with each block of 12 was a work ticket, which told you the name of the shoe and what it looked like together with a perforated list of the various operations which were needed to make the shoe. Each perforated section was known as a coupon. The operator took the coupon relating to a task when he completed it and put it in his tin. The tins were then collected on a daily basis, and in the office we worked out how much each operative had earned.'

In general, new entrants would be paid a fixed wage until they were up to speed, but once on piecework each worker's 'average' would be calculated over a period (normally six months). This would be used to calculate the amount owed for holiday pay, and also to determine how much wages had been lost if machines were down for long periods. It would also be used to calculate how much was owed to youngsters who had been given study leave.

Although the unions did much to regulate pay agreements and ensure workers received the correct pay for the job, no system is infallible, and inevitably there were a number of pros and cons to the system.

One of the main advantages of piecework was also one of its main disadvantages – namely if you were quick you could earn a lot of money, but if you weren't you didn't. This led to a number of paradoxes. Arthur Holmes (cost accountant at Start-rite, 1950 – 1986), remembers that the two highest paid factory workers at Start-rite were the girls who boxed the shoes. He recalls: 'You couldn't see their hands move because they were going so fast. They were like greased lightning. You could hardly bear to look at them.'

But speed did not always depend on your own ability, it was also affected by the job you had been allocated, but there were ways around this. For example, when Nigel Rudling reviewed work practices at the CWS factory in the 1970s, one of the first things he discovered was that if the girls in the closing room were sent a difficult job, they'd send it back to the overseer without doing anything. They then ordered more work hoping that it would be easier!

Shaft-driven machinery, Walter Edwards, c1925

Although in general there was much camaraderie in the work place, and there are numerous examples of colleagues helping each other, piecework could generate a work ethic best described as 'every man for themselves'. For example, trainees in the machine room at Norvic in the late 1970s recalled there was a tendency for some of the older women to allocate the youngsters the work which took longer to do. Whilst Bob Drake, who worked in the making room at Sextons in the 1960s, recollects: 'If you ran into trouble the only person who would help would be your supervisor...everyone was on piecework, so even your mates wouldn't stop because if they did they lost money.'

Another flaw with the piecework system was that in a bid to increase their output, workers often ignored health and safety regulations. This covers a whole range of situations. For example, Muriel Critten recalls that when she joined Edwards & Holmes in 1942 she worked at their temporary factory based in Starling Road. As was typical of many factories the machinists all worked in a row, and a line shaft was used to distribute power via a belt which rotated a wheel on their individual machines. Muriel recalls that if the belt that fed your machine slipped off the wheel you wouldn't dream of stopping your colleagues, who of course were all on piecework. Instead, the girls would just get a stick and bend down and slip the belt back on whilst it was still whizzing around at great speed. Meanwhile, in the press room many men lost fingers because they depressed knives when their hands were under the cutting edge, simply because they were trying to get the work out as quickly as possible.

Some jobs, such as designing, paid a daily rate. Similarly if you were promoted to the role of foreman or manager you would be paid a set rate, which paradoxically was often less than an individual could earn under the piecework system. Nevertheless, some wanted the promotion as it meant they were moving on, and they also saw the advantage of both earning sick pay and taking part in the company's pension scheme. But as Arthur Holmes observes: 'It was often the case that workmen who were really good at their jobs and earning a lot for doing them didn't want to be foremen. You see on piecework they could earn more doing the job than overseeing others and of course they had a lot less hassle. This could create friction if the workers thought they were better at the job than the foreman was.'

The other advantage of being on an annual salary was that you knew how much you would be earning. In the shoe industry work was cyclical throughout the year. So typically at Start-rite, which made children's shoes, the factory would be very busy from March to August and you could earn overtime, but from September to February it was much quieter. As Keith Richardson, who started work as a clicker in 1982 reflects: 'In

Stockroom, Start-rite, c1970

the quiet months we'd be given a reduced amount of work, which meant that we could only earn about three-quarters of our normal money. It was great when I was single and finishing on a Wednesday evening… but not so good when I had a mortgage and a family.' As much as possible, the factories did not lay off workers in the quieter months, instead they were put on short time. This arrangement suited the employers, who didn't want to lose good staff, and the workers who didn't want to lose their jobs. Additionally, if one factory was on slow time but another had lots of work, they helped each other out. This was often achieved by either 'lending' workers (with their agreement) to another factory, or simply by transferring the work between factories.

Piecework generally died out in the early 1990s, by which time the majority of shoe factories had closed. Peter Metcalf, factory manager at Florida, believes that prior to then levels of payment had failed to take full account of greater productivity brought about by improvements in technology. For example, by the early 1960s the clickers in most factories were cutting uppers with presses. They were always well paid, but in the early 1960s their wages escalated relative to their workmates. This anomaly occurred because the unions had set a rate for cutting by hand which was based upon the complexity of the upper. Put simply: the more difficult it was to cut, the longer it took and the more you were paid. When presses were introduced the clickers used press knives, which were just placed on the leather and depressed. As a result it didn't matter how complex the design was, each upper took the same amount of time to cut, and so they should have been paid a set amount to cut an upper. But they weren't, as explained by Peter: 'Clickers using presses got a third of the original rate, which meant that they were still paid a lot more for cutting intricately shaped uppers which could now be produced in the same time as a simple job. Although they were paid less for each upper they were working much faster, and as they were on piecework their wages went up and up. As a result, a technological advance which could have reduced costs significantly only had a marginal effect.'

Janet Metcalf recalls that piecework was discontinued at Florida around 1992. By then she had no doubt that it was outdated. She reflects that: 'Management wanted to do away with it because the rates agreed were just too high. They still paid a good wage but we didn't have, say, one person earning £50 more than everyone else.'

Piecework played an important part in the history of Norwich's shoe trade. As with any payment system it had its good and bad points. In particular, if you worked hard you could earn an excellent wage. However, piecework was synonymous with manual factory workers who despite being skilled and industrious, were not always given the respect they deserved.

Maybe the position is best summed up by Betty Barnard, who worked in the footwear industry between 1940 and 1956: 'In the 1970s I went for an interview for an office job at Jarrolds…and got it. I worked there until I retired in 1985. I liked the work but it was very different to my time in the shoe trade. When I worked in the factories we were on piecework, and so we'd arrive and start work straight away. But in the office everyone arrived, had a cup of tea, smoked a cigarette and then they had a chat. I sat there twiddling my thumbs wanting to get going. I used to think: "All us factory girls used to look up to you. Why didn't I know this then, because it would've made me feel better with myself." You see there was a real stigma attached to being a factory girl. You'd hear people mutter: "Well of course she works in a factory", as if you were nothing. But in the factories I worked with great people who worked really hard and took real pride in doing an excellent job.'

Betty Barnard (back row left), Great Yarmouth, Meadows, c1955

Lasting Memories

Jenny Perry recalls her mother Trixie Bussey who worked at Bally (Haldinsteins): 'Although not the best mathematician in the world when she came home with her "coupons" she sat down and worked out how much she'd earned to the last farthing.'

Brian Lambert worked at Bally until 1982, when he headed up their Technical Department: 'I started at the Bally factory in 1953 doing quite menial jobs and was paid a fixed wage of £2 5s. for a 48-hour week. After about five months I was given my first "proper" job, which involved applying natural latex to the fore-part of the shoe. There were two of us on it when I began but the other man left and I was asked to do it on my own – which I did. After a few weeks, once I'd mastered the job, I went onto piecework and I remember the foreman coming after me a week later and saying to me: "Do you know that you've earned £5 this week? That's a man's money." It seems incredible today but piecework was calculated down to the last farthing and in fact for that job I was earning 1¼ d. per dozen pairs. At the time we worked a five-and-a-half day week. Eventually I was moved on to the heeling department. By now I was on £15 a week, which to me was a huge sum. I was able to earn such sums because I was so fast.'

Bob Drake recalls the shortcomings of piecework: 'In the 1960s whilst working at Sextons I was given a job on the double-pot seat laster. The laster got its name because at the top of the machine were two pots and each one did a different sized nail. I was now working on the track where we made the highest quality shoes in the factory. For example we worked on Mary Quant's Charlie Boots. It was my worst nightmare because nobody could train me how to do it. I was doing a thousand pairs of shoes a day, and each 12 pairs of shoes were different and you had to keep changing the machine. The fellas working on the other two tracks were doing shoes that were already moulded so all they had to do was put them in the machine, the nails would come down and that was the finish. But on this machine I couldn't earn a great deal of money because I had to do a lot of pincer work by hand, which slowed me up.'

Janet Metcalf started doing piecework at Florida in the 1960s: 'I couldn't believe it. I was earning really good money but not only that, if we wanted extra time off we were given it. I remember on one occasion I had Friday afternoon off just to get my hair done. I thought it was great. That said there was a lot of give and take. The Goodman family were very fair to us and allowed us time off if possible, but at the same time if we had lots of extra work to do, and needed to work on a Saturday, we would all go in.'

Janet Metcalf (with flowers) retiring, 2004

Lasting Memories

Jean Woods worked in the shoe industry between 1956 and 1995: 'When I was on piecework, every night I'd come home and work my money out. We had no basic pay it was all piecework, so if we did nothing we got nothing. The only time I got paid other than under the coupon method was when I did repairs and recuts on work that someone else had messed up. If this happened the supervisor would sign me on and I would get my average piecework rate for the time it took me.

'About every six months your average would be recalculated. It was important to keep it high because it was used to calculate your holiday pay and things like that. So when you couldn't work because your machines were down it was quite annoying. Although to be fair if it was down a long time they'd give you other jobs such as table work. Even though the rates for such jobs were much lower than my normal pay I'd still get my average and I'd be quite happy with that. You had a set rate for different jobs and even in the 1980s it was calculated in farthings, which made it quite difficult to work out how much you were owed.'

Jean Woods with her twin girls, c1968

Training

Shoeworkers were trained at Norwich City College and Art School and of course in the factories themselves.

College

'When I left school in 1945, at the age of 14, I started work as a trainee pattern maker at Edwards & Holmes. I used to go to Norwich City College and Art School, which was where the Norwich University College of the Arts is now, on day release to study shoemaking. I was entitled to go because I'd left school at 14. We did a bit of English and then had trade training. At the time there was a big boot and shoe department there. The machines they taught on ran on a line shaft and belt system, and so there was a great big engine at the end of the row that ran all the machines.' (Bruce Rampley)

In 1892 Norwich had become one of the first centres in Britain to give technical education, outside the factories, in the theory and practice of shoemaking. At this time the City did not possess a technical college, and so classes were held in hired rooms. By 1899 work had started on the City's new Municipal Technical Institute on St George's Street (the building now houses the Norwich University College of the Arts), and by 1901 classes were held here. The new institute incorporated a boot and shoe department which offered students courses that covered all aspects of footwear manufacturing. The aim was to provide theoretical instruction to supplement workplace training.

By the late 1920s it had become the normal practice for the principal shoe firms in the City to release selected apprentices and students for two half-day attendances each week of the term. By 1941 the institute had been rechristened as the Norwich City College and Art School.

During WWII classes were discontinued and machinery was taken from the college to replace that lost in the blitzed factories. Nevertheless, after the war, under the direction of George Burrows, classes were soon underway again so that Bruce and his colleagues were able to resume training. At this time a small factory within the college buildings, known as the monastery, was equipped with the latest equipment manufactured by the British United Shoe Machinery Company Ltd (the major supplier of machines to the industry).

The college provided excellent training and in 1965 received particular praise from the British Footwear Manufacturers' Federation for its use of analytical training methods (developed by Arthur Nobbs and Brian Austin) in the lasting and making departments. Arthur was just one of many excellent tutors employed at the college who are still remembered by their pupils today. Others include Wilfred Sparks and George Brandish.

Plaque, Technical Institute, St George's Street, 1899

Norwich University College of the Arts, 2012

Like Wilfred Sparks, a number of lecturers continued to work in the factories whilst teaching evening classes. These included Brian Lambert, who started work at Bally in 1953 at the age of 15. Having left school with few qualifications he discovered that doing well at college was an ideal way to impress his managers. He recalls: '… I quite excelled considering I was a lad from a secondary modern school.' Initially Brian went on half-day release to the college where he had the opportunity to do all aspects of shoe work. At college Brian not only learnt about technical shoemaking skills but also studied a wide range of subjects including the history of shoes and about the shoemaking areas. When he was 18, Brian's half-day release came to the end, and so he made the decision to attend night classes for two or three nights a week, eventually progressing to study for his BBSI (British Boot and Shoe Institute) exams, which were considered the equivalent of a degree in shoemaking. It was a hard graft as Brian was also working 45 hours a week in the factory, and for a time instructed on practical shoemaking skills at the college. Despite these challenges when he was 33 Brian became an Associate of the BBSI. Brian recollects that: 'Doing well in college brought me to the attention of the management, and when I was about 19 I was asked, if I wanted to work in the technical department.' This move started him on a path which in 1974 led to him being appointed as the department's head.

Although in the 1950s Avis Brown recalls that Edwards & Holmes paid for her to attend college one day a week, women often had less chance to extend their education. Janet Metcalf, who started work in the Florida shoe room c1960, was disappointed that shoe-room workers weren't entitled to day release. She remembers: 'The machinists all went, but it was thought that our jobs weren't skilled enough, something that I really disagreed with.'

As the numbers employed in shoe manufacturing fell, so did the demand for courses. In the academic year 1969/70 the number of hours taught fell below 40,000 for the first time since 1948/9. In 1972 the Footwear Department ceased to exist as an independent unit. Subsequently at the end of the 1974/5 academic year all provision for footwear education was discontinued at the college.

The former 'monastery' building, 2012

Lasting Memories

Bruce Rampley, recalls studying in the late 1940s: 'One of the tutors who taught at the college in the evening was Wilfred Sparks. I remember that he was always immaculately dressed. He even wore spats, which was quite unusual after WWII. He was meticulous. He was the technical director at Sextons, where it was reported that once he came in first thing in the morning and noticed something wrong with a shoe on a rack. He went over to examine it and was still there late in the afternoon wearing his outdoor coat. He was dedicated to his work and was even spotted at the Hippodrome Theatre, on St Giles' Street, reading the "Shoe and Leather News" in the interval.'

Derek Rye started training as a clicker at W. H. H. Clarke in 1964: 'Once a week I went on day release to college at St George's where I was taught with other trainee clickers. We had a very good teacher there, called Mr Brandish, who was very tolerant. You had to go to the factory to clock in at 8 o' clock and then you had to be at college by 9 o'clock. That was the easy part. Problems started after the morning break when we went to a little café along St George's that had a pinball machine. You had to get so many points on this machine to claim a monetary prize, and so if we were trying to work up our points we sometimes overstayed and were late back to college...but Mr Brandish was very forgiving.'

John Thain trained at Norvic as a trainee pattern maker in 1966: 'We used to go to City College on day release to learn the technical part of the job. You used to go back in the evenings if you wanted to do the more practical side of things, such as pattern cutting. The youngsters went there from most of the factories so it was a great place to make friends. I still work with a chap I met at the College. When I was there one of the teachers was called George Brandish, who also worked in the pattern room at Norvic. His son, also called George, and daughter-in-law both taught in the department…it was quite a family affair.'

Mike Copland worked at the Bowhill & Elliott slipper factory in the early 1960s: 'In the evenings I studied for all of my diplomas in shoemaking and even won a prize for being the top of the class – I think it was the only time it had been awarded to someone who worked in a slipper factory!'

Arthur Nobbs, 1976

John St Quintin, designer in the shoe industry 1948 – 1981: 'When I was training [late 1940s to the early 1950s] I went to college in the evenings. At the time it was on St George's. On a Friday night we used to crowd down there. So many of us wanted to learn the trade there was real competition for places. I was initially taught by Mr Wilfred Sparks, who was renowned for being very particular. He would arrive at the college wearing spats and a pin-striped suit and carrying a little briefcase, he always looked very smart. He was very strict, but was very good. Another excellent tutor, George Brandish, not only taught me how to design shoes but also how to cut a pattern so that my designs could be made into shoes. I went back after I finished my national service in the Air Force [1955/6] when I remember being taught by Arthur Nobbs who was a lovely man and a great teacher. I can still see him at the front of the class bouncing the skeleton of a foot up and down and teaching us about the structure of a foot. As a footwear designer it was essential that I knew about both the function of a shoe and how it was constructed. To be a good designer you have to be both an artist and technician.'

'I spent about six months being trained to be a folder in the [Norvic] factory in Norwich on St George's. The training was good. They had one of their best folders show us what to do. There was a lot to learn. Not only how to operate the machine but also how to do things like hand folding. We were overseen by supervisors who were more than strict, in fact they were very severe. Where I learnt folding the supervisor was lethal. If you were just one little bit out, even when you were training, she'd prod you really hard. She really did lay into you, I still remember how painful it was. But they could do that then [1956]. You didn't go home & tell your parents…they'd just say that you probably deserved it anyway.' (Jean Woods)

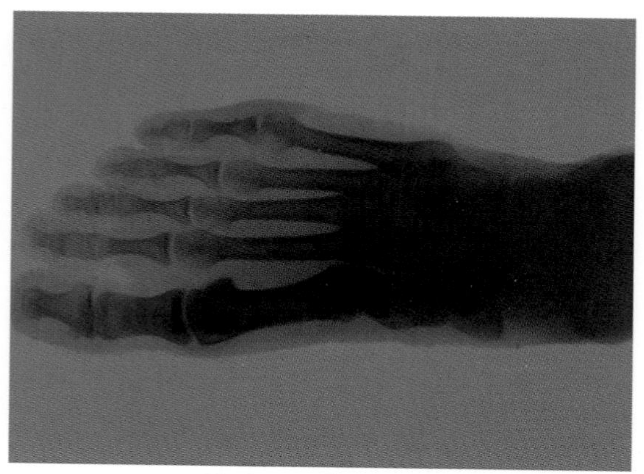

Understanding the structure of the foot

Whether or not workers attended college, workplace training was an essential part of their education. Jean's experience was fairly typical of factory workers but was very different to those taken on at higher levels. For example, in 1948 Martin Miller, who was in his early 20s at the time, began a marketing job at Norvic. He recalls that Norvic wanted all of their staff in sales and management to know everything possible about producing and selling shoes. Hence he started his career by spending time in all of the production departments, followed by a six-month stint split between three Norvic shops and with the travellers (salesmen who sold shoes to independent shops and stores). Similarly Peter Holmes, whose family owned Edwards & Holmes, spent his first year going around different departments. He recollects: 'I spent all year making one pair of shoes. They looked a bit of a mess, but they were all my own work, so I was very proud of them!'

Pattern-making machine

Some entrants who came from less privileged backgrounds were trained in a similar manner. For example, John St Quintin joined Barfield & Richardson in 1946 when he was 16 years old. He subsequently spent his first years going through all of the departments, including pattern making, clicking, the machine room and the trimming room, at the end of which he became a trainee pattern cutter and designer. To this day John is very grateful that his mentor, Len Waspe, gave him the opportunity to train in this way. John subsequently worked in the industry until 1981 during which time he designed many beautiful shoes including the white-silver dance shoes worn by Olivia Newton-John when she starred in the 1978 film 'Grease'.

A post-sewing machine

Norvic In-House Training Programme

The illustrations in this section come from slides used by Norvic in the 1970s as part of their comprehensive staff training scheme.

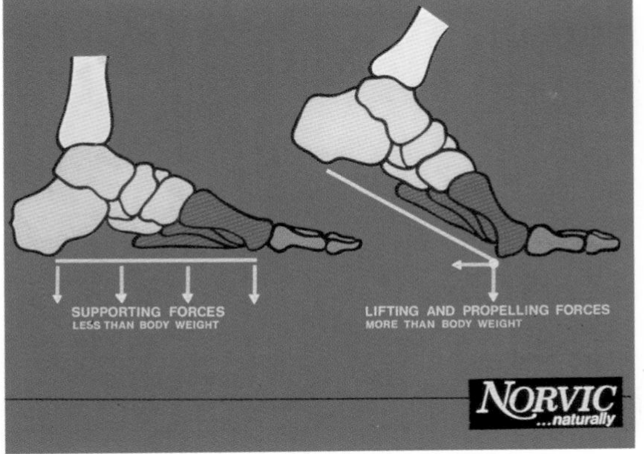

Appreciation of the forces involved in walking

Selecting materials

Clicking using a two-handed press

Closing the uppers

Lasting

Moulding soles

Machine room, Haldinsteins, Christmas 1921

'Christmas in the Florida factory was fantastic. No man would ever dare go in the closing room. The best that happened was you lost your tie and the worst was you lost your trousers. We had congas around the factory. Somebody used to dress up as Miss Piggy complete with pigs' trotters. The tinsel paper hanging around everywhere was the gold foil we used to write Van-Dal on the sock. It was real gold…so was probably the most expensive tinsel in the world. We used to gather it up at the end of the festivities and sell it as reclaimed gold.' (Simon Goodman)

Howlett & White brass band, c1910

Fun in the workplace, the works outing, the social club and the warning given to all young lads that they entered the machine room with its female operatives at their peril...were all an inherent part of working in the shoe factories.

In the workplace itself the radio would often be on. Jean Smith remembers that at Edwards & Holmes in the 1940s: '"Music While You Work" was played on the radio for half an hour. We used to pay sixpence and then write the name of a song on a piece of paper and put it in a tin. If your song came up you won all of the money.' At Norvic they went one better and their club room, which was located at 54 Pitt Street, played host to 'Workers Playtime' (a variety programme transmitted three times a week on the radio by the BBC between 1941 and 1964, from a canteen 'somewhere in Britain'). Mike Quinton recalls: 'We had people such as Charlie Chester perform there. When the show was transmitted the social club was packed with around 400 people.'

The major factories all had social clubs which organised a range of activities for the workforce. These ranged from Howlett & White's brass band (which had been established by the end of the 19th century) to darts leagues and of course the factory football team. For those less active, Start-rite had a horticultural club or you could go to watch the football rather than play it.

Which neatly bring us on to an important part of factory life – namely the 'works outing'. John St Quintin recalls his time at Barfield & Richardson (1948 – 53): 'We used to go on great outings to places like Skegness and Clacton. We all headed off in three coaches. One would take the men from the making and finishing rooms, another was for the ladies who worked in the machine and trimming rooms and the third was for the office staff together with the pattern cutters and designers. It was very much "Upstairs Downstairs".'

Norvic Social Club, Pitt Street, 1938

Meadows, Great Yarmouth, c1954

Bally, summer outing, c1960

Barfield & Richardson, Skegness, 1949

Meadows, Peacock Street, c1952

Kirbys, summer outing, c1924

Barfield & Richardson, Clacton, 1952

Ponds, summer outing, 1905

Southalls, Southend, c1953

Meadows, Great Yarmouth, c1955

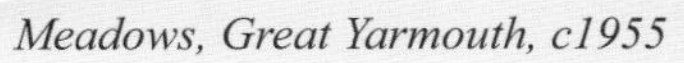

Meadows, Great Yarmouth, c1955

Start-rite, Santa Susana, 1992

Edwards & Holmes, 'Miss Esdelle' & Lady Holmes, 1949

R. Roberts, Christmas party, c1960

Florida, Norwood Rooms, 1961

Florida, 'Miss Florida' with David Goodman, c1960

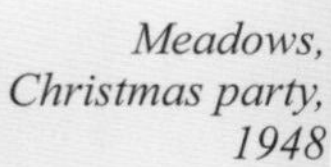

Meadows, Christmas party, 1948

Sextons, Miss Sexton, 1961

Sextons, children's Christmas party, c1959

Although trips to the coast or to the theatre were the most favoured destinations, Jean Smith recalls that in 1952 eight coach loads went from Edwards & Holmes to visit the Festival of Britain. Jean also recalls meeting up with chums from work to go dancing at the Samson & Hercules (Tombland) or the Lido (Aylsham Road). In the 1960s when Jean was at Norvic they even used to go to Blackpool for the weekend. Then in 1989 trips at Start-rite reached new heights when Nigel Brown and his wife Avis organised a week's trip to mainland Spain. Nigel recalls: 'In the end 42 people went. People used to say: "Why do you want to go on holiday with him?" But it was great because you saw a totally different side of your workmates. When we went everyone always wanted to stay together which sometimes made it difficult to find a big enough space on the beach.' The trip was much enjoyed and the couple subsequently organised several trips including a few coach tours and more visits to Spain.

The Start-rite club building was based on Romany Road. Although the building was no longer used after 1986, the social club survived until the end of 2011. Keith Richardson, who joined the firm in 1982, recalls that as a young lad he often went to the club house after work, not only for a drink but also to play snooker and table tennis. Additionally once a month a disco was held here. Although the smaller factories didn't have the same facilities they still hosted social events. Betty Barnard recollects meeting her husband at such a gathering: 'At the side of Shorten & Armes was an old building like a Nissen hut. When we returned to the factory after the war [c1945] the girls used to get hold of a record player and organise dances there, and that's where I met my husband George. You see George's uncle worked at the factory, and not only did he use to supply a lot of the records but he also roped in all the lads he knew into coming.'

Other social events organised by the shoe companies included an annual dinner dance, often held at the Norwood Rooms. This was the perfect opportunity to 'crown' the company's beauty queen. For many years the larger factories, including Norvic (Howlett & White), Florida and Edwards & Holmes, all ran beauty competitions for their female workers. At Christmas a number of factories held parties for their employees' families, whilst some even took over the Theatre Royal for an afternoon. Maurice Land, whose father worked at Sextons recalls: 'Around 1960 I recall seeing Mother Goose and at one rather sad point in the performance one little boy shouted: "I want my mummy." Of course this was why you only went to the pantomime when you were over eight years old. Before this you went to a Christmas party where they served orange squash in bottles and trifle in those little individual greaseproof cartons.'

The camaraderie of the shoe factories is rarely found in today's world, as nostalgically recalled by Keith Richardson: 'The factory workers were a close-knit group, and you just don't get that sort of community feel in workplaces today. I miss a lot of the banter and even most of the wind ups...but not all of them!'

Florida (Van-Dal) v Edwards & Holmes, 1990

Lasting Memories

Nigel & Avis Brown, Start-rite, 1997

Nigel Brown remembers Start-rite's social club: 'I started in the making room at Start-rite in 1974. I hadn't been there long when I joined a trip to see Norwich City away. There were around 65 men working in the making room at the time and around 53 of us went. We used to go at least twice a year to league games. The clicking room used to do the same. On Friday nights we used to have between 100 and 120 people at the club on Romany Road and they were all members of the internal darts' league. Every department had at least one team. It was packed up there. It was very much a part of Start-rite.'

Betty Barnard (front row left), Meadows, 1954

Betty Barnard still remembers days out in the 1950s: 'The factories used to organise annual works outing. We often went on a coach to the coast and then got taken to a show in the evening. We looked forward to going all year. We worked together closely so when we had the trips we were like kids out of school.'

Health and Safety

'I remember going into the press room in my early days [1950s] and saying to a chap: "You've lost the top of your finger." He replied: "Yes, everybody who works here has lost the top of their finger." I looked around and they really had. You see they used to put the knife under the press then as the press came down they tried to adjust it and caught a finger. They did it once and they never did it again.' (Arthur Holmes)

One of the biggest changes in workplace legislation since the 1970s has been the increased emphasis on health and safety issues. Before the legislation was widely adopted factories could be lethal places to work. Not only were shoe factories exceptionally noisy and smelly, the buildings they occupied were often antiquated. Moreover, the workforce used dangerous chemicals, whilst much of the machinery was inherently unsafe. When you also consider the fact that operators were on piecework, hence working as quickly as possible, it is no wonder that accidents frequently occurred.

It was in 1949, when he was 15 years old, that Ron Green first experienced many of the health and safety deficiencies of the shoe factories. At the time many still used a line shaft to distribute power to the machinery, which itself could be dangerous, as explained by Ron: 'When I worked in the press room [at Bally] the first person in often started up the machinery. We had one big motor and a steel pole ran across the top of the room on which were drums or wheels. From these ran wide leather belts, around two-and-a-half-inches wide, down to each machine. Some belts were well over 20-feet long. You couldn't get leather that long so each shorter portion of leather was sewn together with catgut, which passed though wire reinforced holes (eyes). That became my job. There were four or five joins in each belt. If one broke and you were anywhere near you could get torn skin from the flying belts. Those long belts with all those joins would make a rhythmic noise "click, click, click" as they went over the drum above and the wheel on the machine. Then there was the "bang, bang, bang" of the eight presses. My hearing now suffers because of it.'

But the hazards associated with the cacophonous sounds of the press room were just the beginning. This really was the most perilous room in the factory, as again illustrated by Ron: 'At Ballys, towards the Tombland end, a whole new department was built with a glass roof. All down both sides were big presses around eight-feet long, big enough to place a whole hide under. In front of each was a table which was

Press room, Walter Edwards, 1925

the same length. There was a platform in between on which the operator stood. I got a bang over the lug because I stepped on one of these platforms and saw several innocent lads receive the same. You see at the side of each platform, and level with it, was a long treadle which operated the press. Put one foot wrong and a man could lose parts, or all, of his fingers. We used to call these machines "Big Jumping Presses". There was a ruddy great bang each time one came down on the cutter, which was a cast iron thing the shape of a sole; it was something like the pastry cutters my mum used. You had to place the cutters on the leather to make sure you got the most out of it. The cutters had a rubber guard on the top, but not on the bottom, so if you accidentally stood on the treadle, which operated the press and pushed down the cutters, you can see why you'd lose a digit.'

The jump press was particularly dangerous. Mike Copland, who has been making footwear since 1963, recalls one such press was used by Syd Thompson at his small manufacturing unit on Golden Dog Lane. The press stood on a table and two operators would stand on either side. Each operative had a round block of wood and worked with press knives that were made out of solid-cast steel and were around six inches deep. As described by Mike: 'When the press came down on one side it would go up on the other, a bit like an oil pump. When yours went up you'd put your knife under quickly and hold it in place until it had been pressed down. Meanwhile the guy on the other side would be doing the opposite. If you left your finger under the knife it was gone.'

Mike still works with a press at his Norwich-based factory (Broadland Slippers in Renson Close). However, current legislation decrees that all presses are operated using two hands, an approach that guarantees your hands cannot be under the press when it comes down.

If you worked in a shoe factory you couldn't avoid its tumultuous din. Despite the racket no one wore ear muffs. One of the noisiest machines in the making room, and indeed in the entire factory, was the pounder which was used to flatten all of the pleats around the bottom of a shoe after it had been lasted. It was a wheel with washers on it. You'd hold the shoe against it as it rotated around at a terrific pace and it vibrated onto your hands. Lenford Laband, who worked in the industry from 1946 until 1990, recalls that you could stand in Colegate and hear their 'dreadful scream' from the Norvic factory on St George's. Even worse was that when the operators finished working on the machine their hands continued to vibrate and their fingers tingle because it had stopped the blood circulation. Eventually its use was banned.

Although the women's rooms were generally safer than the men's making and press rooms, horrendous accidents did occur. One of the worst accidents seen by Jean Woods was caused by a toe puff machine when she worked at Start-rite in the 1990s. Before operating the machine a girl would put the toe puff in position on the upper and place it on the machine. She then pulled a handle down which applied pressure and heat for a predetermined number of seconds, the heat

Making room, Walter Edwards, c1925

being necessary to stick the toe puff onto the leather. As Jean recalls: 'On one occasion a girl got her hand caught in the machine, and because it was on a timer she couldn't get it out until the time was up. It was horrendous. I still remember her screaming. After that she was off for a very long time.' The mechanism was subsequently altered so that it couldn't lock if anything thick, such as a finger, was caught in it.

Another big issue for the industry was the use of solvents. Avis Brown recollects that when she started at Edwards & Holmes in the 1950s, health and safety didn't extend much beyond the provision of fire extinguishers. In the finishing room they always had four Bunsen burners lit. This was despite the fact that they also worked with flammable liquids which were used, for example, to make final repairs on shoes. Avis still vividly remembers a colleague who put some wax on her knife and took it over to a Bunsen burner to heat it up. She then accidentally dripped the hot wax into a jar of flammable liquid and it blew up into her face, hair and clothes. Avis recall: 'She was completely alight. She just ran around until someone caught her and threw a coat over her. Her daughter worked upstairs and she came down screaming. It was horrendous, but there was no question of compensation because she knew that the liquid was highly inflammable, and she shouldn't have taken the boiling hot wax near it. Although she recovered, her face was badly burnt. She never returned to work. It was lucky that the whole factory didn't burn down because all four tables were alight.'

On top of all this, many of the buildings themselves were dilapidated. Although a number of the factories were rebuilt after WWII some companies were located in very old premises that simply were not fit for purpose. One such property was the CWS footwear factory located on St John's Street (Mountergate). Nigel Rudling, who started to work there in the 1970s, recalls that factory maintenance costs were horrendous. In particular there was a lot of asbestos in the building especially in the heating system, which was bad enough, but it was even worse if you were of a slight build. Nigel recollects: 'Every summer we used to find the smallest person in the factory and send them to work with the maintenance engineer. Their job was to climb through a tiny hole, around 15 inches across, and scrape it out.'

However, the shoe factories would not have been any more dangerous than other manufacturing companies operating at the same time. Health and safety policies have greatly improved the factory environment of today. The huge clunking presses have gone as have the screaming machines. Nowadays machinery guards and protective ear muffs are mandatory whilst the use of chemicals is strictly controlled. Although many bemoan the bureaucracy of the legislation few would want to return to the days when accidents were such a common part of working life.

Clickers using two-handed presses, Norvic, c1965

Lasting Memories

Simon Goodman describes the constant din in a shoe factory: 'The two things that epitomise a shoe factory are noise and smell. The biggest changes in factories today are those two. Health and safety policies have made a huge improvement to the factory environment…but even though noise levels have reduced you have to get used to them. When I go around the factory today I still half lip read. On top of the machine noises we also used to play music in the factory and we also had a Tannoy system. It all added up.'

Ron Green remembers a lucky escape: 'In the 1950s I was once on a huge sandpaper roller. A lever would dislocate the machine from these belts but momentum meant that the machine would still keep rolling. On this occasion I'd lifted up the guard while it was still moving and my pullover sleeve was caught on the roller. It took the sleeve right off at the shoulder so quick that I didn't feel a thing. This clogged up the machine which stopped it just before the sandpaper roller made contact with the under part of my wrist.'

Brian Lambert recalls working with 'flesh-eating latex' in 1953: 'My first "proper job" involved applying natural latex to the fore-part of the shoe. In those days we never wore protective clothing in the factories so I soon found out that I was allergic to latex. It used to get down my fingernails and stripped my flesh back. It got so that I was going to see the nurse, who we had in the factory, every day to get my hands dressed. So in the end she said that I'd have to come off it. I never thought about putting on gloves. In any case it was quite fiddly work so I don't think I'd have been able to do it wearing them.'

Billy Critten describes a common industrial injury: 'Many workers suffered from carpal tunnel syndrome which was caused by pressure on the median nerve [the nerve in the wrist that supplies feeling and movement to parts of the hand] which often resulted in weakness or muscle damage in the hand and fingers. It particularly affected workers in the making room where part of the job was to push the shoes up for them to be stitched. They could only do the job for a short period of time because once the wrist went they had to be taken off. That said whilst doing the work they could earn terrific money, and afterwards at least they could claim for an industrial injury.'

Brian Lambert explains why it was not much safer working at home: 'At Bally in the 1960s we had some heel covering done by outworkers in their own homes. Nobody seemed to question having inflammable solvents in their kitchens in those days! We relied on people using their common sense – although I do know people who used to smoke whilst they were doing it. It doesn't bear thinking about now.'

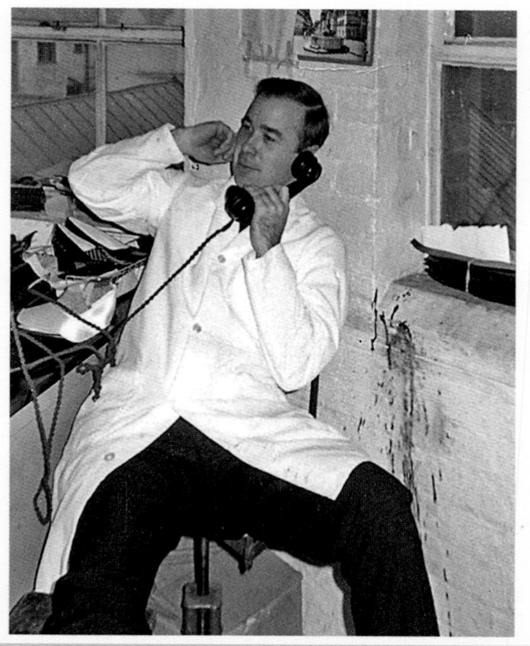

Brian Lambert, Queen Street factory, Bally, c1960

The Unions

In the latter half of the 19th century, the combined effect of Norwich's isolation from other industrial conurbations and the plentiful supply of labour from the countryside, resulted in Norwich wages being below the national average. The bargaining power of workers in the shoe industry was further undermined by the fact that much employment was seasonal, and so the manufacturers supplemented their factory staff with outworkers who could be hired and fired at will. In such an environment attempts by trades unions to exert any kind of power met with little success.

Nevertheless, the National Union of Boot and Shoe Operatives (NUBSO) was founded in February 1874. By April they had opened 35 branches in all major shoemaking centres, which of course included Norwich. Although their formation initially had little impact on the City, during 1890 – 91 they were one of a number of organisations that contributed to an upsurge in union activity in Norwich.

In 1891, in response to such activity, the Norwich shoe manufacturers followed the example already set in Leicester, and formed the Norwich Footwear Manufacturers' Association (NFMA). Its aim was to give manufacturers, like operatives, the ability to deal with disputes and settle wage problems collectively. As a result, in 1897 they were ready to fight the shoe operatives who joined together to strike for a minimum wage, a 54-hour week and 'constraint' on the part of employers in the employment of boys (i.e. cheap labour). The strike, which lasted from March to September, not only ended in failure but it cost the union £15,000 and a huge loss of influence amongst the operatives. It was not until 1908, after the national union had committed around £100,000 to the cause, that a minimum wage was finally agreed in Norwich.

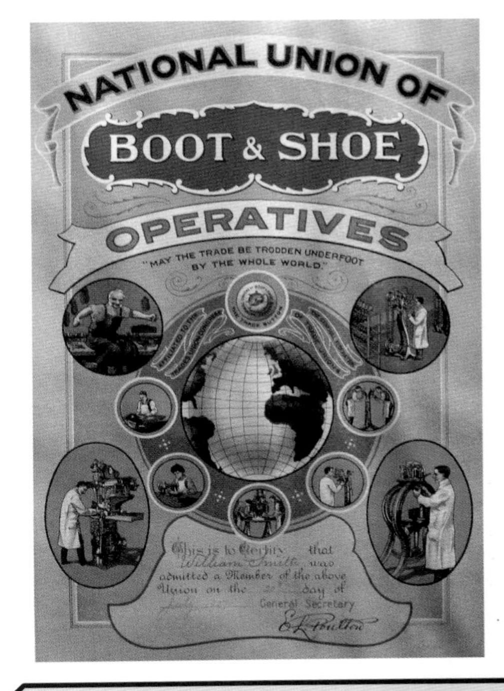

Did you know?

In 1877 the Select Committee on Intemperance was puzzled by the fact that although Norwich had one of the highest proportions of public houses per head of population in the country, it had the lowest incidence of drunkenness. Simms Reeve, a city magistrate at the time, believed that the phenomenon was explained by the simple fact: 'The men do not earn enough money to buy spirits.'

Did you know?

James Southall was elected the first president of the Norwich Manufacturers' Association, a role he held until his death in 1920 when he was 90 years old! Subsequently the office passed on to A. G. Howlett, and from then on it was held for one year.

Did you know?

On one occasion during the 1897 strike the operatives did not receive their strike pay from union headquarters, without which many would have starved. The local-union official, James Mason, approached Sir George White, director of Howlett & White (pictured), who guaranteed the payment. At the end of the strike no one would employ Mason until Sir George White gave him a post.

NATIONAL UNION
OF
BOOT & SHOE OPERATIVES.

NORWICH BRANCH.

NORWICH & DISTRICT
Finishing Statement
AS ADOPTED BY THE
ARBITRATION BOARD,
July, 1919.

Norwich
The Caxton Press, Maddermarket.

BENCH WORK. DAMPDOWN WORK.

				Per Doz.
Sandpapering bottoms				2d.
Dampdown with flannel.	Ladies'	4d.	7 x 1	3½d.
Brown bottom	,,	4d.	,,	3½d.
Black waist and brown and white	,,	5d.	,,	4½d.
Marking over				¾d.
Painting bottoms, 1 colour	,,	2½d.	,,	2d.
,, ,, 2 ,,	,,	3d.	,,	2½d.
Top-pieces only				½d.

BENCH WORK. BLACK BOTTOMS.

Fill up channels and holes in heels	Ladies' 3½d.	7 x 1	3d.
Cleaning nails in heels			½d.
Brown or white bottoms, fill up channels and holes in heels	Ladies' 3½d.	7 x 1	3d.
Marking over second time			1d.
Turnshoe, filling holes in heels and cleaning nails			1½d.
Foreiron waist on painted and dampdown bottom			2d.
Ladies' black waist M.S., filling in channels in waist, holes and heels			2d.

LASTING UP.

All classes	1d.

Lasts to be properly sorted.

8

HEEL PADDING AND SEAT WHEELING.

		Per Doz.
Wood heels		2½d.
Heel padding	(½d. extra ink)	1¾d.
Tan ,,		1½d.
Faking		½d.
Girls		1d.
Seat wheeling		1d.
,, Louis		1½d.
Black heels on coloured uppers (padding)	extra	1d.

BOTTOM SCOURING.

Buffing out sole at front of heel	¾d.
,, covered heels	1d.
,, Louis	1½d.
Breast scouring	½d.
Rough ,,	½d.
Fine scouring and naumkeg	1¼d.
Scouring top-piece only	½d.

INKING.

Edges	1d.
Black edges on coloured uppers	2d.
Heels	1d.
Fronts of heels	½d.
Black bottoms	1d.
,, waists	1d.
Top-piece only	¼d.
Black heels on coloured uppers	2d.

9

Footwear finishing statement, 1919

NUBSO continued to represent the shoemakers until 1971 when it merged with other unions to form the National Union of Footwear, Leather and Allied Trades (NUFLAT). In the 1970s Nigel Rudling recalls: 'Annually NUFLAT issued what was called a "Footwear Statement" (see above for an early example issued by NUBSO) which outlined pay levels. A few factories made the odd amendment, but otherwise it was applied across the board. In Norwich NUFLAT and the NFMA mutually agreed the pay structure which applied in all factories.' Subsequently the role of local union officers, including Billy Critten, was to make sure that the right price (rate) was paid for a job. He remembers: 'The shoe trade was predominantly piecework and an industry price was set for each job which would enable the worker to earn a decent income. Initially the price was set as a percentage above the minimum wage, basically the more skilled the work the higher the percentage. Later on we introduced a time study system. The rate was agreed by the general union when we went to conference, where I represented Norwich.'

Although no major dispute involving all firms occurred in Norwich during the 20th century, a number of 'skirmishes' took place in the individual factories. In the first instance these were normally dealt with by the union rep. Janet Metcalf undertook the role at Florida. Although the rep's role was to stick up for the workers, she notes that in general the unions and the managers worked well together. If any dispute couldn't be sorted out by the individual factories they would be referred to the NFMA who were responsible for resolving outstanding issues. Their aim was to regulate the way the industry was run in Norwich, with local members also representing the City on a national federation.

Executive Committee, Norwich Footwear Manufacturers Association, January 1959

Disputes arose over many issues including wages and working conditions. Probably one of the most unusual occurred just after the end of WWII. In November 1947 300 girls in the closing room at Sextons threatened to spend Saturday morning away from work so they could buy nylon stockings! The problem arose after local store, Henry Jarvis & Sons Ltd, obtained over 1,500 pairs of this scarce commodity and advertised a sale. Disaster was averted after arrangements were made to put away 300 pairs for them.

It is widely accepted that the union gave extensive support to workers locally, and did much to protect them, but as the industry started to decline, at times their approach seemed to be archaic. For example, even in the 1970s piecework wages were calculated in farthings. They also supported an arrangement whereby every factory in Norwich closed for the same summer break, which was often impractical, not least because children's shoe manufacturers had different trading peaks to the ladies' fashion shoe manufacturers.

As the industry faltered, the union continued to try to negotiate the best possible deal for their members, but as firm after firm folded, it was observed that their actions were potentially making UK producers uncompetitive. For example, Peter Metcalf recalls: 'When clickers started to use presses the unions introduced a pay system which meant that they were still paid more for cutting intricately shaped uppers which could now be produced in the same time as a simple job...as a result, a technological advance which could have reduced costs significantly only had a marginal effect.'

Derek Rye recalls that in the mid-1980s the operatives at Clarkes could see: '...that the industry was in decline and the constant push to increase wages was putting pressure on the factory owners. At one time we actually spoke out and said we didn't want the pay rise, but the union insisted that we should get it.'

In the 1970s the Association of Scientific, Technical and Managerial Staffs (ASTMS), which represented white-collar workers, was very active in the Norwich shoe factories. Ian Gibson, who was on the National Executive of ASTMS at the time, recalls that shoeworkers were joining the union in droves, because they were seeing their incomes reduced relative to their blue-collar colleagues. In fact shop-floor workers often earned more than their managers. ASTMS were heavily involved when Sextons announced their closure in 1972. On 1 March they had a meeting in St Andrew's Hall, where it was agreed almost unanimously (the vote was 646 – 6) to refuse redundancy notices and also to occupy the factory and to prevent machinery being moved out. Subsequently, Mr Jack Taubman, a property developer and manufacturer, negotiated an agreement with the receiver that resulted in around 400 jobs being saved, at least initially, in the Norwich factory.

Ian Gibson was also closely involved in the plight of the girls who had worked in Sextons' closing room in Fakenham, who started a sit-in when they realised their factory was going to be closed. He recalls: 'I visited them on numerous occasions and supported them on their sit-in, which lasted 18 weeks. On the first day I helped them barricade the factory and make a handwritten notice to hang outside which said "This Factory Is Under Workers' Control". Then my two young daughters and myself slept in the factory with them for the first night the factory was under occupation. The ladies eventually formed themselves into a co-operative called "Fakenham Enterprises" producing leather goods. It lasted a few years as a co-operative, but by 1976 had become an outpost of a local clothing manufacturer.'

As factory after factory closed the unions tried to support their members. However, they could do little to prolong the life of the shoe firms. Across the country the trade was contracting and as workers left union membership similarly fell. Eventually in 1991, after their national membership had fallen to 22,900, NUFLAT merged with the National Union of Hosiery and Knitwear Workers to form the National Union of Knitwear, Footwear and Apparel Trades.

In some quarters there has been criticism that the unions (NUBSO and NUFLAT) and the NFMA were 'too cosy', but others admired the mutual respect and support that existed between them. Whatever the rights or wrongs, there is little doubt that for many years the organisations jointly ensured the smooth running of the shoe trade which in turn strongly influenced the prosperity of the City.

NUBSO badges and ladies' clip

Lasting Memories

Billy Critten explains why shop stewards recommended that their members accepted reduced hours of work: 'At times production needed to be cut back. Rather than reduce the workforce, which would have resulted in companies losing skilled workers, factories went on slow time. If this happened you were guaranteed three-quarters of your average income. If it got worse you would be laid off. The unions and members had to agree any changes. When I was a shop steward I represented the clickers at Ballys. If the company had to go on slow time, because the clickers were at the start of the production process we were first hit. So I used to say to them they either had to accept that someone had to be stood-off, or to work to a certain wage.'

Billy and Muriel Critten, c1980

Mike Quinton describes how industrial relations were managed: 'We had the NFMA and union officers, and whenever there was any likelihood of problems they got together to sort things out. From that point of view it was a very well organised industry. Each company had a representative at the NFMA which had its own offices and full-time secretary. The various firms took turns at being president and any disputes with the unions, which couldn't be sorted out by the individual factories, were referred to the Association who got together to resolve outstanding issues. The aim of the Association was to regulate the way the industry was run in Norwich. There was also a national federation on which Norwich had three delegates.'

Jean Woods became a shop steward in the late 1970s at Start-rite's closing room in Wymondham: 'As shop steward I had to look after my colleagues. The mechanic could be slow mending machines so I had to chivvy him along. It was a bit awkward but I was paid to do it. If it was perishing cold in the factory I used to tell the boss that I'd give him an hour to get the heating going and if he didn't we would down tools.'

Arthur Holmes recounts how disputes were dealt with at Start-rite: 'The shoe trade always had a reputation of having very good industrial relations. On a couple of occasions I was called on to stop a strike and I had no problem at all. I remember once I was sitting in my office and was told that the machine-room girls had walked out and were standing in the road, and I was asked to talk to them. So I went out and said: "What's the problem?" There was some minor issue around wages and I said: "Well that can soon be sorted out." So little old Gertie Moore shouted to the rest: "Mr Holmes says he's going to sort it all out, so back you go." It was as easy as that. When these little tussles were sorted the girls went back with no ill feeling and everything just got back to normal. There really wasn't any griping. I was a liaison between the directors and the factory because I was friendly with both the directors and everybody in the factory. Also as cost accountant I was on the balcony adjacent to the workrooms, so my office was easily accessible to all parties. I got on extremely well with the union people. On the odd occasion that one of our employees raised a complaint with the union stewards in the main office, they'd come to see me and we could talk it through in a very reasonable, amenable way. Similarly if one of our workers came to see me with an issue I'd refer them to the union official and say that's who they should talk to. The union did the workforce a lot of good in establishing fair levels of pay and holidays.'

Nigel Rudling recalls that some systems put in place by the unions were archaic: 'When I joined, in 1970, pay rates and working practices were set by the union across all the factories. Many practices were old-fashioned and prevented the industry from modernising. As a small example, when I joined piecework wages were still being calculated in farthings and even after decimalisation many factories didn't change. Even at CWS we didn't change straight away. The last to accept the new currency were the clickers, who always thought they were above the rest of the workforce.'

4. Technological Changes

It was not until the latter half of the 19th century that shoe production became mechanised, which in turn led to the growth of factories.

In the years that followed a combination of factors, including new materials, mechanical innovation and the introduction of computers, have all combined to transform production techniques. Yet despite all these changes the basic way to construct a shoe, i.e. shaping an upper around a last and attaching a sole, remains unchanged.

Heathside factory, Norvic, 1964

Technological Changes before 1950

In 1856 Charles Winter became the first Norwich manufacturer to use a sewing machine to close uppers. A few years later there were over 400 upper-closing machines in the factories and 300 in private homes. Their introduction had two major effects on shoe production. Firstly they significantly reduced the amount of time to make a pair of shoes and secondly, by making the process less physical, women could replace men. In Northampton their use led to a strike which lasted for two years, but in Norwich there was no serious industrial action. This is not entirely surprising as sewing machines resulted in high-quality, durable shoes being produced at affordable prices, which increased sales and hence the numbers employed in the trade.

In the years that followed numerous machines were introduced. As a result shoemaking was transformed from being a handicraft to a mechanical, factory-based process. Major inventions and innovations include:

- The Blake, or Mckay, sole-sewing machine was invented c1858. It stitched waxed thread which meant that it could be used to sew a sole to the shoe. By 1861 at least two Norwich factories were using the machine
- The Consolidated lasting machine was invented in 1884 by J. W. Matzeliger, an American mechanic. Prior to its adoption all lasting operations were performed by men who were known in the trade as 'hand-tappers'. Fifteen years later Edwards & Holmes introduced the machine to Norwich. It proved to be so efficient in terms of production costs and quality of work that soon most of the other Norwich shoe manufacturing firms had followed suit. That said some factories still hand last today, and even where the process has been mechanised many operatives continue to insert tacks manually, as noted by Ray Carpenter who works at Florida: 'The governor [Simon Goodman] sometimes comes around and sees me hand lasting and he asks me: "Why aren't you putting that in the machine? It cost me a lot of money", and I always tell him it's because I can do it better by hand. It's only for certain styles and I only do a bit of tweaking here and there, but I've been in the business so long I know which designs need the extra care. He knows that and we have a laugh and a joke about it.'
- Sole-cutting presses were used in Norwich by the end of the 19th century. Before their introduction soles and insoles were punched out by hand after the leather had been dampened, which was both slow and costly. The new machines considerably quickened the process.

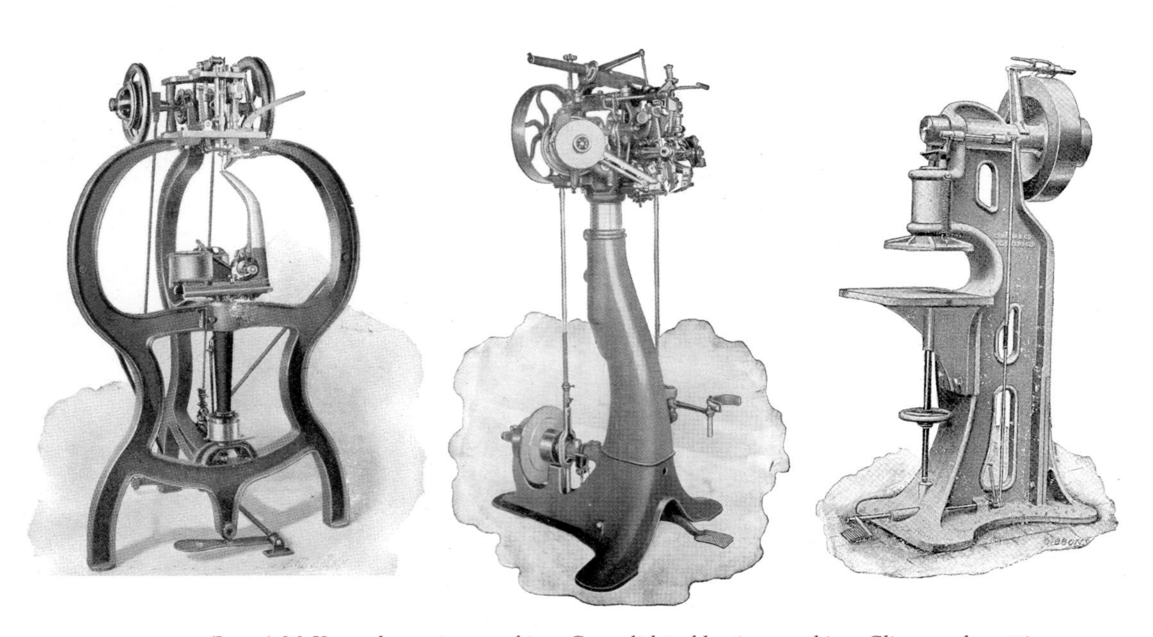

(L to r) McKay sole-sewing machine, Consolidated lasting machine, Climax sole-cutting press

In the 20th century the mechanisation process was accelerated by the widespread introduction of electricity. This energy source was in its infancy in 1900. Over the next 50 years this simple method of powering factories facilitated increased mechanisation, which in turn promoted the manufacture of ornamental, yet practical, footwear.

Improvements included:

- Patterns for ladies shoes were traditionally made in a size four. Subsequently they had to be reproduced for every size of foot. The Hartford grading machine, enabled patterns to be graded (i.e. increased and reduced in size) more accurately. In 1900 Howlett & White was one of the first factories in the country to introduce the machine. In the following year an improved model was brought out which was installed at both Southalls and Chittocks. The machines improved the uniformity and accuracy of patterns and hence the footwear produced from them
- The Rex, or Consolidated, pulling-over machine, was invented in 1901. It further enhanced the lasting process and, because it brought uniformity to the operation, it also resulted in the production of better-fitting footwear.

At the same time progress was also being made in methods of shoe construction. For example, in 1925 Fred Lee, a foreman at Haldinsteins, invented an adhesive material for cementing the sole to the shoe. The firm can thus claim to have been the pioneers, if not the actual inventors, of the cemented shoe in this country which they called 'Turnstyles'.

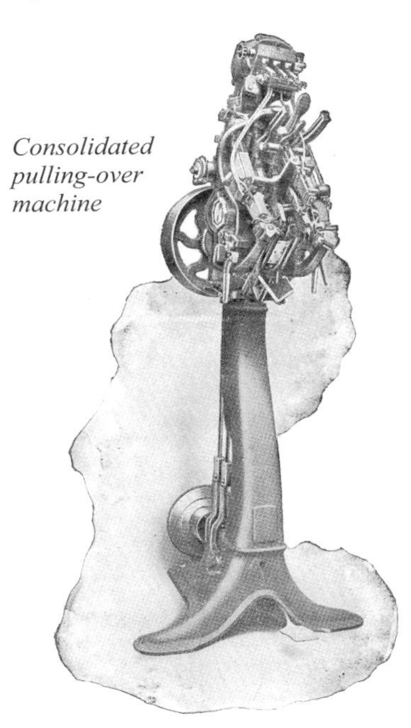

Consolidated pulling-over machine

Pattern grading machine, Walter Edwards, 1925

One of the big debates, which started in the early 20th century, centred around the best way to transport partially completed footwear between different departments. Traditionally this was done on racks (trolleys), but in 1932 a party of Norwich shoe men visited Batá of Zlin, a shoe manufacturer in Czechoslovakia, who used a conveyor-belt system. In particular, it was noted that if shoe designs were relatively simple, Batá used the conveyors as more than just a means of transport. In such cases operators were lined up with their machines along the conveyor, and each performed their individual task as the work progressed from station to station.

The Norwich manufacturers were impressed, and concluded that if they adopted the system it would improve efficiency in their factories and reduce costs. One of the first firms to install a conveyor belt in Norwich was Edwards & Holmes, and to facilitate the innovation a new plainer shoe was designed. The adoption of conveyor belts was not an unqualified success. Operatives were unable to spend as much time on the shoes as when shoes were transported on racks, and the footwear produced on it was decreed as not having the extra touches which gave them the 'Norwich look'.

By the end of the 1940s conveyors were mainly used to transport work swiftly between operations. Some factories, such as Edwards & Holmes, reverted back to using racks, whilst others continued to experiment. Post WWII there remained ambivalence about the use of conveyor belts. Factories that did adopt them tended to take a dual approach, whereby in the closing room they were generally used to transport work to the ladies and then back to the overseer, whereas in the making room the work was sent around on a track, and each operative did their job before it was sent on to the next operator, and so on. Nigel Rudling explains: 'You could use this system in the making room because every shoe went through the same process. In the closing room different styles underwent different procedures so you couldn't implement the same type of track.'

Shoe racks, Edwards & Holmes, 1965

First conveyor belt in a Norwich shoe factory, Edwards & Holmes, c1930

Lasting Memories

Ron Green recalls what happened when W. H. H. Clarke tried to replace racks: 'I think that it was around the late 1960s that the bosses wanted to install a conveyor belt system to transport partially completed shoes between sections. The first operator had to pare the edges on the sole, the next stamped the size etc. The problem was if anyone went off for a fag the others stood there waiting for the shoes. One morning we all put up big cardboard signs. The first stop was "Thorpe Station", I was "Brundall Gardens" and the inker was "Acle" etc. One day the bar on the buffer at the end got loose. Someone undid the nuts and several trays went off the rails...we all knew it was sabotage. We were soon back to using the old trusty trollies [racks], even though some of them were well over 100 years old.'

Bob Drake describes the conveyor belt at Sextons: 'In the 1960s, when I was in the making room at Sextons, the shoes were transported on three tracks which went around in a circle. Each track was around 15 metres long. The shoes were on hangers and they'd clank around and stop at every operation. Each week between 5,000 and 6,000 pairs of shoes were made on each track. It was mass production on a huge scale. I'd never seen anything like it.'

Nigel Rudling explains how a typical conveyor belt worked in a closing room: 'In the 1970s in the closing room at CWS we had a little conveyor belt which was run on a red and green light system. There were two belts, one above the other. When the machinist was ready for work they put on a green light. Work was put on the top belt which carried it to the machinists. When the work was completed it was put back onto the bottom belt and it was then carried back to the overseer. I soon found out that if some of the girls were sent a hard job they sent it back without doing anything, and ordered more work, which they hoped would be easier.'

Simon Goodman considers the pros and cons of using conveyor belts: 'At the Florida factory we eventually installed two conveyor belts in the closing room. The idea of the belt was that a machinist had work beside them, and when they moved their work from the left to the right it tripped a switch which showed a light on a feeder. The person on the feeder knew what type of skills the machinist had, so they put her next piece of work on the conveyor belt, pressed a button, and it travelled along the belt and stopped beside the machinist, who was supposed to take it off the belt and turn the switch off. Unfortunately it didn't always work because the machinist didn't take her work off the belt, so it travelled away from her eventually falling off the end...normally to the sound of much cheering. It was more efficient then the trolley system because as the machinists worked on one job they had another beside them, so the down time was much less.'

Making room, Riverside factory, Norvic, 1961

Technological Changes 1950 – 1980

By 1950 the factory system was well developed. In the years that followed the introduction of new materials, improved adhesives, mechanical innovation and the introduction of computers all combined to revolutionise production methods. Changes resulted in increased efficiency such that between the mid-1950s and the early 1970s the numbers employed in the Norwich footwear industry fell by around 38%, whilst output increased by over 40%, reaching an 'all-time record' in 1972 when the Norwich firms produced over 10.8 million pairs of shoes and fashion boots.

Brian Lambert and Peter Metcalf, both senior managers in the industry, consider that major technical changes in the shoe factories up until the 1970s included:

- ***Combination machinery:*** where one piece of kit did five or six jobs at a time, which simplified the process enormously. For example, Brian recalls that the pulling-lasting machine, which was introduced into Bally in the late 1950s, replaced six operations in the lasting room: 'I was one of the first people in Norwich to use it, and subsequently I trained the operatives at Bally. The new machines not only replaced manual jobs but, because they were so accurate, they also reduced the time we had to physically spend measuring and checking. Additionally, because we had fewer processes, we also needed fewer foremen and supervisors.' Similarly, Peter reports that at Edwards & Holmes in the early 1970s: 'We brought in a four-part laster, which would pull the upper over and cement all of the front in one go. So basically one guy with one machine replaced four hand lasters.'

Ray Carpenter at his multi-purpose lasting machine, Florida, 2012

- ***Lasting:*** Shoes used to be on the last for up to a week, until the leather could hold its shape. As a result a lot of capital was tied up in a factory's last collection. But in the 1950s a heat setter was introduced which basically acted like an oven. As noted by Brian: 'Lasted shoes would spend five minutes in a setter, which had been heated to 125 degrees centigrade, after which the last could be removed.' This not only quickened the amount of time it took to make a pair of shoes, it also reduced the investment that factories had to make in stocks of lasts.
- ***Prefabrication:*** Previously, after soles and heels were attached to the uppers, an entire department (the finishing room) was given over to tidying them up and 'finishing' them off. This all changed in the 1960s when improvements in synthetics allowed companies, such as Bally, to start making prefabricated soles out of resin which could be cut to an exact size, and completed before they were attached to the upper. At the same time wooden and leather heels, which had been made in the factory, were replaced with plastic heels, which were bought in. Once companies started to use prefabricated bottom stock, finishing rooms became obsolete. Many more job losses were generated in the smaller factories where they started to buy-in soles. In the 1980s it became more economical for even Bally to follow this route. By that decade soles and heels could be made in one unit, which further simplified the process.

Sole and heel unit, Florida, 2012

Plastic lasts, Florida, 2012

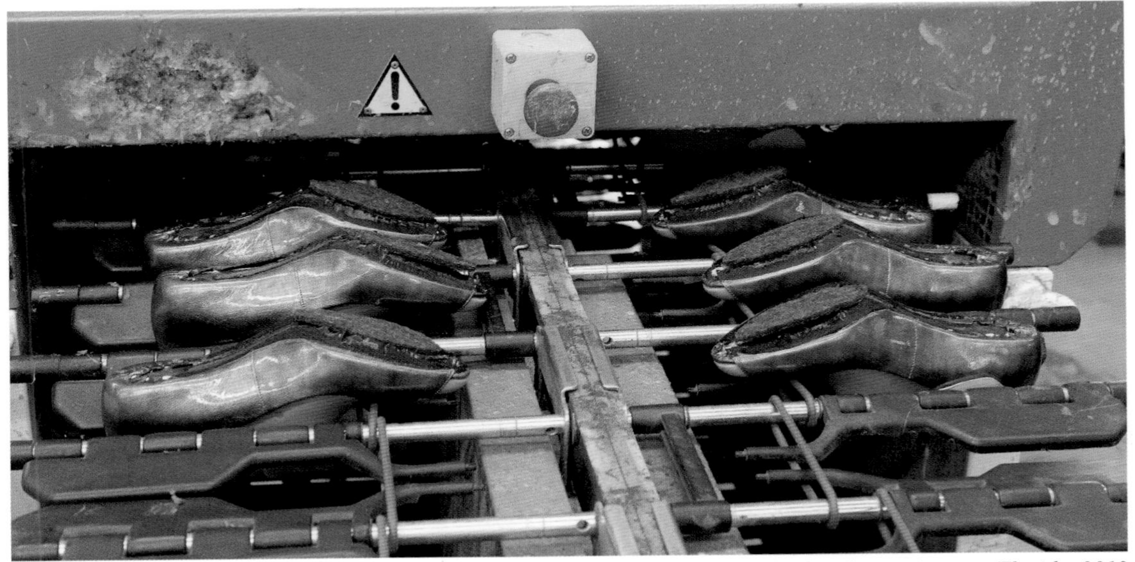

Lasted uppers about to enter a high-velocity air oven, Florida, 2012

- ***Improvements in presses:*** Unlike Bally, Edwards & Holmes continued to make soles out of leather. Like other factories, to get around the need for cutting different shaped soles, which would have involved an astronomical investment in press knives, they used a composite sole to which you could attach a variety of designs, which meant that they still needed their finishing room. However, in the 1960s presses became more refined and lighter. As a result you could now use light-weight steel press knives, which were significantly cheaper to produce. So for the first time it became cost efficient to cut pre-finished leather soles, which meant that the sole could be cut to the exact shape and totally finished before it was stuck to the upper. As noted by Peter Metcalf: 'Unsurprisingly this change led to many redundancies. Whereas before you had a dozen or more presses you could get away with half that number. Additionally [similar to synthetic prefabricated soles] you didn't need all these guys in the finishing room doing the edges of the soles. For example, under the old system you could only ink one sole at a time, and because it was already attached to the shoe you had to be really careful. With pre-finished soles you could spray a whole stack together.'
- ***Adhesives:*** As adhesives improved they became a more viable replacement to tacks. In the 1950s neoprene was employed, but this deteriorated with age. As a result, soles which had been stuck on had a tendency to peel off. By the 1970s polyurethane was being used, which was more reliable and gave a better finish.
- ***Clicking presses:*** As noted previously, by the end of the 1960s most factories were cutting leather uppers with presses. This meant that intricate designs could be cut in the same time as simple patterns.
- ***Synthetic materials:*** Artificial leathers such as Porvair and Corfam came onto the market in the second half of the 20th century. Neither they, nor plastics, were widely used to make uppers at the quality end of the market. However, even Edwards & Holmes started to make linings out of synthetics in the early 1970s, because by then the materials were so good that few would have noticed the difference.

Hytronic press with knives, Florida, 2012

Lasting Memories

Brian Lambert observes that modern machines were not always reliable: 'The downtime on some of the new integrated machines, many of which were hydraulic, was quite high. Obviously this gave us [Bally] problems. The vast majority of our machines were leased from the British United Shoe Manufacturing Company [B.U.] who had offices on Starling Road, and so if we had problems we called them in. Many of the Norwich factories also leased machinery from the B.U., so their engineers were often busy and we had to wait quite a time for them to arrive.'

Lenford Laband describes how machinery quickened even the simplest of processes: 'For a style of shoe called "I. Miller" Sextons had a girl handwriting details such as the size and brand name in the shoe, which was a very long process. Most manufacturers had a printing machine to do the job. Later on she gave us [the Standard Engineering Company Ltd] a copy of her writing and we made a special block so that when they printed the lining the writing still appeared to be handwritten.'

Ray Carpenter describes how lasting processes have changed: 'It used to be a sackable offence if you didn't leave a shoe on the last at least overnight. This gave it a chance to set into shape. We now heat them then cool them off in the chiller and it takes ten minutes. The chiller contracts the material which means that it fits really tight to the last. The new technologies mean that we don't need the same last banks that we had when I first started in 1960.'

CAD demonstrated to trainees, Bally, 1986

Technological Changes post 1980

Since the 1970s many of the major changes in shoe production have been related to developments in IT and automatic process controls, rather than to improvements in the machines themselves. Similar to earlier innovations, these have combined to improve uniformity and efficiency and hence reduce costs. Examples include:

- ***Computerised stitching:*** John Thain recalls that computerised stitching was introduced at Start-rite in the mid-1980s: 'Previously uppers had been marked so that when decorative stitches were being applied to the shoes the machinists knew where to sew. My new job involved programming a computer so that an upper could be fed into a sewing machine on a pre-designed pallet, and be automatically stitched in the correct place. This not only meant you didn't need a team of people marking the leather, but also that the stitching was more accurate and uniform.'
- ***CAD/CAM (Computer-Aided Design/Computer -Aided Manufacturing):*** This was introduced in the late 1980s as an aid to shoe design and pattern making. K Shoes installed such a system, which they called 'Shoe Master', at Clarkes during 1989. The dimensions of a last would be fed into a computer so that the last itself could be viewed from different angles. The designer was then able to draw his design on the screen, including colour, and subsequently view it from all angles. Once the designer was satisfied with his creation the system produced a pattern from which a sample could be made. If the style was adopted for bulk production a fully graded sets of patterns were then produced. Computer-aided techniques enabled patterns and designs to be produced more quickly and accurately. Today at Florida most of the machines are computerised.
- ***Clicking:*** One of the main skills of the clicker was his ability to achieve the greatest value out of a hide. Today you still need the human eye to highlight flaws in a skin, but then a computer can work out how to cut the maximum number of uppers. In the past this was the clickers' role and it made them some of the most important and highly paid operatives in the factory. When a computerised system is used clickers are generally paid the same as other machinists.

The above changes, coupled with the general decline of the industry, led to significant changes in how factories were structured. Of course by 1990 few of the old traditional shoe factories remained in Norwich, and those that did were in a highly competitive market dominated by foreign producers, who could generally make shoes at significantly lower costs. Both Bally and Florida responded by totally revolutionising the factory structure. Basically, out went the rooms (departments) and in came teams (modules). Staff in these teams were trained to be multi-skilled and they were overseen by coaches rather than supervisors. Bally, led by directors Bob Marston and Ivor Whitbread, based their new structure on Nissan factories. Teams, with up to 18 members, were responsible for making one style of shoe, from the cutting of the leather to putting it in the box for sale. At the same time piecework was scrapped and replaced by a pay structure based on experience rather than speed. Using the new system the directors estimated that they could get shoes 'from leather to shop' in

Mike Fisher, Florida: (l) Pattern grading mechanically, 1987; (r) Pattern grading using CAD, 1991

less than 48 hours, when at one time it would have taken 28 days. Around 1996 Peter Metcalf introduced a similar system at Florida. As had been done at Bally, teams were set up who were responsible for producing a shoe from start to finish. Also a new payment system was introduced under which wage levels were linked with a weekly production target. Once that target had been reached, subject to quality standards being met, people could go home. Peter Metcalf noted: 'This became the incentive for people to work hard. So we often had everyone finishing on a Thursday afternoon, which meant that the factory could be shut down early, which also reduced overheads…it also gave a huge incentive for workers to learn each other's skills.' Today Florida still run a modular system of production with multi-skilled staff at their factory on Dibden Road.

Start-rite did not adopt the modular system of production, instead they took the decision to reinvent themselves. The firm no longer manufacture shoes. Instead they design, develop, distribute and market shoes for the developing foot of a child. They work closely with factories, mostly based in India, who produce their shoes on a conveyor belt, one pair of shoes at a time. As described by Keith Richardson: 'When you see them you can see how labour intensive the work is. On each conveyor belt, depending on the complexity of the shoes, there are between 30 and 60 operatives making one pair of shoes. Each has a different job and the shoes basically are built as they move around the belt – a bit like putting a jigsaw puzzle together.'

Of the other factories that still produce footwear in Norwich two of the most traditional, Bowhill & Elliott and Broadland Slippers, still send their footwear around their factory 'departments', albeit there may be only one person in each! They use minimal machinery, some of which is more than 50 years old. They hand last and, depending on the material used, they may still cut uppers with a clicking knife, rather than with a press knife. However, even traditional factories sometimes need to depend on modern methods, as wryly noted by Mike Copland: 'At Broadland Slippers we use many of the traditional methods, including using a gold-leaf imprinter to stamp names into the in-sock. My previous machine blew up but I managed to buy a replacement on eBay!'

Florida, 2012

Supplement to 'NORVIC' Way, August, 1915

'DIPLOMA.'

D 26

Selling Price 17/6

Black Cloth Bal., pat. golosh cap, short front, and high Cuban heels.
D 25. Same Boot in Button.

D 27

Selling Price 17/6

All Black Velvetta Calf Derby, self cap, short front, high Cuban heels.

D 107 *and* 108

Selling Price - 10/11

Glace Kid Court Shoe with covered buckle, short front, high Cuban heels.
D108. Same Shoe in Blk. Velvetta

D 55

Selling Price - 13/9

Box Calf Derby Shoe, with imitation golosh.

D 106

Selling Price - 10/11

Glace Kid One Bar House Shoe with paste and silver buckle.

'MASCOT.'

M 102

Selling Price 14/6

Glace Kid Derby Boot, with Adelaide golosh and patent cap on smart American Toe.

The 'Mascot' Ward Shoe
illustrated on page 34
'NORVIC' Way.

M 88

Selling Price 10/6

Glace Kid Gibson, with patent cap (for Maids).

Supplement to the 'Norvic Way', Howlett & White's in-house magazine, August 1915

5. 20th-Century Norwich Shoes

By the early 20th century, Norwich had a national reputation in the manufacturing of high-quality shoes for women and children. An extensive collection of these shoes are on display in the City's Bridewell Museum.

In the following pages we show a selection of shoes produced by Norwich firms. These range from the elegant boots favoured by the Victorians through to the glittered platforms worn by all dedicated followers of fashion in the 1970s.

Please note:

- The date given in the description of the shoe refers to when it was made
- All footwear held in the Bridewell Museum collection is labelled 'Bridewell' whilst that owned by the Florida Group is labelled 'Florida'. All other images are reproduced by kind permission of Start-rite.

The Bridewell Museum, Bridewell Alley, 2013

Norwich Fashions: 1890-1920

Norwich Fashions: 1920-1929

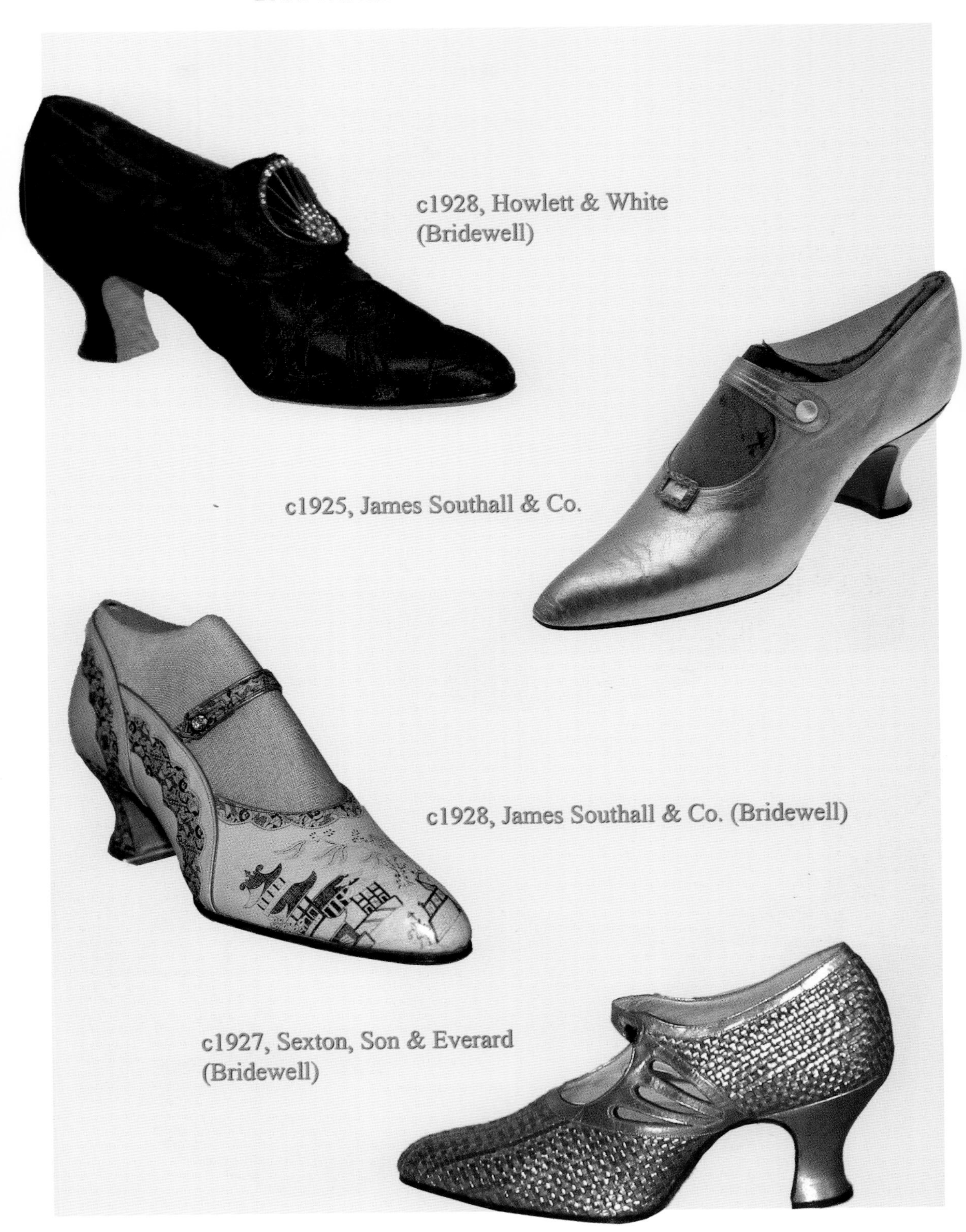

c1928, Howlett & White (Bridewell)

c1925, James Southall & Co.

c1928, James Southall & Co. (Bridewell)

c1927, Sexton, Son & Everard (Bridewell)

Norwich Fashions: 1930-1949

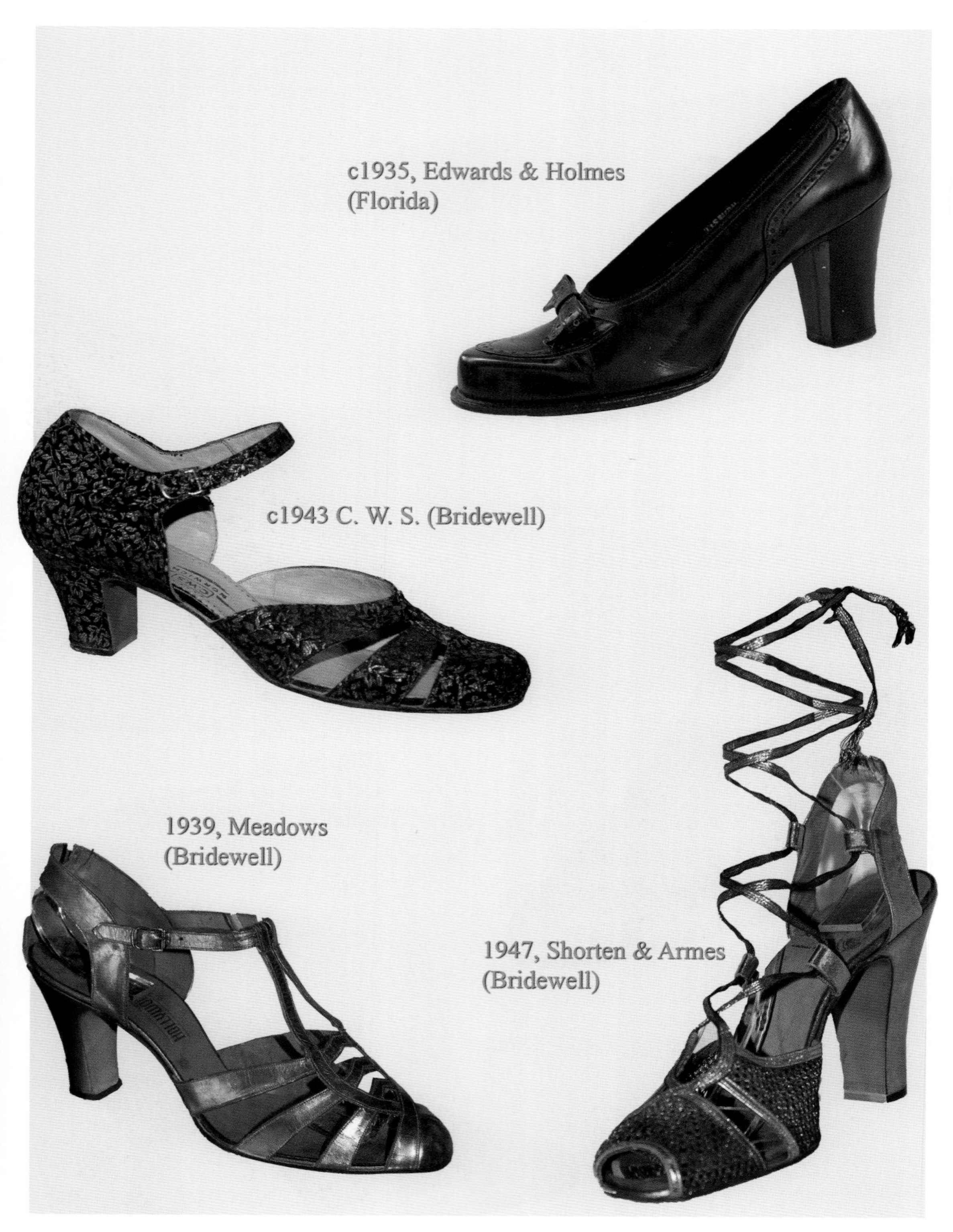

c1935, Edwards & Holmes (Florida)

c1943 C. W. S. (Bridewell)

1939, Meadows (Bridewell)

1947, Shorten & Armes (Bridewell)

Norwich Fashions: 1950-1959

c1955, Edwards & Holmes
(Florida)

c1958, Edwards & Holmes
(Bridewell)

c1955, Norvic
(Bridewell)

1957, W. H. H. Clarke
(Bridewell)

Norwich Fashions: 1960-1969

c1965, Shorten & Armes
(Bridewell)

c1960, John F. Kirby
(Bridewell)

c1963, Edwards & Holmes
(Bridewell)

c1965, John F. Kirby
(Bridewell)

1968, Edwards & Holmes
(Florida)

1961, Bally
(Bridewell)

1969, Edwards & Holmes
(Florida)

Norwich Fashions: 1970-1979

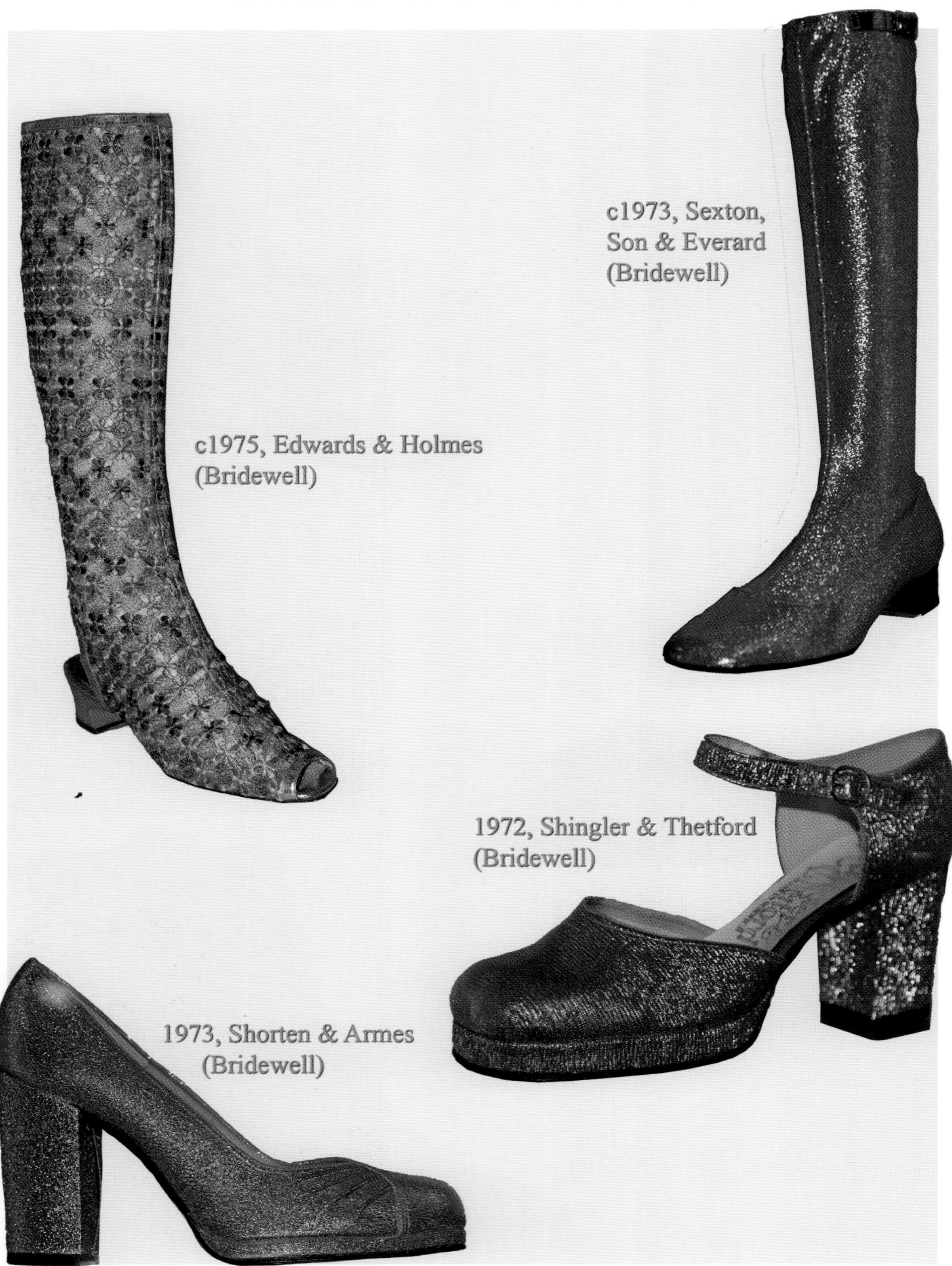

c1973, Sexton, Son & Everard (Bridewell)

c1975, Edwards & Holmes (Bridewell)

1972, Shingler & Thetford (Bridewell)

1973, Shorten & Armes (Bridewell)

Norwich Fashions: 1970-1979

c1975, Edwards & Holmes (Bridewell)

c1973, Edwards & Holmes (Bridewell)

c1975, Edwards & Holmes (Bridewell)

1979, Shorten & Armes (Bridewell)

start rite
1920s to 1930s
1940s to 1950s
1960s to 1970s
1980s to 1990s
21st century

6. Shopping

Gentleman's Walk, Norwich, c1975

Shoe retailing has totally changed over the last 60 years. In the 1950s footwear was generally purchased from specialist retailers which were often small family firms. Today you are more likely to buy shoes either from a supermarket or online. Competition also comes from clothes retailers, who now often have their own footwear ranges. This has led to some footwear manufacturers, such as L. K. Bennett, fighting back and expanding their range to include clothes.

Although the majority of the Norwich factories had seconds' (or reject) shops, relatively few had their own full-price stores. Those that did included Norvic, Edwards & Holmes and Start-rite.

The obvious advantage of a company owning its own chain of shops was that it gave a ready outlet for the footwear produced in its own factories. For example, by 1970 Norvic owned over 140 outlets which sold around 25% of their shoes. In 1972, after they had been taken over by Drakes, the chain was sold to William Timpson Ltd. As part of the deal, for the next three years, Timpson was obliged to take the same value of Norvic shoes that had historically been sold through the outlets. However, at the end of this period they stopped stocking Norvic footwear. It proved impossible for Norvic to replace this level of sales, and in 1981 the company folded.

In contrast Edwards & Holmes had a very different approach to retail. Peter Holmes recalls that when he joined the company in 1949, approximately 85% of their production was sold in the UK to around 40 retailers, including Dolcis, Saxone and Lilley & Skinner. Peter recalls: 'Other Norwich firms supplied the same chains, and when their buyers came to Norwich they'd visit all of us and try to drive our prices down. They were very fierce in their approach. So in 1952 my father [Geoffrey] took the decision to change tack and sell to all of the individual department stores and outlets throughout the UK. As a result we split the country into six regions and appointed a team of salesmen. We aimed to have outlets in every market town. In Norwich we dealt with three retailers, including Bowhill & Elliott and Ponds.' It was not until around 1970 that the company decided to develop a string of shoe outlets in department stores around the country, and by 1981 they had 60. Although this expansion gave the firm a solid basis for selling their own shoes, the loans that were taken out to finance the growth coincided with escalating interest charges which eroded profits. In 1987 the business was sold.

Historically, Start-rite sold the majority of their production through traditional, family-owned shoe shops, which had professionally trained fitters. However, in 1964 they purchased their first retail outlet, and by 1992 they had built a chain of 25 'Domani' shops which only sold Start-rite products.

Meantime in 1987 Boots the Chemist came up with the idea of running stores entirely for children, selling items such as shoes, clothes and toys, which they called Children's World. They opened 52 branches very quickly, and Start-rite and Clarks each supplied the footwear for around half of the stores. In 1996 Boots sold the business to Mothercare who decided to sell only one brand of shoes and, as Clarks was the biggest, Start-rite suddenly lost about 26 outlets. Around the same time they made the decision to sell the Domani chain.

With the loss of so many traditional shops and the growth of the internet, Start-rite has had to adapt. As explained by Peter Lamble, chairman and MD: 'First of all we formed strong relationships with chains that placed the same emphasis as us on service; the obvious ones being John Lewis and Russell & Bromley. Both fit shoes using methods which are suitable for a Start-rite product. Today we supply about 450 outlets in the UK mostly through large national chains.' Recently Start-rite has backtracked and bought an established chain called 'One Small Step'. Unlike the Domani chain the shops and concessions, which include an outlet in Harrods, not only sell Start-rite shoes but also complementary brands.

Lasting Memories

Martin Miller remembers his early days working at Norvic in the late 1950s: 'During my training the first shop I worked in was in the Holloway Road (London), where we sold our cheaper shoes. Once I was considered competent I had a short spell working in our most elite shop at 302, Upper Regent Street. We sold our most expensive shoes there. Some cost up to six guineas. To put that in perspective at the time I earned £500 a year. They didn't have fitting stools in this shop, instead shop assistants would serve customers standing in a trench. This meant that they could stand whilst helping customers to fit shoes. It was a gimmick…but it worked. People who went to the shop demanded a high level of service and had the money to pay for it.

'Part of the idea of Norvic having its own stores was to ensure continuity of production. The onus was on the shops to order shoes from our [Norvic] sales department but they also sold shoes produced by other companies. Norvic had its own window dressers who dressed all of our shops although they also offered the service to independent retailers as well.'

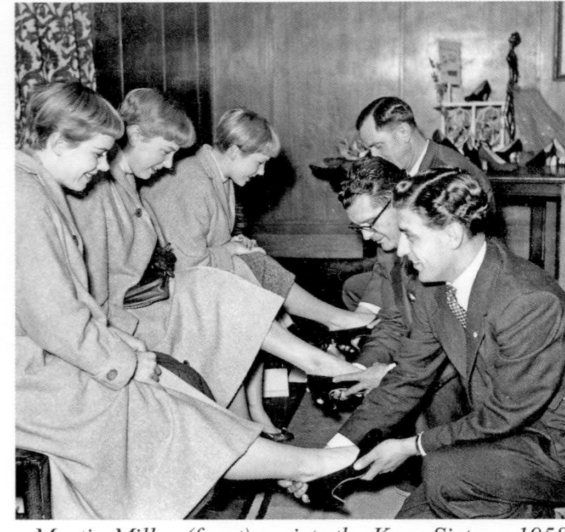

Martin Miller (front) assists the Kaye Sisters, 1958

In 1915 Norvic ran a window-dressing competition which was won by W. Rogers & Son of Letchworth (below) The runners up were E. Armitage of Rochester (above right) and Denny & Co. of Biggleswade (below right).

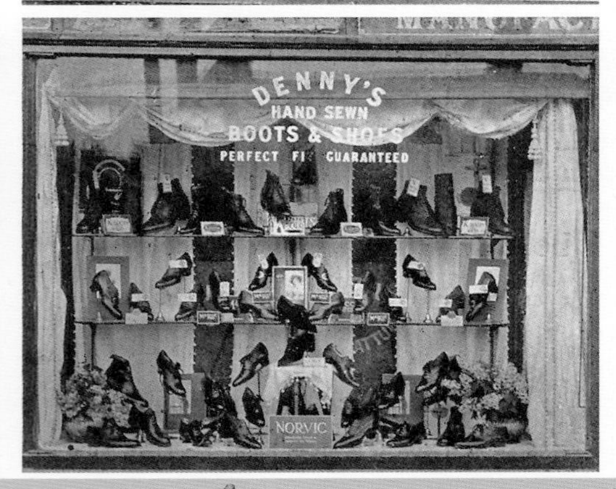

Norwich Shoe Shops

It would be an omission to write a book about the Norwich boot and shoe trade without reference to the City's independent shoe shops. Here we look at three of our local family stores: Bowhill & Elliott, J. Buckingham & Sons and Ponds.

Freeman, Hardy & Willis, London Street, c1969

Bowhill and Elliott Ltd

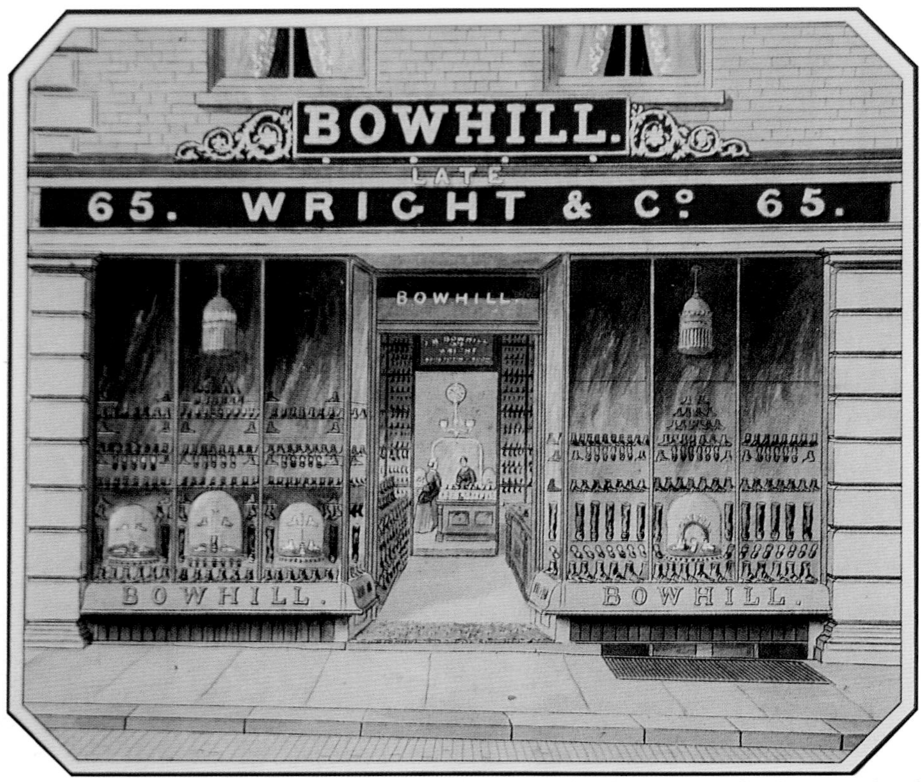

Late 19th-century shop front, 65 London Street, undated

A footwear business was first established at 65 London Street in 1843 by Robert Wright. Subsequently in 1874 it was purchased by Obadiah Henry Bowhill who already had considerable experience in the making of footwear.

Obadiah Henry had four children. Of these, three became involved in the footwear industry. Namely:

- Obadiah Herbert who in 1897, together with his brother-in-law Thomas Baines Elliott, bought the London Street business which incorporated a shop and workrooms, from his father
- Thomas who in 1890 established the footwear manufacturing firm of Thomas Bowhill & Hubbard
- Walter who managed his father's business, Bowhill & Co, in Swan Lane which supplied the shoe trade with findings (i.e. small tools and supplies such as uppers and bottom leather).

In 1910 Obadiah Herbert died. Subsequently, in 1929 the private company of Bowhill and Elliott Ltd was incorporated, with Thomas Baines Elliott as governing director and Mr W. E. Hastings (an employee) and Agnes Elliott (Thomas' wife) as directors. In 1941, two years before her death, Agnes appointed her daughter, Agnes Youngman, and Mr Sydney Jury as directors. Today the Jury family continues to own and run the firm.

Until WWII, similar to both Ponds and Buckinghams, boots and shoes would have been manufactured on the premises. In particular a lot of bespoke work was carried out. Today, at the rear of the shop, footwear is still made in a small slipper factory which evolved from the Osoeasie Slipper Company, bought by Bowhill & Elliott in 1960.

Amazingly 170 years since Robert Wright first set up his shop it remains a small family business that sells high-quality footwear. That said over the years it has

Bowhill & Elliott, London Street, 1951 (left) and after refurbishment, 1952

witnessed many changes as explained in memoirs written by W. E. Hastings in 1966: 'I recall back to 1904 when wearing a black apron and holding a duster in my hand I was instructed to go through the stock. It soon became evident that the firm had been engaged in supplying the mounted and infantry services fighting in the Boer War, which had ended in 1902. Leather and cloth puttee leggings, which had come into considerable usage during the conflict, were still a part of the usual stock. Indeed we did extensive business with the military during the time that Norwich was a garrison city, the mounted regiments being stationed at the Cavalry Barracks [Barrack Street] and the infantry regiments at Britannia Barracks [Britannia Road]. We did much trade with the officers...generally bespoke order, made to measure.

'It was during WWI that I realised the extent of the firm's clientele. Orders came in daily from the Colonies from those gentlemen, the pioneers of the age, who were returning to join the Forces. Many of these customers one could remember fitting out as youths to go abroad to seek their fortunes, or join the Empire Services. Much of the footwear was handmade and of the finest quality. The lasts were fitted at London Street, the uppers being made at the Swan Lane establishment [Bowhill & Co]. They were then given to outworkers for completion. All the bottom stock was cut at London Street, and was of the finest English and bark-tanned leather.

'When the war of 1939 started, it was the firm's experience of things military that soon brought an avalanche of business, which continued throughout the hostilities. Following the entry of the U.S.A. into the war we were inundated by US troops stationed in England, who had become aware of our reputation as suppliers of high-quality military footwear. Rationing of footwear by coupon of course tightened up supplies, but military permit forms enabled the firm to cope with the demand for such supplies successfully.'

Lasting Memories

Elizabeth Glover: 'I've worked in the shop for the last 20 years. When I first arrived as an assistant in the 1980s it was all terribly twee and old fashioned. In years gone by, before my time here, we didn't put the price on the shoes as it was deemed that if the shoe fitted well and was what was required, the cost didn't matter. Then we had a huge brigade of staff who either worked in the gents' department [downstairs] or the ladies' department [upstairs], and neither could do the other's job. You didn't move between floors. I now manage both and we are all interchangeable.

Bowhill & Elliott staff, c1955

'It is impossible for us to generalise about our customers. We get mothers bringing in their sons for their first pair of decent shoes when they are 13 years old. Similarly we get carers bringing in elderly ladies and gentlemen who have bought their shoes from us since they were children.

'We have cards recording customers' details, such as their size and what they bought, that go back many years. We still have records relating to customers who bought shoes from us when they were performing in local variety shows in the 1950s and 1960s, including Bob Monkhouse, Tommy Trinder, W. H. Dainty (Billy) and Norman Wisdom. In the ladies' department we still use the system today. For the gentlemen we have a computerised database, but in many ways I think the old card system worked better.

'I believe we have survived because not only do we give a high level of service but we also sell good-quality shoes for a fair price.'

Bowhill & Elliott, 2012

J. Buckingham & Sons (Norwich) Ltd

G. S. Buckingham, his wife and 14 children, 1908

Jonathan Buckingham was born in Colchester in 1796. As the son of a bootmaker he learnt his trade from his father, and around 1821 set up his own boot and shoe business in Westgate Street, Ipswich. Subsequently, in 1835, he moved to larger premises in Gothic House, Tavern Street (still in Ipswich). When Jonathan retired in 1862 his youngest son George Somerset Buckingham came to Norwich where, with £300 of capital, he established a shop at 27 London Street which he named J. Buckingham & Sons (Buckinghams).

Interestingly, the first circular that advertised Buckinghams to prospective customers in Norwich and Norfolk describes it not as a shop but as a boot and shoe manufacturer. In fact, George sold both made-to-measure footwear as well as holding an extensive stock, including items as diverse as gentlemen's wellingtons and ladies' French dress slippers.

To manufacture his made-to-measure goods George acted as a garret master. Uppers and soles were cut in workshops at his London Street premises before being sent out to be sewn and lasted by outworkers. In his book celebrating Buckingham's centenary, Eric Fowler noted that early order books for such footwear revealed as much about the character of customers as their orders: 'Mr Bales – a plain and practical man – wanted a pair of light wellingtons, easy to get on, wide across the tread, with low, wide heel and three rows of nails. Miss Trevor, of the Plantation – seeking to combine fashion with durability – ordered a pair of patent-leather shoes with light double soles but high tapering heels.' Despite having an extensive order book George was not tempted to develop a factory, a decision no doubt influenced by the success of the shop which was located on one of the best retail streets in the City.

Employees at Buckinghams became like members of the family. Many worked there for years, such that in 1962 there had only been three heads of their men's department. The first was Everett Gaze (pictured on page 108) who joined the firm as an errand boy when the shop first opened in 1862, and subsequently served at Buckinghams all his long working life. When he retired he was succeeded by Mr Bertie Bumfrey, after whom came Mr Reginald Hollidge, who joined the firm in 1923 and was still there at the time of the firms centenary. George himself never retired, continuing to work until 1913, when he died at the age of 74.

George had 16 children. Two of his sons, George Herbert and Horace Clifford, succeeded their father as joint managing directors. 'Mr Herbert' and 'Mr Clifford' ran the business until 1951, when they retired together at the ripe old ages of 84 and 74 respectively. One of their earliest acts was to incorporate the

Everett Gaze: (l) errand boy, 1862, (r) at his retirement c1915

business as a private limited company. Then in 1922 they expanded the flourishing retail business by moving the shoemaking and repairing department to premises in nearby Bedford Street, which enabled them to convert the old workrooms above the shop into fitting and stockrooms. Despite this they still needed more space, and so in 1923 J. Buckingham & Sons (Norwich) Ltd acquired W. B. Rutland's premises in Davey Place. The original proprietor of Rutlands had been a hand-sewn bootmaker named Silvanus Smith. In 1899 he was succeeded by his son-in-law, W. B. Rutland, who built the shop and a 'commodious four-storey' factory behind. The Buckingham family converted the entire building to shop premises. Despite the change of ownership, the premises continued to be known as Rutlands.

Clifford's sons Maxwell and Maurice joined the business in 1926 and 1941 respectively, and together they contributed significantly to the expansion of Buckinghams when, in 1949, they acquired the old family firm of Ivatts of Aylesbury (Buckinghamshire). In 1951 they took over as joint MDs. They both made extensive contributions to civic and business life for which they wered duly recognised. In particular, in 1959 Maxwell Buckingham was elected chairman of the Norwich branch of the British Boot and Shoe Institution, becoming the first retailer to head a branch of the Institution. Then in 1962, in Buckinghams' centenary year, Maurice Buckingham had the honour of being Mayor of Aylesbury.

(L to r) Mr Herbert and Mr Clifford, retiring, 1951

W.B. Rutland, Davey Place, c1950

Meanwhile Peter Buckingham became the sixth generation of his family in the trade. After two years' training with Clarks of Street and Lotus of Stafford, he joined the business in 1958, subsequently taking over as MD. In the years that followed he expanded the chain to nine shops.

In 1970 the London Street shop had a lucky escape when its neighbour, Garlands department store, suffered a disastrous fire. Firemen used the shop to reach the blaze, which inevitably resulted in it suffering from water damage, but luckily it survived more or less intact.

In 1981, with no one in the family wanting to continue the business, Peter decided to sell the chain of shops to Clarks. In the 23 years since he started he had seen major changes in both the way shoes were sold and bought. He reflects: 'At the beginning, stores such as Marks & Spencer did not sell shoes. As they and others entered the market, competition became very tight. At the same time customers generally wanted to buy shoes that were relatively cheap and more or less disposable. As an example, just before I retired I was given the opportunity, that I didn't take up, to buy shoes from Russia, which were boxed and delivered at a cost of £2 a pair! In such a context there became less of a demand for small independent firms, such as us, that sold and fitted quality shoes. That said I thoroughly enjoyed my time in the trade and was sad to sell.'

J. Buckingham & Sons, London Street, c1950

Ponds Foot Fitters Ltd

Outing, Bessie Bone (middle), Herbert and James Pond (centre), Percy Mainwaring (front), Edith Pond (right), 1903

In 1861 James Pond, who was 'devoted to the service of providing comfortable shoes to the people of Norfolk and Norwich', founded his own business. Over time he established a profitable venture which included a shop at 22 – 23 Castle Meadow, with workshops above where handmade bespoke footwear was made, and a small factory at 24 – 26 St George's. At the factory he manufactured non-bespoke footwear together with various appliances to keep feet comfortable, such as foot supports, which he patented. At one time he lived above the shop, but eventually he did so well that he was able to buy a house on Newmarket Road.

James' agent in America for the various foot supports and appliances was a certain Mr Scholl, who came to Norwich once a year. The young lad at the end of the front row in the photograph above was Percy Mainwaring. As a junior in the firm he was responsible for meeting Mr. Scholl at Thorpe station and escorting him back to James Pond's house, carrying his luggage in a barrow. As a reward for his endeavours Percy received a sticky sweet, which Mr Scholl fished out from the depths of his pocket. During WWI the various patents ran out and Mr Scholl, who then styled himself Dr Scholl, took over sales in America...and the rest is history. It's amazing to think that Percy was still making shoes in the workshop above the shop in the 1960s.

James Pond died in 1906 and the business was taken over by his son Herbert who had worked with his father since 1891. Under Herbert's leadership the firm continued to prosper, and in 1920 he purchased 21 Castle Meadow, which enabled him to extend the shop premises. Interestingly, number 21 used to house the prison warden who worked in the Castle, and for many years a tunnel (which is now blocked) linked the two buildings.

By now the firm had 200 employees which meant that it employed the largest number of hand-sewn-boot makers of any firm in the City. The firm also made 'Pond's Arch Supports and Surgical Appliances' which were recommended by many eminent surgeons and members of the medical profession as giving 'comfort and ease to tens of thousands in all parts of the country'.

Blocked tunnel to the Castle, c2000

Ponds' shop, Castle Meadow, undated

Ponds' shop, Castle Meadow, c1955

It was in 1919 that the Gascoyne family started their long association with Ponds when young Reginald Gascoyne joined the firm as Herbert Pond's personal assistant cum factory manager, a role he undertook until 1927 when Herbert died.

Following Herbert's death his daughter Laura, who was a pharmacist in London, took over the business. By the early 1930s the factory on St George's had been sold although bespoke shoes were still made in the workshops above the shop. Unfortunately the shop was struggling, and as the manager was of retirement age Laura asked Reginald together with the firm's secretary, Bessie Bone, to manage it on behalf of the family.

Peter Gascoyne (Reginald's son) recollects: 'Although we sold shoes made by a number of Norwich firms our major supplier was Norvic. So when my father, who had no experience in retailing shoes, started to manage the shop he went along to the Norvic factory on St George's to ask for help. My father was advised to target his marketing at customers in trades who would wear out their shoes quickly, such as publicans or farmers! When the Cattle Market was still located in the City the shop was well placed to sell shoes to the latter. They would visit us on market day and demand: "The best pair of boots." '

In 1945 Reginald Gascoyne and Bessie Bone bought the business, including the freehold of the shop premises (21 – 23 Castle Meadow). At the time they still had four hand-sewn bootmakers upstairs. Peter remembers: 'To measure a person's foot for bespoke footwear we used strips of paper which we wrapped around the foot and bottom of the leg in five places. We also drew the outline of a person's foot. We particularly needed to know if the customer had corns, bunions or other deformities. We even had a form that customers could use to measure their own feet. We didn't normally make a new last for each customer but would adapt an existing one by adding bits of plaster, leather etc. The main reason people bought bespoke shoes, rather than shoes off the shelf, was because shoes often weren't well graded. At this time Ponds was seen as high-class. I remember people saying: "You have to pay half a crown to go across the doorstep." That said we weren't in the same class as Buckinghams or Bowhill & Elliott, and so when customers were sent across from either of those firms because they couldn't fit them up, they could be somewhat miffed. We had a particularly good reputation for making shoes for people with bunions!'

Ponds' shop, Castle Meadow, 1959

Ponds, shop interior, 2002

Peter joined the firm in 1947 and took over as MD around 1960. Although they had passed on the batten neither Reginald nor Bessie Bone could keep away. In fact Reginald worked part time in the business until he was in his late 80s whilst Bessie continued until she was 92!

Jane Gascoyne, Peter's wife, recalls how shoes used to be fitted: 'From around 1930 until the early 1970s shoe shops X-rayed customers' feet using a pedoscope with the aim of ensuring well-fitted shoes. They were phased out when the dangers of radiation were held to outweigh the benefits of comfortable footwear! We stopped using our machine in 1971.'

Peter ran the business with the help of Jane until 2004, when it was sold. During that time they had many regular customers, including a Mr Shuffery whose first pair of shoes had been bought from Ponds when he was a few months old and who was still buying his shoes from them when he was 100. In fact he bought a special pair for his hundredth birthday party.

During his time in the trade Peter witnessed many changes: 'I saw the rise of the fashion guru and their encouragement to customers to constantly change and move on. When I started if someone found a shoe they liked they'd buy the same shoe, or one with a slight variation, the following season. Today customers are encouraged never to buy the same thing again. To put it in perspective, I remember in the mid-1950s when new colours came out it was quite exciting, even though the colours in question were beige and grey!' Peter has no doubt as to why Ponds survived for so long: 'It was because we had a niche. Our customers tended to be quite conservative, so we tended to ask ourselves: "How far behind should we follow?" We had many regular customers. Lots wouldn't go anywhere else for their shoes, so when we retired they were quite bereft.'

Ponds still trades on Castle Meadow in 2013. One of the few independent shoe shops operating in the City.

Peter and Jane Gascoyne, c2000

7. Royalty and Celebrities

Norwich was renowned for making beautiful footwear, and so it is not surprising that it has many links with the rich and famous.

Princess Anne meets Terry Norman, Start-rite, 1990

Princess Elizabeth accompanied by Geoffrey Holmes, closing room, Edwards & Holmes, 1951

The Norwich shoe factories have played host to many eminent visitors, the most important of whom was the Queen who toured the Edwards & Holmes' factory on the 18 June 1951, when still Princess Elizabeth. The visit is still imprinted on Jean Smith's memory: 'When Princess Elizabeth visited she stood behind us kids as we were machining, and I broke a needle and thought: "Oh no!" I still remember exactly what she wore...' When leaving she was presented with a pair of hand-made, gold-kid evening sandals. Although these were possibly the first shoes manufactured by Edwards & Holmes that the princess had worn, when Prince Charles visited Start-rite in 1992 everyone present knew that he had worn a great many of their shoes. In fact many of the operatives he met could proudly tell him that they had made them!

Princess Elizabeth, Edwards & Holmes, 1951

Princess Elizabeth meets Geoffrey Holmes

Leather store

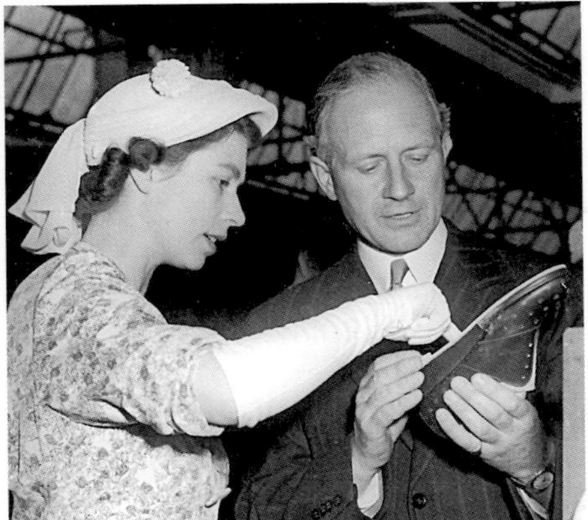

Examining a sole

Princess Elizabeth meets a clicker

The lovely photos on this page were all taken when Princess Elizabeth visited Edwards & Holmes' factory in 1951.

They clearly show that the Princess enjoyed meeting staff and that even at a young age she was able to put people at their ease, a quality in evidence throughout her long reign.

Forty-one years later Prince Charles exhibited the same characteristics when he visited Start-rite's factory, during their bicentenary celebrations in 1992.

Prince Charles visits the closing room, Start-rite, 1992

Prince Charles visits the leather store, Start-rite, 1992

Prince Charles, Start-rite, 1992

It was in 1955 that Start-rite (or James Southall & Co. as it was then) was first granted a Royal Warrant for supplying shoes for Prince Charles and Princess Anne. By the time of Prince Charles' visit, to celebrate the firm's bicentenary, they had fitted hundreds of pairs of children's shoes for the Royal Family, including pairs for Prince William and Prince Harry. It was always the best operatives who were given the opportunity to work on these specially-made shoes, one of whom was Jean Woods who recalls: 'It was a real honour to be selected to work on shoes for the Royal Family, but making them was a nightmare because they had to be absolutely spot on. Goodness knows how many times a pair went around before it was let out of the factory.'

Unfortunately in the year after the bicentenary the Royal Warrant was withdrawn from Start-rite. There was no disgrace in the loss as by then Prince Harry had celebrated his 18th birthday, and so there was no demand for children's shoes amongst the members of the Royal Family who could grant the Warrant, namely the Queen, the Prince of Wales, the Queen Mother and Prince Philip.

Prince Charles chats to Avis Brown, Start-rite, 1992

Prince Charles, Start-rite, 1992

Wedding photo of Princess Mary to Viscount Lascelles with King George V and Queen Mary, 1922

A souvenir given by George Haldinstein to staff who made Princess Mary's wedding shoes, 1922

Not only has Norwich footwear been worn by royalty for everyday occasions, but it has also graced royal weddings. For example, back in 1922, preparations were being made for the marriage of Princess Mary (daughter of King George V) to Viscount Lascelles. At the time Haldinsteins were renowned for the quality of their satin and brocade shoes. Somewhat fortuitously, a friend of Mr Haldinstein was asked by an acquaintance at Buckingham Palace where the best satin shoes could be found. George Haldinstein subsequently explained: 'My friend was kind enough to introduce me to his acquaintance and we arranged to take Princess Mary's measurements and make a special last for her foot. We made four pairs of shoes on this last to ensure a perfect pair. They were made of white satin and put in a beautiful casket lined with velvet to be presented to the Princess.

'I was invited together with the people who helped to make them to the palace to meet Queen Mary and Princess Mary. We travelled in my Hispano Suiza, and I remember that we were very nervous. The Queen put us at our ease very quickly, but poor Princess Mary was so terribly shy she could hardly speak. She found the shoes a perfect fit, so much so that she told me she was going to wear them when she appeared in public again.'

In 1956, when Grace Kelly married Prince Rainier in Monte Carlo, S. Thompson & Son were appointed to make their pageboys' shoes. For the occasion they created a pair of 'Cromwell' shoes (thus called because of the period when the style was popular) out of white buckskin embellished with a unique buckle specially made for the occasion. Forty-five years later Broadland Slippers were similarly delighted to make the evening pumps with gold buckles worn by the pageboys at Prince William's wedding to Catherine Middleton.

Wedding-shoe casket and Hispano Suiza, 1922

Evening pumps, Broadland Slippers, 2012

Celebrities

Norwich footwear has long been favoured by celebrities both on and off the stage. Edwards & Holmes in particular had a reputation for supplying shoes for West End shows, including 'South Pacific', that ran at the Theatre Royal on Drury Lane between 1951 and 1953, 'I Am A Camera', a play which opened in 1954 with Dorothy Tutin as its leading lady, and 'My Fair Lady', which opened at the Theatre Royal on Drury Lane in 1958 and starred Julie Andrews. Peter Holmes remembers: 'We arranged to have free advertising in all of the programmes and in exchange we supplied all of the shoes without charge. The slight problem we had was that 'My Fair Lady' ran for five-and-a-half years and the chorus girls kept changing, so we were forever making new shoes. But it did help to make our name. We in fact had quite a battle with the Queen's shoemaker, Edward Rayne, who wanted to take the contract from us, but we didn't give way. It was a great feather in our cap at the time.'

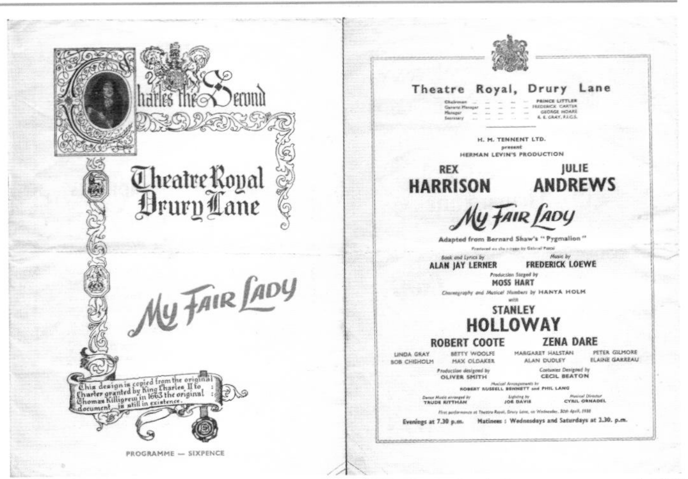

Charles the Second

Theatre Royal Drury Lane

My Fair Lady

This design is copied from the original Charter granted by King Charles II to Thomas Killigrew in 1663 the original document is still in existence.

PROGRAMME — SIXPENCE

Theatre Royal, Drury Lane

Chairman — PRINCE LITTLER
General Manager — FREDERICK CARTER
Manager — GEORGE HOARE
Secretary — R. E. GRAY, F.I.C.S.

H. M. TENNENT LTD.
present
HERMAN LEVIN'S PRODUCTION

REX HARRISON — JULIE ANDREWS

My Fair Lady

Adapted from Bernard Shaw's "Pygmalion"

Book and Lyrics by ALAN JAY LERNER — Music by FREDERICK LOEWE

Production Staged by MOSS HART

Choreography and Musical Numbers by HANYA HOLM

with

STANLEY HOLLOWAY

ROBERT COOTE — ZENA DARE

LINDA GRAY, BETTY WOOLFE, MARGARET HALSTAN, PETER GILMORE, BOB CHISHOLM, MAX OLDAKER, ALAN DUDLEY, ELAINE GARREAU

Production designed by OLIVER SMITH — Costumes Designed by CECIL BEATON

Musical Arrangements by ROBERT RUSSELL BENNETT and PHIL LANG

Dance Music arranged by TRUDE RITTMAN — Lighting by JOE DAVIS — Musical Director CYRIL ORNADEL

First performance at Theatre Royal, Drury Lane, on Wednesday, 30th April, 1958

Evenings at 7.30 p.m. Matinees : Wednesdays and Saturdays at 2.30. p.m.

'My Fair Lady' programme, 1958

Harold and Alice Johnson (couple on right), Drury Lane, c1958

Local firms also made many shoes for ballroom dancers. For instance Wards made shoes for world ballroom-dancing champion Peter Eggleton (a title he held in 1966, 1969 and 1970 with partner Brenda Winslade). Additionally, whilst working at Shorten & Armes (1963 – 82), John St Quintin can still recall the day he returned to the factory after lunch to find that they were being visited by Dimitri Petrides and his wife Nina Hunt, renowned Latin-American dancers and coaches. John takes up the story: 'They told me what they were looking for, and so I ran them up a pair of pullovers [roughly made shoes without fixed outer soles] which Nina tried on. It was just what they wanted, and after that I made them and their pupils thousands of pairs of mainly white-satin shoes and sandals. I often went to see them at their dance school in London with its huge hall with mirrors all around the edge. I used to see them on television in "Come Dancing", where they were judges and held up the numbers to score the competitors.'

John already had experience of designing shoes for celebrities during his time at Kirbys (1956 – 1963), where he recalls a visit by pop star Alma Cogan who asked him to make some lacy, theatrical shoes to match her bouffant dresses. He recalls that days later the smell of her perfume still lingered in the sample room. John's other claim to fame is that he made and designed white-silver dance shoes worn by Olivia Newton-John in the film 'Grease' (1978).

Peter Eggleton, undated

Alma Cogan, c1958

Norwich shoes were also popular with dancers when they were not performing. For example, in the late 1940s and early 1950s, whilst working at Barfield & Richardson, designer Len Waspe made shoes for many famous ballerinas, including Dame Margot Fonteyn, Moira Shearer (who starred in the film 'The Red Shoes') and Nadia Nerina. In fact in 1952 he designed all of the shoes worn offstage by the Sadler's Wells Ballet Company during their American tour. His daughter Margaret Brawn Meek recounts: 'I still have a photo of him with Dame Margot Fonteyn and Pamela May after the fitting where he looks slightly dishevelled. On the back he's written: "Yours truly shattered after fitting an entire company." Ballerinas have very distorted feet as a result of being on pointes from a very early age. As a little girl I used to go to his workshop where he had wooden lasts everywhere. When he made shoes for ballerinas, whose feet were covered in lumps and bumps, he used to mould bits of plaster and stick them on to the lasts so that they accurately reflected the shape of the ballerina's feet with a bunion here or a lump there. It would have been very expensive to have shoes personally fitted and made like that. Margot Fonteyn sent me a signed pair of ballet shoes. Sadly when the shoe trade failed dad sold them to raise money...but I wish I still had them.'

(L to r) Pamela May, Margot Fonteyn, Len Waspe, c1952

Nadia Nerina (centre), Len Waspe (r), c1952

(L to r) Moira Shearer, Len Waspe, c1952

Richard Todd stands to the right of Victor Scarlett (in the white coat), Bally, 1962

Similar to royalty, celebrities also toured around the shoe factories. The above photograph was taken in February 1962 during a trip to Norwich by Richard Todd. Ostensibly he came to attend the Norfolk & Norwich Press Ball, but during a hectic day after arriving on an old locomotive, called the Norfolkman, he managed to squeeze in visits to both the Bally and Mackintosh Caley factories, lunch at the Maid's Head, tea at the Regent Café and a meal at the Samson & Hercules!

The staff very much enjoyed such visits as recalled by Jean Woods, who was a supervisor in Start-rite's machine room in 1994 when the Crome Road factory played host to Ruth Maddoc, better known as Gladys Pugh from the sitcom 'Hi-De-Hi!'. Ruth had come to collect a cheque on behalf of the Paul O'Gorman Foundation, which helped children with leukaemia. Jean recounts: 'We'd been told in no uncertain terms that we were to stand there and say nothing to her. I was at one end of the factory and she came in the other and walked all the way up the factory. When she got near to where I was standing the girls looked at me and I gave them the nod and they all shouted out: "Hi-de-Hi!" Well she thought that was wonderful. We had great fun.'

In 2013 dance shoes are still made in Norwich at Freed of London's factory on Mason Road (off Mile Cross Lane). In particular pointe shoes are made for many prestigious ballet companies including both the Royal and Northern Ballets. In 2010 they made the shoes for Natalie Portman when she appeared in the film 'Black Swan'.

Ruth Maddoc, Start-rite, 1994

Lasting Memories

Mike Copland recalls an early footwear order he made for a well-known celebrity: 'Years ago I made a pair of slippers for Dean Martin and we've recently been approached by an American guy who asked us to make an identical pair from a photograph he had. He was flabbergasted when he found out I'd made the originals.'

John St Quintin remembers his time at Barfield & Richardson: 'At Barfield & Richardson we made outdoor shoes for the Sadler's Wells Ballet Company. Len [Waspe] used to go to London to measure their feet and we made bespoke shoes. I recall that in his office he had a pair of ballet pumps on the wall which had been worn and signed by Margot Fonteyn. Although we mainly made ladies' shoes we did make shoes for Robert Helpmann, a dancer and choreographer, and other male dancers.'

As a cost accountants Arthur Holmes needed to take a balanced view: 'When we made shoes for the Royal Family we invoiced a London firm and we charged the normal price for a "special", which was 50% above the cost of a mass-produced shoe. In the 1960s I would think the shoes would have cost around £50 a pair to make, equivalent to around £500 today. The cost was high because our fitter, Billy Peake, went to the Palace and then the shoes were made individually on a special last. This meant we were making a loss but obviously we were very proud to have the order which gave great kudos and publicity to Start-rite.'

Janet Metcalf: 'At Florida we made a pair of shoes for the Queen Mother for her hundredth birthday and I was thrilled because not only did I help make them but I was the person who put them in the box.'

June Whitfield visits W. H. H. Clarke, 1975

1954
NORWICH
MANUFACTURERS
seen at their annual luncheon
by the
'NEWS' ARTIST
Eric Sexton,
Sexton Son
& Everard
Geoffrey Barrett,
Shorten & Armes
Jim Hanly,
Start-rite
Arthur Howlett, Batson & Webster
Richard Parker,
Norvic
Paul Moll,
Bally
T. C. Jones,
Secretary
NFMA
Ralph Colman, Norvic
Geoffrey Holmes,
Edwards & Holmes
D. P. Hurrell,
Hurrells

8. The Norwich Footwear Manufacturers

In his book 'Shoemaking in Norwich', published in 1949, Wilfred Sparks included a separate section giving information on five of the 'oldest and largest' Norwich shoe firms. At the time these were: James Southall & Co. Ltd, Bally Shoe Factories (Norwich) Ltd, Sexton, Son & Everard Ltd, Norvic Shoe Co. Ltd and Edwards & Holmes Ltd.

In the pages that follow we have charted the rise and, in the vast majority of cases, the decline of more than 30 firms of varying sizes. We have concentrated mainly, but not exclusively, on firms that were in existence after WWII. Where possible we have included personal memories, newspaper reports and photographs to bring the story of each firm alive.

The names of many of the companies changed over time, which presented some challenges in deciding the most appropriate way to list them. Please note the following:

- Generally we have listed a firm under its final name. For example, information on James Southall & Co. Ltd is found under Start-rite Ltd. However, where a company was known by a name for many years and this was changed for the last few years of its existence, we have listed it under its original name. For example, Shingler & Thetford Ltd, which was founded in 1901, is not listed as Burlington International who owned the firm for its last three years of trading.
- We are conscious that many firms are also better known by their 'local' names rather than their official titles, which may give problems when trying to trace a firm. Please use the table below to locate specific firms.
- On occasion we have included information on a new firm, which was set up by directors of a failed one. Information on both companies appears together. Again please use the table below to locate specific firms.

For the following:	See
Bowhill & Hubbard	Thomas Bowhill & Hubbard Ltd
Burlington International	Shingler & Thetford Ltd
A. Chittock & Co.	Chittock & Sons Ltd
Clarkes	W. H. H. Clarke Ltd
CWS	Co-operative Wholesale Society Ltd
Haldinsteins	Bally Shoe Factories (Norwich) Ltd
Howletts	Arthur Howlett Ltd
Howlett & White Ltd	Norvic Shoe Company Ltd
Hurrells	W. Hurrell Ltd
James Southall & Co. Ltd	Start-rite Ltd
K Shoemakers Ltd	W. H. H. Clarke Ltd
Kirbys	John F. Kirby Ltd
Magdalen Shoes Ltd	Freed of London Ltd
Norwich Shoes Ltd	Shingler & Thetford Ltd
Osoeasie Slipper Company Ltd	Bowhill & Elliott Ltd
P. Haldinstein & Sons Ltd	Bally Shoe Factories (Norwich) Ltd
Rudards Ltd	Co-operative Wholesale Society Ltd
Seggers	P. Segger (Norwich) Ltd
Sexton Shoes Ltd	Sexton, Son & Everard Ltd
Shinglers	Shingler & Thetford Ltd
Southalls	Start-rite Ltd
Van Dal (previously Van-Dal)	Florida Group Ltd
Wittons	S. L. Witton Ltd

When captioning photographs we have included as much information as possible about workers, machinery and the department/room that is depicted. Please note that where images were produced before WWII the rooms may differ from those described on pages 25 to 46. Where little is known about a picture but we think it is interesting it has been reproduced despite the lack of particulars.

Principal Sites of the Shoe Trade in Central Norwich c1960

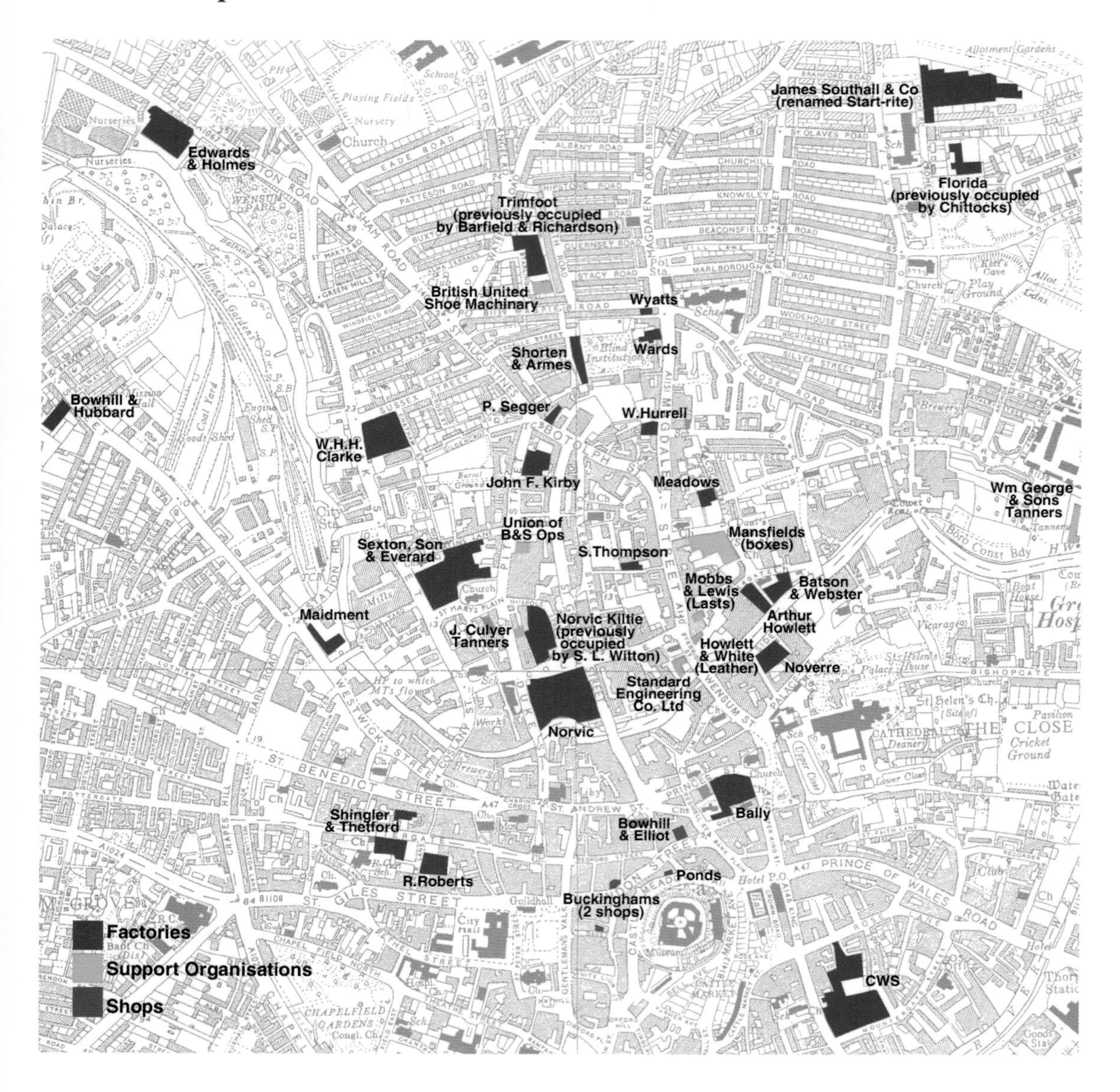

This map shows the location of:

- The main factories occupied by the companies described in this chapter. Please note that a number had factories outside the area shown on the map. Additionally in 1959 Thomas Bowhill & Hubbard relocated from Heigham Street and took over part of John F. Kirbys' factory on Pitt Street, but here they are shown as being located at their earlier site.
- Support organisations mentioned on pages 231 to 238, which were located within the area shown on the map.
- The retail outlets occupied by Bowhill & Elliott Ltd, J. Buckingham & Sons Ltd, and Ponds Foot Fitters Ltd.

Arthur Howlett Ltd

The firm of Arthur Howlett Ltd was founded on Fishergate in 1947.

At the time Arthur Howlett was a director at Batson & Webster, a firm that he had joined as 'the boy' in 1913. Here he had worked his way up to the position of manager, and subsequently married Fred Webster's daughter, Blanche. In the late 1930s he took on the role of MD. After WWII, although business was good, Batson & Webster had too many families to support. As explained by Arthur's son Graham Howlett: 'My father and uncle were directors, but both had two sons who wanted to go into the shoe trade. So in 1947 my father and brother Eric, who was 12 years older than me, started a small business in a renovated building on the corner of Fishergate and Hansard Lane called Arthur Howlett Ltd. In the mid-fifties I joined the business.' Howletts produced children's shoes whilst Batson & Webster mostly made ladies' shoes, hence the firms weren't in competition. Although Arthur had shares in the business it was run by his sons.

In 1968, when the firm was producing 12,000 pairs of shoes a week, the business was sold to Norvic. Graham explains why: 'Our decision to sell was largely based on the fact that between us my brother and I owned 90% of the shares in the company. If one of us had died the death duties would have been horrendous, and it is likely that the company would have gone bust. Additionally, Eric was a very capable man and Norvic offered him the opportunity to run their children's division. A challenge he was eager to take up.'

Both brothers went to work for Norvic, where in 1971 Eric was appointed MD of the children's division. Two years later Howletts was sold to Start-rite and Eric made the decision to move with it. At the time of his death in 1977 he was still Howletts' MD.

(L to r) Graham, Eric and Arthur Howlett, 1958

Between 1975 and 1986 Start-rite closed a number of its ancillary factories until production was concentrated at Crome Road and Arthur Howlett's former factory on Fishergate.

When Jean Woods worked for Start-rite in the early 1980s she was based at the Fishergate premises. She recalls: 'The factory was on two floors and stretched from the road through to the river. When I went there, on the ground floor they dealt with the "bottom stuff", which were the soles. On the first floor the clickers were at the end near the road and the rest of the floor was taken up by the closing room. It wasn't posh but the atmosphere was good. We couldn't really hear the noise from the bottom floor but the clickers made a lot of noise.'

In 1995 the Fishergate factory was finally closed down although the building still stands in 2013.

The former Arthur Howlett factory, Fishergate, 1985

Bally Shoe Factories (Norwich) Ltd

David Soman, undated

Philip Haldinstein, undated

In 1934 Bally, a Swiss-based shoe-manufacturing firm, came to Norwich. Around 1880 the company had developed substantial exports to Britain, and in 1892 they had even opened their first shop in London. In the early 1930s, when the UK government imposed heavy import duties on many products, including shoes, it made sense for Bally to seek a partnership in England with a high-grade manufacturer who would make shoes that bore the Bally name. At the time Norwich had a reputation of making top-quality shoes for ladies, and so it was natural for Bally to seek a partner here. P. Haldinstein & Sons Ltd (Haldinsteins), one of the City's largest manufacturers, was particularly attractive to Bally because George Haldinstein, who ran the business at the time of the merger, had no heirs who wanted to retain their interest in the firm. The partnership agreement was made between the two companies at the end of 1933, and was put in motion in the following year.

Haldinsteins had been founded in 1799 by David Soman, a French emigré, initially to make caps, although he eventually began manufacturing boots and shoes. In 1846 Philip Haldinstein married one of David Soman's daughters and was taken into partnership with his father-in-law. In 1853 the partnership was dissolved and the business was carried on solely by Philip Haldinstein, who in 1870 took his eldest son, Woolfe Haldinstein, into partnership. By the time of Philip's death in 1891, when he was 82 years old, the business had grown considerably and even had a branch in London.

Following Woolfe's death in 1896, his son Alfred became sole proprietor. By 1904 the firm employed around 2,000 people, and had extended beyond Norwich and London with factories in Leicester, Kettering and Wymondham. At the time it was reported in the publication 'The Men Who Have Made Norwich', by Edward Burgess: 'At each of the branch factories there is a constant output of boots and shoes of all kinds – from ladies' and girls' lightest evening-dress shoes to men's heavy boots.'

By then the company occupied extensive premises comprising seven blocks of buildings which ran between Queen Street, Princes Street, Redwell Street and Tombland. In 1904 the building was subdivided as follows:

- Adjoining the churchyard of St Michael at Plea was a five-storey stockroom. The basement of the same building was used as a leather room
- The original four-storey premises occupied by Haldinsteins was in Queen Street, located next to the warehouse. It contained offices, sample rooms, drying rooms and the export department
- Central to the site was a large six-storey factory, built of white brick, in which the actual manufacturing took place. It included: the bottom-stock room (ground floor), the clicking room (first floor) and the finishing room. On the top '...was a large airy, well-lighted machine room, where at least 100 women and girls were occupied in fitting and machining the uppers of boots and shoes and gaiters and leggings'
- From Redwell Street was a path leading to the entrance to another factory where the 'nursery works' were located. Also produced here were patent oxford and court shoes
- Next to this was another block where items such as tennis shoes and slippers were produced.

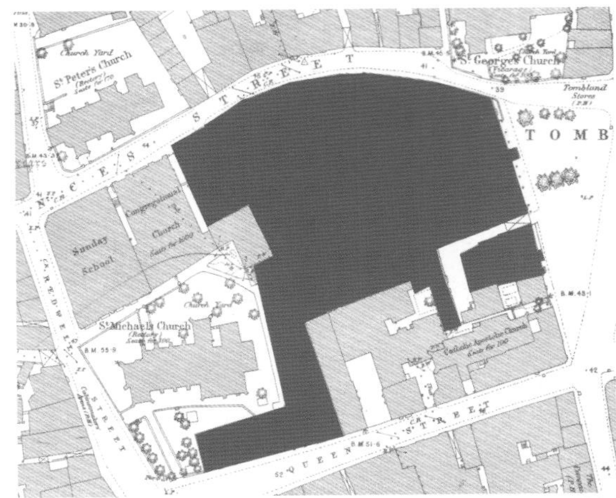

Approximate location of the Bally shoe factory, c1904

From Princes Street one could also enter a block housing an engineers' shop on the ground floor and a carpenters' shop above. Edward Burgess explains: 'The engineering department has a wider scope than is generally implied by the term. It is here that knives for cutting are turned out for use in larger numbers than many a small workshop, devoted exclusively to the work, could produce. In the carpenters' shop, in addition to urgent repairs, all the export cases required by the firm are made.'

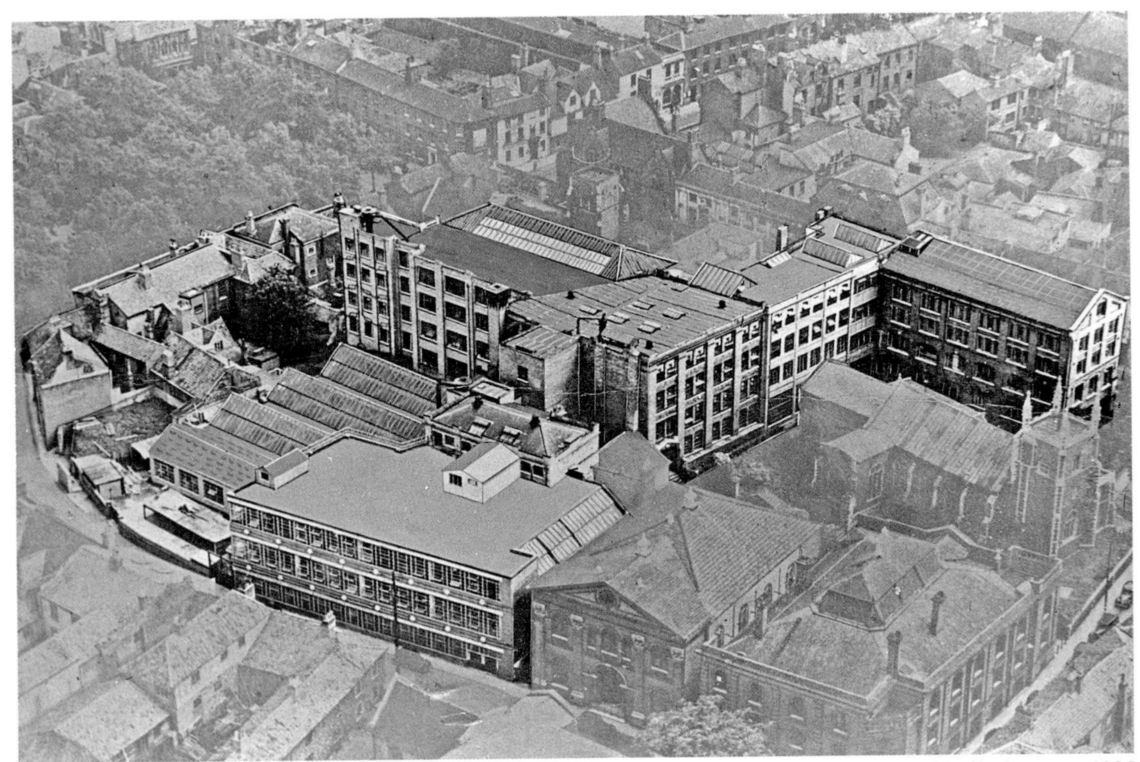
The former Haldinstein and Bally factory, c1935

George Haldinstein, 1934

Paul Moll, c1965

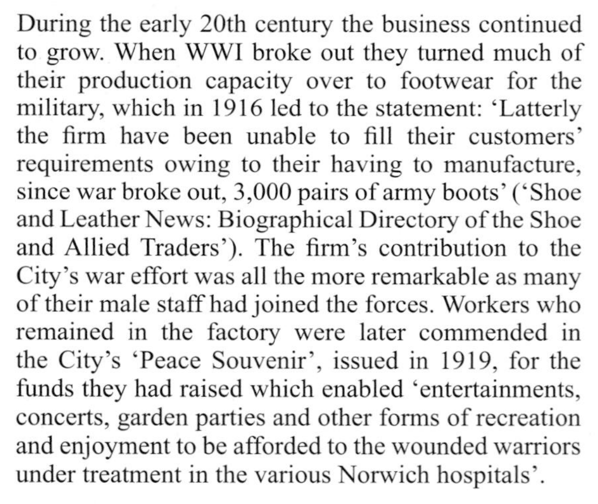

During the early 20th century the business continued to grow. When WWI broke out they turned much of their production capacity over to footwear for the military, which in 1916 led to the statement: 'Latterly the firm have been unable to fill their customers' requirements owing to their having to manufacture, since war broke out, 3,000 pairs of army boots' ('Shoe and Leather News: Biographical Directory of the Shoe and Allied Traders'). The firm's contribution to the City's war effort was all the more remarkable as many of their male staff had joined the forces. Workers who remained in the factory were later commended in the City's 'Peace Souvenir', issued in 1919, for the funds they had raised which enabled 'entertainments, concerts, garden parties and other forms of recreation and enjoyment to be afforded to the wounded warriors under treatment in the various Norwich hospitals'.

By then George Haldinstein, Alfred's son, was head of the firm (although he did not take over full control until his father's death in 1923) and the factory in Norwich had been reorganised and reconstructed to enable them to produce high-quality footwear for ladies and children. This strategy was so successful that in 1922 Haldinsteins' reputation for making satin and brocade shoes resulted in them being invited to make wedding shoes for Princess Mary, the only daughter of King George V and Queen Mary, when she married Viscount Lascelles. The same reputation drew the firm to the attention of Bally, and led to them initiating the partnership agreement. Paul Moll was sent over from Switzerland to establish the collaboration. Paul's family (which included his nine-year-old son Walter who later became a director of the Norwich business) arrived in Norwich in April 1934. Walter recalls: 'Ironically, although Bally had been established as early as 1851 Haldinsteins could trace its origins as far back as 1799, so in some quarters my father's arrival here was seen as a case of teaching your grandmother to suck eggs! Despite this he was made welcome by George Haldinstein.'

Between 1934 and the outbreak of WWII the partnership of Bally and Haldinstein, based in the old Queen Street factory, successfully developed their business. However, the war brought about two major management changes. Firstly George Haldinstein, who was Jewish, was worried about a Nazi invasion and moved to South Africa leaving Paul Moll to run the company. Subsequently, because Paul was a German-speaking Swiss subject, he was deemed a potential danger to the country if an invasion occurred on the east coast. As a result he had to move from Norwich, but only as far as Thetford, from where he managed the business. Eventually in April 1942, by which time Bally was producing footwear for the forces, the authorities let him move back.

After the end of the war George Haldinstein, who still owned 51% of the company, returned to Norwich. Initially he wanted to take over the reins again but after his prolonged absence Paul Moll felt the time was right for Bally to buy him out, which is what they did, and in 1946 the company became Bally Shoe Factories (Norwich) Ltd. Paul Moll was the first Managing Director, a role he held until 1968, although he continued as chairman until 1971.

In the mid-1940s the firm was producing 620,000 pairs of shoes a year. By 1958, which marked the 25th anniversary of Bally and Haldinsteins entering into partnership, output exceeded one million pairs. The increase in production was partially attributable to the strength of the export market, which absorbed around 12.5% of output. It could also be ascribed to the opening of a new factory in Lowestoft, which had taken place in 1955. Prior to that the company only had a closing room in the town, but Bally used the new premises to make cheaper footwear out of synthetic materials.

Bally shoe fountains at a shoe exhibition, 1957

Bally shoes with mannequins at a shoe exhibition, 1957

Shoe display room, Bally, 1957

Picture Gallery - Former Bally Factories

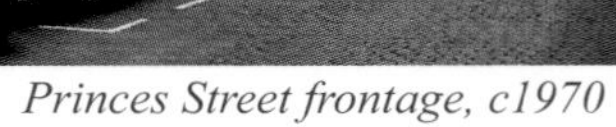

Princes Street frontage, c1970

Overlooking St Michael at Plea, c1970

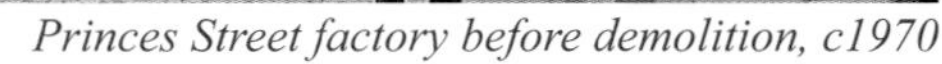

Princes Street factory before demolition, c1970

Hall Road, c1970

By the 1950s the City-centre location of the factory was problematical for both the company and the City authorities. The factory had grown in an ad-hoc fashion, which hindered production, whilst the traffic generated by workers was quite mind blowing, as explained by Walter Moll: 'The thing I remember well about the 1950s was that nearly everyone came to work on bicycles. When you think that at one stage we had over 1,400 people working in the factory it was quite a sight to see them come and go. Not only at the start and end of the day but many also went home over their 90-minute lunch break.'

Between 1961 and 1969 Bally relocated to a purpose-built factory, warehouse and administrative centre on Hall Road. Brian Lambert recalls when the main part of the factory was finally transferred from the City centre: 'It was August 1969, during the staff holiday period, when we moved the main part of the factory across to our new building on Hall Road. You can just imagine how traumatic it was to pack up the entire factory. We had lorry after lorry transporting machinery and stock.'

Walter Moll explains the advantages of the move: 'We became a lot more efficient, not least because the new factory was on one floor. We had occupied about three-quarters of the area between Queen Street and Princes Street, we even had offices on Tombland, and manufacturing was spread across five levels. The place was like a rabbit warren...if you wanted to go and see a colleague it could take five minutes. Production at Hall Road was a lot more efficient. The layout of the factory was much better than at the old factory, to the extent that we cut the time it took to make a pair of shoes by one third. The new layout also enabled us to reduce management numbers. We introduced a conveyor system in the making departments, which was quite revolutionary at the time.' Following the relocation, improvement in productivity resulted in staff numbers being reduced to 750. However, within a few years demand for Bally footwear outstripped supply, and in 1973 the firm opened a new closing room in Dereham.

A rare view of St George Tombland and the Cathedral from the demolished Bally factory, Princes Street, c1970

In 1974, the decision was made to restructure Ballys' operation in the UK. Until then there were three distinct companies each of which had its own board of directors and management structure. These were:

- Bally Shoe Factories (Norwich) Ltd, which manufactured footwear for the group
- Bally Shoe Company Ltd, which was the wholesaler for the group
- Bally London Shoe Company Ltd, which was the retailer for the group.

After rationalisation, the firms were amalgamated into the Bally Group (UK) Ltd. This enabled many functions that had previously been triplicated, including warehousing, computer services and financial control, to be centralised in Norwich. Ten years later, in 1984, the firm celebrated 50 years of shoemaking in Norwich. In the same year the group turnover approached £35 million. Despite the problems facing the footwear industry Geoffrey Marshall, the Bally Group managing director, was confident enough to announce: 'We next plan to mark the 200-year anniversary of the company's original foundation by David Soman, which comes up in 1999.' He also somewhat mischievously added: 'It is a nice point that this event will precede the bicentennial of Bally Switzerland by 52 years!'

In the same year Walter Moll was invited to lead an international delegation of shoe manufacturers to India. They had been invited to the country by officials who were aware that they had a lot to learn from Europeans about all aspects of shoemaking. He notes: 'Largely as a result of my visit, Bally started to buy-in components from India. The Indians produced leather, mostly kid or buffalo, which they cut into uppers. So rather than import hides we imported uppers at a much lower price than we could produce them here. At the same time we started to buy other components, such as leather soles, from Italy. Consequently, we changed from undertaking every aspect of shoe production to being an assembly plant, and as a result we employed fewer people.'

As little as five years later Geoffrey Marshall's conviction that Bally would survive the next 15 years appeared to be in doubt, when in April 1989 the *Eastern Evening News* carried the chilling headline: 'Bally to axe 100 jobs and factory.' Luckily the position wasn't as bad as implied as the factory in question was the Dereham closing room. Nevertheless it marked a decision by Bally to slash manufacturing by another 15%, which not only resulted in the loss of 53 jobs at Dereham, but also led to additional redundancies at Lowestoft and Norwich. As a result the production workforce was reduced to around 500 personnel, with a further 200 people employed locally on wholesale and central services.

Walter Moll, c1965

In the years that followed the numbers employed by Bally continued to contract. Then in 1997 the Lowestoft factory was closed and the Norwich manufacturing division was split from the UK group and sold to a management buy-out team, headed by Bob Marston and Ivor Whitbread. The couple renamed the famous old company Eaton International Ltd, and continued to employ over 200 staff at Hall Road (which was still owned by Bally).

Sadly in 1999 bicentennial celebrations were not held – but a wake was – as in August of that year Eaton International called in the receivers and shoe manufacturing ceased.

In October 1999 the Hall Road premises were put on the market by Bally. In 2012 planning permission was granted for a development scheme incorporating both retail and leisure facilities.

Meanwhile in September 1999 Bally's Swiss-based owner, Oerlikon Buhrie Holding, sold the company to the Texas Pacific Group. It was subsequently purchased by the LABELUX group, a Vienna-based luxury goods holding company. Today the name of Bally is still synonymous with quality footwear.

Lasting Memories

Brian Lambert recalls his time at Bally: 'The City-centre building was huge. It faced onto three streets: Queen Street, Princes Street and Tombland. The ladies used to go in through the Tombland entrance with their cycles, just about everyone had a cycle then. I used to have to go up Princes Street and down in the basement where us men left our bikes. Just inside the entrance was the directors' garage, where they parked their cars. The only part of the building that is still there is the front office, including the technical department office where I worked.

'At Queen Street there wasn't a conventional conveyor belt, so the shoes were moved around the factory on metal trays and trolleys. At Hall Road we had tracks in the lasting and making rooms, which really quickened up the shoemaking process. The only problem with the tracks was that if a couple of machines broke down, and a procedure couldn't be done, work often stopped as the shoe couldn't move onto the next process. The downtime on some of the new integrated machines, many of which were hydraulic, was quite high. Obviously this gave us problems.

'In the 1970s we were beginning to assemble some shoes, rather than make them from scratch. For example, we started to produce men's moccasins at our Lowestoft factory. By taking shortcuts, such as buying in our uppers (pre-cut and sewn) from India and our sole units from Italy, it only took about six operations in our own factory to finish them off. At one time we were producing around 2,000 pairs a week. We then moved on to make classic shoes for men in the same manner.'

Ron Green remembers his early years at the City-centre factory : 'In 1949, when I was 15, I started at Ballys' shoe factory in Queen Street. It was a huge building three storeys high that stretched across as far as Princes Street. To the east there was an entrance onto Tombland. Imagine leaving off work in those days. Our bikes were all kept in the cellar – there were hundreds of them all in a tangle. We all poured out of the Princes Street entrance, all in a hurry. We were paid on Fridays and on my first pay day I remember cycling home with one hand on my back pocket, which contained £1 10s. My mother took it and I was left with 2s. 6d.

'As a youngster I'd often go night fishing and get to work tired so I'd get someone to cover for me and get a bit of a kip in the last lockers. The lockers for lasts which were size 9 to 9 ½ were the best 'cos they were up really high.'

Brian Lambert (right) with the technical team, Bally, c1960

Barfield & Richardson Ltd

(L to r) John St Quintin discusses a design with Len Waspe, c1965

In June 1954 it was announced that a receiver had been appointed at Barfield & Richardson Ltd. At the time of the receivership the factory was located on Starling Road.

Even though it was one of the smaller Norwich factories, when it closed it still ran all of the traditional departments, including pattern making, a clicking room, a machine room, bottom-stock preparation and a trimming room. The premises had been used as a boot and shoe factory since 1886, but whilst it was old it was well maintained. John St Quintin started working there in 1948 when he was 16 years old, he recalls: 'The factory was cold. The pipes around the factory were right up high and of course any heat rose, so they were totally ineffective. Windows were draughty, they rattled when the wind blew. So I'd look forward to my break at 10 o' clock when we used to walk over to the canteen for a cup of tea and a cheese roll.' Reg Kilbourn also worked there at the end of the 1940s. One of his lasting memories is of killing mice in the leather room!

Len Waspe began working here in 1931 as 'the boy', where one of his first jobs was to sweep the factory. He joined his father Frederick, who had worked in the trade from 1906, and at Barfield & Richardson had risen to the position of foreman clicker. Despite his humble start Len had an outstanding career during which he won numerous gold and silver medals and 23 diplomas for his shoe designs. His trademark at Barfield & Richardson was the 'Boofers' range, which were stylish, top of the range day shoes for ladies, often designed with a slight wedge. In the 1950s he made shoes for many famous ballerinas, including Dame Margot Fonteyn and Moira Shearer (star of the film 'The Red Shoes'). In fact, in 1952 he designed all of the shoes worn offstage by the Sadler's Wells Ballet Company during their American tour.

Len left Barfield & Richardson to be a director at Trimfoot Ltd, which was formed in 1953. Following the demise of Barfield & Richardson, Trimfoot took over the Starling Road premises and also provided employment for many of their staff.

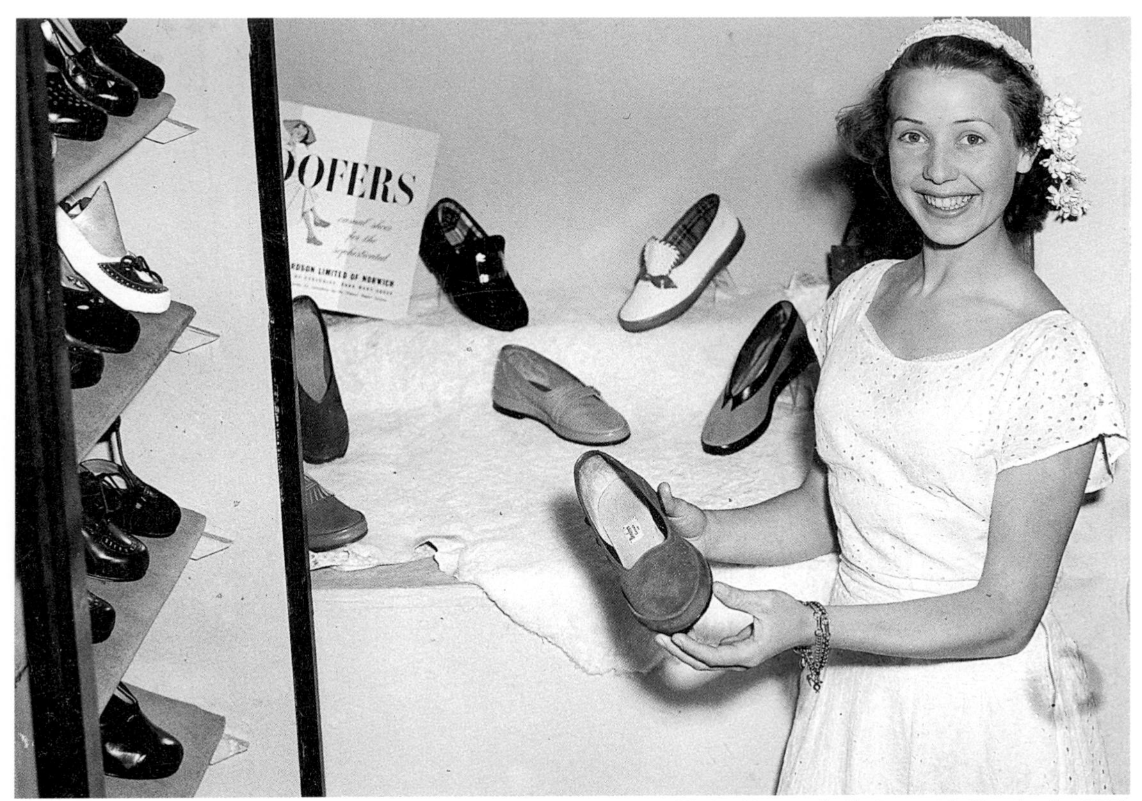

Nadia Nerina, ballerina, with 'Boofers', c1952

'Boofers', spring range, 1952

Batson & Webster Ltd

(L to r) Reggie Batson, Jack Batson, Brian Batson, Mike Batson, c1955

It was in 1913 that Frederick Webster, a pattern cutter at Howlett & White, formed a partnership with his colleague Jack Batson, the foreman of the making room, to set up a shoemaking business called Batson & Webster. As orders came in they established a small factory in Calvert Street with six employees, but soon moved into a new factory at St Edmund's Works on Fishergate.

Graham Howlett recalls that his grandfather Fred Webster was a very big man: 'He had a reputation of being a fierce disciplinarian, and so he could be quite frightening. He'd fire a whole room if he thought it necessary, and obviously in those days there was no such thing as unemployment benefit or redundancy pay. There's a story that in the 1920s a trade union official was sent to see him. The official enraged my grandfather so much that he picked the poor man up by the scruff of his neck, took him over to Fye Bridge and threw him in the river. Fortunately this chap could swim! At the time a lot of the factory owners and managers were despots, but they did have a lot of drive and they needed that to succeed.'

In the same year that the business was formed a 14-year-old Arthur Howlett saw a notice outside the premises which said 'Boy wanted'. Arthur, whose father Robert was a garret master, already had experience in the trade as he had been working part time in his family's business since the age of 11. He applied and got the job and soon proved himself as an accomplished clicker. Fred Webster saw Arthur's potential and put him in charge of the clicking room after which he continued to be promoted until he reached the position of manager. Arthur subsequently married Fred's daughter Blanche.

Until around 1930 Arthur always worked inside the factory, as many considered his Norfolk accent and limited education would prevent him from being an effective salesman. However, he was a very determined man and decided that he needed to know the other side of the business, and so he started dealing with the buyers. Proving his detractors wrong, it wasn't long before his Norfolk accent and sense of humour made him one of the best-known characters in the industry. His ability to get along with people was the secret of his success.

Just before WWII Fred Webster became ill and couldn't carry on and so Arthur took over as MD. By then Reggie Batson, Jack's son, had also joined the business as a director. During WWII Reggie joined the RAF. Arthur was too old to be called up but served as a special constable. Later on he used to speak of the time when he was a 'poor copper'.

WWII obviously put a strain on the industry. Arthur recognised the need to plan ahead and he stored machinery, equipment and materials in a barn at Panxworth. Some of his competitors thought that he

Arthur Howlett marries Blanche Webster, Fred Webster stands behind her, c1920

was ultra-cautious, but the raids came and he was proved right. The Panxworth store was used to help those in trouble. Then on Saturday 5 September 1942 a bomb landed in Batson & Webster's courtyard and blew up a fire-watcher's brick look-out post. Arthur's son Graham recalls: 'My father was very lucky. He'd been working in his office and left his jacket on the back of his chair when he went into the factory. His office was blown up and I still remember him coming home that evening in his short-sleeved shirt, without his jacket.' Sadly two employees, Joan Knights and George Smith, were killed in the attack whilst another 14 were injured. Graham recollects: 'From a young age my father was affiliated to the Labour Party and, especially during the war, he took the view that "everyone was in it together" and so he made sure that the girls who were injured were looked after.'

In 1950, at the age of 15, Mike Batson (whose paternal grandfather was Jack Batson and maternal grandfather was Fred Webster) joined the family firm: 'We made a very unique shoe, which had been created by my Grandad Webster, for mature ladies. We used a machine to prick out holes on the uppers which made intricate patterns. We sold them mainly through Barratts of Northampton. Every year they would give us an order, maybe of around 250,000 shoes, which was the mainstay of the business.'

Batson & Webster's factory has been demolished and replaced by the modern flats below, but a plaque recalls the bombing of 1942, photos 2012

Arthur Howlett, c1910

Meanwhile Arthur Howlett continued to lead the business, only retiring from Batson & Webster a year before he died in 1961.

Although he enjoyed his position he never forgot his poor beginnings. Graham reports: 'As a lad my father was in the Boys' Brigade, where he played the kettle drums. He used to go with the brigade on an annual camp to Trimingham, which he thought was great because it was the only holiday he had. He always kept in touch with them and eventually he became their president. Even then he used to join them at the camp for a couple of nights. Every year he used to take the whole brigade to see the pantomime at the Theatre Royal. He'd ring up and book every seat for one performance. All the boys and officers, with their girlfriends and wives used to turn up for a great night out.'

In 1962, the year after Arthur's death, the company was sold to the Liverpool Shoe Group, a London-based firm. The factory was kept running until 1967 when it was closed down. The building has since been demolished and new residential flats built in its place. The location of the former factory is marked by a plaque which commemorates the deaths of Joan Knights and George Smith during the 1942 raid.

Arthur Howlett officiating as the Boys' Brigade march past, c1955

Bowhill & Elliott Ltd

Although the firm of Bowhill & Elliott is well known in Norwich for its shoe shop on London Street, relatively few people are aware that in a small factory, located behind the retail premises, beautiful slippers are made using traditional techniques.

It was in 1960 that Sidney Jury, whose family own Bowhill & Elliott, bought the Osoeasie Slipper Company, which in turn had been established in 1939 by Jack Hale.

When Bowhill & Elliott purchased the company it was based in the old Enterprise Cinema on Northumberland Street. This resulted in the factory having some rather unusual features, not least of which was a slightly sloping floor. Mike Copland, who started work in the Bowhill & Elliott repair shop, moved across to the slipper factory in 1963 and continued to work there for over 40 years. He recalls: 'When I first went to Northumberland Street the closing department was part of the old stage. What they'd done was cut around it leaving an oblong and the ladies sat on either side with their machines on top. At one end of what was the stage there was one massive motor with a shaft leading from it that ran every machine. In the mornings you had a big electrical thing on the wall that you had to crank up to get the motor going. It used to spark like mad...a real fire hazard. In the end health and safety regulations forced us to change everything and get in individual benches and motors.' In such circumstances it is not surprising that eventually the decision was made to move the factory from the old cinema to Bowhill & Elliotts' London Street premises.

The Osoeasie Slipper Company, and subsequently Bowhill & Elliott, specialised in the manufacture of fine turnshoe slippers made out of leather and suede, which were lined with sheepskin. Meanwhile the Ward shoe company made velvet and leather Albert slippers, many of which were sold through Bowhill & Elliott's London Street shop. In 1957 Wards was taken over by Start-rite. Despite this they continued to make slippers until 1977 when their Magdalen Street factory was closed. Mike Copland remembers: 'When Wards closed we were given the opportunity to purchase, for a minimal amount, their old lasts and start manufacturing Albert slippers. After I'd been along to see how Wards made them we decided to give it a go. In the early days it was a struggle, as Wards lasted by machine and we were going back to a hand-lasting method. But in the end we sorted it out.'

It is amazing that in the 21st century many of the slippers produced in Bowhill & Elliotts' factory are still made using the lasts and patterns purchased from Wards.

Hand lasting, Bowhill & Elliott, 2012

Elizabeth Glover, who has worked at Bowhill & Elliott for over 20 years, reports: 'Some of the machines that the ladies use to sew the uppers are over 60 years old... that said they work very well. Also, all of our slippers are hand lasted. The only difference from traditional hand lasting is that under health and safety regulations the lads can't hold the tacks in their mouths!' Elizabeth explains that using such old techniques is not always easy, especially for such a small firm: 'Historically we have always used brass-bound patterns, which are basically templates that are cut around, but it is proving increasingly difficult to get these made. So recently we have started to use acrylic patterns, which sadly keep breaking. It can also be hard to source items such as raw materials, machinery and tools. We are further hindered by the fact that because of our size we do not need to buy in bulk.'

Today the workforce at Bowhill & Elliott continue to produce some of the world's finest and most exclusive slippers, which the firm is proud to announce are 'treasured by royalty, presidents and connoisseurs the world over'.

Clicking by hand, Bowhill & Elliott, 2012

The 'machine room', Bowhill & Elliott, 2012

Broadland Slippers

D & M Shoes, which trades as Broadland Slippers, was set up by David Cubitt and Mike Copland early in the 21st century in a small factory on Renson Close.

Before starting the business, Mike had worked in the trade for well over 40 years at Bowhill & Elliott. He began in their Northumberland Street slipper factory in 1963, and eventually rose to the position of manager. He recalls his early days in the industry: 'In the evenings I studied for all of my diplomas in shoemaking at St George's, and even won a prize for being the top of the class – I think it was the only time it had been awarded to someone who worked in a slipper factory! I also learnt how to mend and maintain machines.'

(L to r) Shaun Cubitt and Mike Copland, 2012

Whilst at Bowhill & Elliott, Mike was aware that the demand for their slippers exceeded the supply, and so he eventually took the decision to set up in partnership with David Cubitt, who did hand lasting as an outworker from a unit on the Cattle Market. David has since retired and his son Shaun, who trained as a hand laster at Bowhills, is now in partnership with Mike. Broadland Slippers make high-quality velvet and leather slippers and house shoes, together with patent-leather pumps and buckle shoes. Customers for the latter have included the parliamentary official Black Rod and the 'Beefeaters' at the Tower of London.

At Broadland Slippers footwear is produced using traditional machinery and techniques. As noted by Mike: 'Most of our equipment has been bought second-hand. Some I bought in the 1970s and 1980s when a lot of the factories were closing down, whilst some was owned by David. I've always enjoyed mending machines so always had a few on the go in my garage.'

Mike and Shaun, together with their small team at Broadland Slippers, go to great efforts to ensure the high quality and the authenticity of the footwear they produce. For example, heels are brass slugged (a slug does the same job as a tack), whereas nowadays most firms use steel. As explained by Mike: 'The reason being that traditionally the slippers were made for the elite, who lived in luxurious properties which more than likely had a parquet-wood floor. Steel is hard and as the leather wore down it would've scratched the floor. On the other hand brass is softer and wears down with the leather avoiding the problem. Today we still give the same attention to detail.'

(L to r), Ollie Plunkett, clicking; Shaun Cubitt, hand lasting; Julie Hartt, machining, Broadland Slippers, 2012

Patent-leather buckle shoes, 2012

The firm supplies footwear to both companies and individuals. Each pair is made to order, and so they can be personalised to include family crests, monograms or club logos. Motifs are hand stitched onto the uppers and, apart from making the leather soles, is the only procedure not undertaken in the factory. The firm sends full details of what they want, together with the uppers, to their embroiderers and in four to six weeks they get them back. Additionally customers send the firm tapestries that they have sewn themselves which are made into slippers.

Similar to so many of the City's older shoe firms, Mike and Shaun continue the tradition of making footwear for both royalty and celebrities. They were particularly proud when they were chosen to make shoes for the page boys at Prince William and Catherine Middleton's wedding. They received the order just ten days before the big day, after which they worked late into the night to ensure that they met the deadline. Eventually the shoes were rushed to London by courier for a fitting on the Thursday before the wedding so that they could be worn by Tom Pettifer and Jamie Lowther-Pinkerton for the dress rehearsal. The shoes had black patent uppers, a satin quilted lining, leather sole and heel and gold buckles. More recently Mike recalls: 'In 2012 Richard James, who has a shop on Savile Row, sent some velvet in various colours. We made them up in a couple of weeks and then they stuck on diamantés. They featured in their fashion show and apparently they were a roaring success. When they sent us photos of the show we saw that Sir Elton John was sitting on the front row, and we're really pleased that he ordered several pairs.'

The firm remains a living testament that there is a huge market for high-quality footwear that is made not only in England, but also in Norwich.

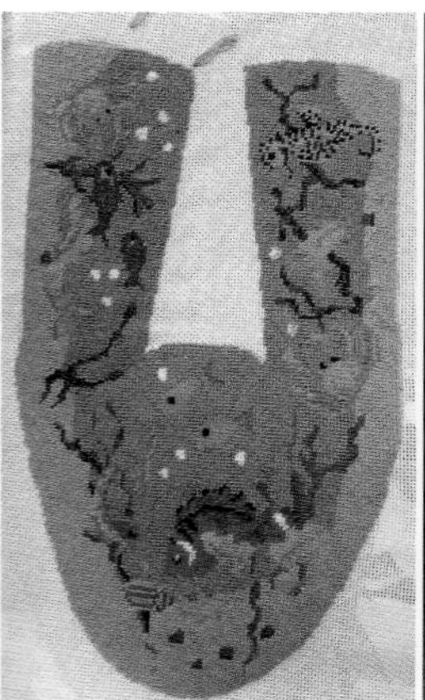

A selection of embroidered uppers, Broadland Slippers, 2012

The original Eagle Shoe Works on Dibden Road, together with Chittocks' directors, 1916

A. Chittock & Co. was founded on Calvert Street c1885 by Mr Arthur Chittock. The firm later relocated to Whitefriars' Bridge where it flourished to such an extent that in 1912 the directors built a splendid new factory, the Eagle Shoe Works, on Dibden Road. This premises was expanded in 1920.

In 1959 Florida purchased Chittock & Sons Ltd and Chittocks (Norwich) Ltd and in so doing acquired the Eagle Shoe Works. Over the next two years Florida transferred their entire operation across to the Dibden Road site, and are still based there today.

The former 'Eagle Works', now the Florida Group factory, Dibden Road, 2012

Co-operative Wholesale Society Ltd

The Boulton & Paul factory, Mountergate, c1900

The CWS factory, Mountergate, 1986

The Co-operative Wholesale Society (CWS) was founded in 1863. Today it is known as the Co-operative Group. The CWS began in small premises in Manchester from where it expanded to produce CWS branded goods for co-operative societies throughout the UK. These included food, furniture, clothing, household products and of course footwear.

In Norwich the Co-operative Wholesale Boot and Shoe Works (CWS) was opened in 1923 on St John's Street, Mountergate. It was located in a building bought from Boulton & Paul Ltd (the engineering company) which was concentrating production in their Riverside premises. It was one of a number of footwear factories owned by the CWS across the country. The CWS footwear group headquarters were in Leicester, where they also made ladies' shoes. Other members of the group included: Buckfastleigh (Devon), which produced moccasins; Haslington (Cheshire), where they made slippers; Rushden (Northamptonshire), which produced men's industrial footwear; Heckmondwike (West Yorkshire) where they made industrial footwear and sportswear. Initially all of the footwear produced by these factories was supplied to the Co-operative Society retail division.

In its early days the CWS paid 'over the odds', i.e. more than the agreed day work rate for a job, which made it a popular place to work. By 1938 CWS employed around 900 and the weekly output was around 12,000 pairs of shoes. In 1943 the Norwich factory stopped producing footwear for men and children, after which output and employment contracted.

In 1970, when Nigel Rudling started working for the company as a work-study engineer, the Norwich operation employed around 330 people. They still occupied the factory on Mountergate, which by then was showing its age. He recalls: 'It was a really old building which was quite dilapidated, the maintenance costs were horrendous. There was a lot of asbestos in the building, particularly in the heating system. Every summer we used to find the smallest person in the factory and send them to work with the maintenance engineer. Their job was to climb through a tiny hole, around 15 inches across, and scrape it out. I don't think that we'd be allowed to occupy the building today. In fact I don't think that it was ever fit for purpose.'

The building on Mountergate had four floors, but the factory only took up the ground floor. On the first floor was the factory shop, which was some 60 feet by 40 feet. Here you could buy rejects and end of lines, together with shoes that had been manufactured out of surplus materials left at the end of a job. The top two floors were used for warehousing.

Deliveries came in at the entrance which was nearest to the top of Mountergate, at the back of Valori's fish and chip shop. Nigel recalls that it gave him a few problems: 'Goods came through an old archway, which really got in our way. So I ordered new doors and one weekend we went to pull the archway down. It was only then that I found out that it was listed, and so it stayed.'

The factory was set up in a traditional fashion with a making room, clicking room etc. In the closing room

Finishing room, CWS, c1935

was a little conveyor belt, which was run on a red and green light system. There were two belts, one above the other. When the machinist was ready for work they put on a green light. Work was put on the top belt which carried it to the machinist. When the work was completed it was put back onto the bottom belt and it was then carried back to the overseer. Nigel soon found out that if some of the girls were sent a hard job, they sent it back without doing anything and ordered more work, which they hoped would be easier. A different system was utilised in the making room as explained by Nigel: 'Here the work was sent around on a track where each operative did their job. It was then sent immediately on to the next operative who did theirs and so on. You could use this system in the making room because every shoe went through the same process. In the closing room different styles underwent different procedures so you couldn't implement the same type of track.'

Around the 1970s CWS started to reduce their manufacturing operations across the country, and their retailers were allowed to purchase from other producers. In turn the CWS factories started to sell on the open market. In 1975 the Norwich factory had a boost when Pell Footwear closed, and the CWS took over their contract with the British Shoe Corporation. Nigel notes that: 'Profit per pair of shoes was minimal. So to make any money we had to be both efficient and sell in high volumes.'

CWS, children's Christmas party, 1938

On 16 January 1987 the *Eastern Evening News* carried the shock announcement that the factory would close in the next 90 days, leading to the loss of 134 jobs. The newspaper reported that CWS officials blamed the closure on a number of factors, including declining orders, caused by cheaper foreign imports, and poor trading conditions in the spring and summer, which resulted in a 'sizeable' operating loss. Nigel believes that CWS was faced with the option of closing either the Norwich or the Leicester factory: 'The Norwich factory was an old building which needed a lot of money spending on it. In particular the roof was in a horrendous state. The Leicester premises was a lot newer, and so we were sacrificed.'

After the factory closed in 1987 Nigel Rudling went on to set up a new company called Rudards Ltd, which was based on Hellesdon Park. He was allowed to buy any of the old CWS machinery which wasn't on lease. He employed eight of the employees from CWS and manufactured court shoes and dance shoes for ladies. The company lasted around two years, after which he sold out to a competitor.

Brocade fabric shoe, CWS, c1940

The old Mountergate factory has since been demolished and in the late 1990s 87 flats were built on the site for the Cotman Housing Association. In memory of the old factory part of the development is named Parmentergate Court (a parmenter being a leather worker). Nigel will also be pleased to note that the old archway which led into the factory still stands.

The wall and arch outside the former CWS factory, 2012

Edwards & Holmes Ltd

Esdelle Works, Drayton Road, pre-1942

In 1891 Henry Holmes and W. C. Edwards began a shoe-manufacturing business in a four-roomed cottage on Pottergate. Over the next five years the business expanded so rapidly, the growth largely fed by exports to the Commonwealth, that it moved premises twice. Eventually in 1896 a new factory was built on Esdelle Street. Three years later Edwards retired from the firm.

Despite losing his partner Henry Holmes continued to expand production, and soon the Esdelle Street factory was no longer capable of handling the firm's orders. Hence in 1912 work began on building a three-storey, red-brick factory on Drayton Road, on the outskirts of Norwich. Unfortunately it was also located near the River Wensum. Peter Holmes recalls: 'That was the year that Norwich was badly flooded and my father [Geoffrey, Henry's son] told me that when the waters were high, men rowed in and out of the spaces left for the ground-floor windows, which hadn't yet been inserted!'

Notwithstanding this mishap, manufacture began at the new 'Esdelle Works' in 1913. At the time it was reputed to be the most up-to-date factory, in terms of both structure and internal layout, in the country. At the factory Edwards & Holmes produced a diverse range of footwear which encompassed everything from infants' shoes to men's dress shoes. By WWI the firm was exporting around 75% of its production, one of their larger markets being in South Africa.

In the aftermath of WWI the firm needed to review its business strategy. Not only had their market contracted during the war, but afterwards many of their overseas customers did not return. In response they began to concentrate on the manufacture of ladies' fashion shoes, with the aim of replacing their lost export trade with increased sales in the home market. It would seem they were successful in this task, as in 1919 a single-storey extension was added to the Drayton Road factory. In order to boost production, around 1933, they installed a moving conveyor belt, one of the first Norwich shoe manufacturers to do so.

Henry Holmes continued to be governing director (i.e. in overall control) of the firm, until his death in 1940, when he was superseded by his son Geoffrey. Henry was twice Lord Mayor of Norwich (in 1921 and 1932). He was knighted for his services to the City.

Sir Henry Holmes, 1922

During WWII Edwards & Holmes was badly affected by enemy action. They were first bombed on Wednesday 29 April 1942. On that evening the Holmes family had been out for dinner and on their way home they stopped at Ketteringham Cross, where they had a full view of the City. Already Geoffrey Holmes was expecting the worst, as he realised that one of the huge fires raging in the City was his factory. Peter Holmes still remembers what happened the next morning: 'My father went into the factory as usual, where he found that there was nothing left of the huge, red-brick, three-storey building but rubble, twisted girders and molten machinery. When he saw it his hair literally stood on end. Everything was destroyed including stock, fixtures, lasts and patterns.' Undeterred the firm re-established itself in two small factories, one in Westwick Street the other on Starling Road. About six months later, in October, a lone German raider dropped a bomb on the Westwick Street factory, demolishing half of it and leaving the rest unusable. Luckily this raid took place at lunchtime and the workers were all outside, and so there were only a few minor casualties. Notwithstanding this setback the firm continued producing footwear in the Starling Road factory and did eventually manage to repair the damaged half of the premises on Westwick Street, which they initially used to cut and prepare their bottom stock.

In 1943 Mr W. D. Forrest (Bill) joined the firm as a general manager. Bill's father owned a leather tannery, and that is where his career had begun. Bill next worked at H. & M. Rayne Ltd, one of the country's top shoe manufacturers that specialised in making high-quality shoes for ladies. Here he had started in the leather room before working his way through the business. As a result he knew the shoe trade inside out and at Edwards & Holmes rose to the position of managing director (supporting Geoffrey Holmes who took on the joint roles of company chairman and governing director). When Bill arrived, Edwards & Holmes had a reputation for producing good shoes which were simply designed, but under his leadership they became renowned for producing top-quality, elegant fashion shoes for women. In 1945 when Bruce Rampley joined the firm as a boy of 14, Bill Forrest was already making his mark. Bruce recalled: 'Mr Forrest wanted to make high-quality footwear. So Westwick Street was set up on a relatively small scale for that purpose. It was here that they made the really high-class shoes.'

After WWII the decision was made to build a new factory on the site of the bombed premises on Drayton Road. The new two-storey factory had an area of 75,000 square feet. The making, finishing, packing and storage departments were based on the ground floor. The upper materials, clicking and closing departments, together with the offices, were located on the first floor. In the 1950s Avis Brown recalls: 'At lunch times we went out into our yard at the back. As there was no fencing, if it was a lovely day we could put our feet in the River Wensum.'

The newly built Esdelle works, Drayton Road, c1950

Celebrations (above and below) after the opening of the new factory, 1948

Picture Gallery - Edwards and Holmes, Esdelle Works c1965

(L to r) Bill Forrest, Sid Harlow and Maurice Nicholson

Leather sorting

Clicking room

Paul Cracknall, time & motion manager, machine room

Eddie Hurren, 'pull over' laster, making room

A Consolidated lasting machine, making room

Bruce Rampley, 1955

(L to r) David Franklyn and Eddie Hurren, making room

Florence Durrant, shoe room

Shoe room

Harold Johnson (factory director) checking the quality

Shoes ready for boxing

Geoffrey Holmes, 1921

Bill Forrest, c1968

Although the factory was relatively new, around 1958 Mr Forrest decided it was time to review the facilities. Avis Brown remembers the event well: 'Mr Forrest decided he was going to build a new ladies' toilet – we even had an opening ceremony. I think that he must have been on holiday somewhere posh because when it was unveiled, hand painted in pastel colours across the top of the door was written the word "Boudoir". Well of course it was something new to us. We were quite excited. We all went in for a look. In the first section across one side there was a full-length mirror with a shelf. I remember him telling us that it was for us to put our handbags on. There were seats all around and ashtrays on stilts, so that we could sit and have a smoke. In the next piece there were the hand basins and then the loos. I can tell you now that in all of the factories I've ever worked in I've never seen such posh toilets!'

Meanwhile, Edwards & Holmes were building a reputation for making quality shoes. They promoted themselves by making footwear for a number of major London shows including 'South Pacific' that ran at the Theatre Royal on Drury Lane between 1951 and 1953, and 'My Fair Lady', which opened at the Theatre Royal on Drury Lane in 1958 and starred Julie Andrews. In February 1966 'My Fair Lady' was performed at the Theatre Royal in Norwich, and so the firm took a party of 600 to see the show to celebrate the fact that over the years they had made 900 pairs of shoes for the production.

In 1952, in the face of cut-throat competition, Geoffrey Holmes had taken the decision that rather than just deal with 40 major retail chains (such as Dolcis and Saxone) the firm would sell direct to independent retailers and department stores across the country. As a result the firm had to rethink its marketing strategy, which included appointing a team of salesmen. In 1957 Peter Holmes, who had joined the family firm in 1949, took on the role of sales director. He recollects that one of his roles was supporting this team: 'Our London office was based at 23 Grosvenor Street, and 15 of our major customers were based within a mile of the office. So I would travel there and spend a whole day visiting them. I visited shoe shops all over the country with the sales reps. It boosted our sales considerably as our buyers appreciated receiving a visit from the boss's son.' The firm had a number of gimmicks to promote their wares, amongst which was a display called 'the magic birdcage', for which the company made special shoes which were exceptionally attractive, but were hardly wearable. It used to travel around the country to the major department stores which sold their shoes. Some of the beautiful shoes from the 'magic birdcage' are now on display in the Bridewell Museum.

Under Bill Forrest's guidance Edwards & Holmes were producing lovely shoes, but as observed by Peter Metcalf: 'Bill Forrest was brilliant at his job, but he was very conservative in his approach to shoemaking and was slow to adopt modern methods of production. When I was at college [in the 1960s] I visited other factories which made me aware that the Edwards &

Geoffrey Holmes (wearing cap) surveys the damage after a vehicle crashed into the Esdelle works, 1955

Holmes factory was a bit behind the times. That was because he wanted to make shoes the way they always had been. For example, we stayed hand clicking after many other factories had started to use presses.' However, at times the firm could be very go-ahead as noted by Bruce Rampley: 'When stilettos first came out plastic heels weren't available, so they were made of wood. Wood isn't as strong as plastic so the stiletto heels often broke. Somebody sold the manager the idea of copper plating the heels, which we did for our shoes and also for other firms. It worked, but eventually the heels got a little spiky and had to be ground down!'

The firm continued to flourish, but by the 1970s, along with other Norwich footwear manufacturers, it was really feeling the effect of strong foreign competition. In 1975 Bill Forrest died, leaving Peter Holmes at the helm. Despite the climate Peter Holmes describes 1978 as Edwards & Holmes' 'best trading year'. Then Chancellor of the Exchequer Geoffrey Howe's budget of 1981 increased interest rates up to 14%. This was awful timing for the firm who had increased their borrowings to enable them to develop a string of shoe outlets in department stores across the country. They were successful when the rate was 3%, but after the huge hike they began to struggle.

In 1987 Peter Holmes sold the firm to Simon Goodman at Florida. As he now observes: 'By then only Start-rite, Florida and Bally still survived. If I hadn't sold there's no doubt that in the next couple of years we'd have gone bust. It was a terrible time. When I signed the documents on 31 July 1987, I had a huge feeling of relief.'

As reported in the *Eastern Evening News* at the time: 'Florida's move for Holmes was to help its own expansion plans, but was also viewed as a rescue plan for a company which had returned losses of more than £500,000 over the last three years.' Following the takeover the intention was for Edwards & Holmes (whose workforce was reduced by 45 to 123) to continue to operate independently and produce a range of narrow and medium-fitting shoes for ladies. However, with the benefit of hindsight Simon Goodman freely admits: 'In retrospect the takeover was a mistake. When we bought the company our strategy had been to both develop their brand, which catered for ladies with narrow feet, and utilise spare capacity in their factory to make more Van Dal shoes. Then the market turned. The 1980s were worse than the 1970s. We were hit by import penetration combined with recession...we felt it badly. We had to act quickly and in 1990 the Edwards & Holmes factory was closed down and all production was transferred back to Dibden Road.'

Today the factory on Drayton Road has been replaced by residential properties. But it is still remembered in the names of the streets that serve the small development, which include Clickers Road, Boot Binders Road and Finishers Road.

Picture Gallery - Edwards and Holmes, Esdelle Works

Making room, 1965

Factory closed, c1991

Deserted factory floor, c1991

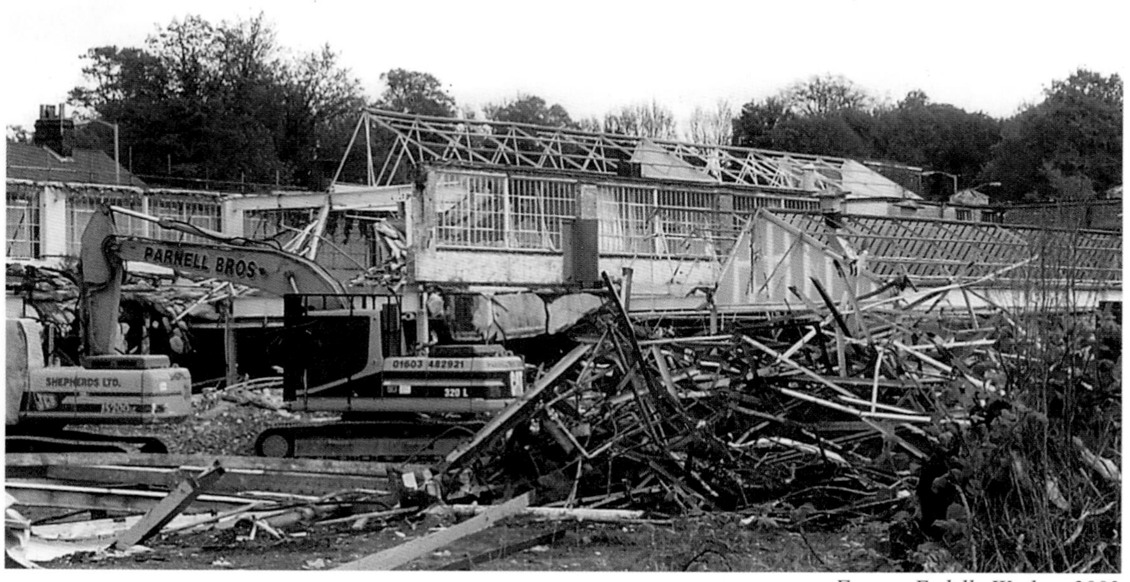

Former Esdelle Works, c2002

A modern housing development now stands on the site of the Esdelle Works. But the old factory is still remembered in the street names.

Photos all 2012, taken by Mike Dixon

The Florida Group Ltd

In 1936 Adelman Goodman came to Norwich and bought the Florida Shoe Factory on Salhouse Road, but his links with the footwear industry had started some 60 years previously.

In 1870 Aldeman, a refugee from Belarus, started work as a clicker in London. He obviously enjoyed the work as in 1910, together with two colleagues, he opened his first shoe factory. During WWI the firm, which was called Goodman, Caiden and Kissin, specialised in making army boots. After the end of the war the business was sold. Subsequently, in 1920, Adelman was joined by his son David, and together they opened a retail outlet called Goodfit shoes at premises in Ealing, London. Five years later they returned to manufacturing with the formation of A. Goodman & Co. Ltd, which was based in the Paragon Works on Paragon Road, Hackney, in London's East End. Here they manufactured shoes for Thomas Lilley, the forerunner of the prestigious shoe retailer Lilley & Skinner. Lilley was so impressed by the quality of their ladies' shoes that he offered to buy as many as they could make. Despite this support, the factory closed down in 1929 and Adelman, joined by his second son Lionel, again entered the retail side of the industry whilst David worked for a time in the gown trade.

Adelman Goodman, undated

It was in 1936 that Adelman bought the Florida Shoe Factory Ltd in Norwich. The small factory which was located at the junction of Salhouse Road and what is now the Ring Road, known locally as 'Florida Corner', had been set up by a German refugee named Mr Herschel to produce ladies' shoes. During WWI the factory had been an aircraft hangar for the old aerodrome located opposite. Although little is known about the earlier factory around 1932 John Alfred Grant (better known as Alf), moved from Leicester to Norwich to manage it and by 1935 two of his sons, Jack and Ron, also worked there.

In an interview given in 1984, Adelman's granddaughter Joan (David Goodman's daughter) recalled meeting one of the employees from the old factory who remembered her grandfather coming to look around when it was on the market. Joan recounted: 'He told me that all of the others who came to look went straight to the books but grandpa was looking at how the shoes were made, and he obviously knew what he was talking about from the way he handled the shoes.'

In 1938 Adelman died and the business, which was now called the Florida Shoe Factory (Norwich) Ltd was continued by his two sons, David and Lionel.

John Alfred Grant with daughter Barbara, c1933

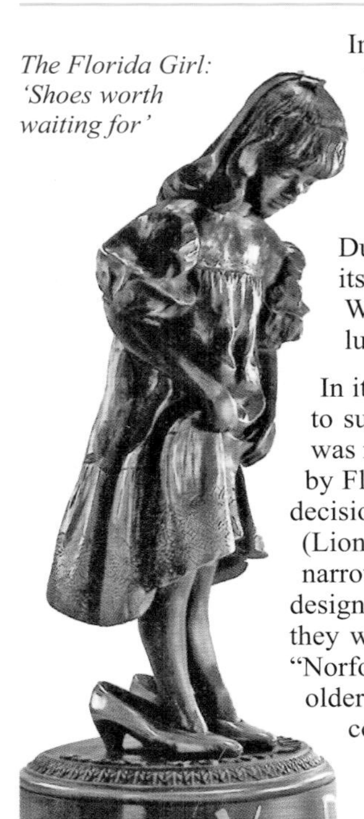

The Florida Girl: 'Shoes worth waiting for'

In those early days the company had around 85 employees. The Goodman brothers took an active role in its running with David taking responsibility for manufacturing and leather buying, whilst Lionel looked after selling and accountancy. Joan Goodman reminisced in 1984: 'I remember my father [David] saying in 1936 when he moved to Norwich and took over Florida, how lovely it was to be back in the shoe trade; the people were so much nicer to do business with.'

During WWII the factory on Salhouse Road was requisitioned and the firm moved its production across to Northumberland Street, where they were allocated space in W. H. H. Clarke's shoe factory. In April 1942 this factory was totally destroyed, but luckily Florida were allowed to move back to Salhouse Road.

In its early years the firm made good-quality unbranded ladies' shoes that were sold to such firms as Lilley & Skinner and Russell Bromley. Then in 1946 the decision was made to form Van-Dal Shoes Ltd to market the Florida range. Today, shoes made by Florida are still branded Van Dal (unhyphenated). Subsequently, in the 1950s, the decision was made to change the focus of the firm's shoe designs. Simon Goodman (Lionel's son and now chairman of the firm) tells the story: 'We started making narrow-fitting footwear named "Norfolk Narrows". The joke is that Billy Waller, a designer, made a small mistake and instead of the lasts coming in as narrow fitting they were made as wide fitting. So rather than making "Norfolk Narrows" we made "Norfolk Broads".' At that time women with wider feet had to buy shoes designed for older women irrespective of their age. Florida introduced the 'Italian look', which was considered to be fashionable, into wider-fitting footwear, which was sold under the Van-Dal brand name. Unfortunately the range had to be renamed after it was exported to South Africa, where the term 'Norfolk Broads' had somewhat sleazier connotations! Despite this slight setback the change in direction was a masterstroke, because it gave Florida a unique position in the market place.

(L to r) Lionel Goodman with brother David, undated

Ray Newman worked in the Salhouse Road factory in the mid-1950s. He recalls: 'To get into the clicking room you used to go up three steps to the door, and then went down three steps on the other side. So the door was about three or four feet above the level of Salhouse Road.' Apart from the offices, which were at the front overlooking Salhouse Road, the factory operated in one large room, which was subdivided by partitions to form the machine room, clicking room etc. This layout allowed Ron and his mates to enjoy their working life a little more than they should have done: 'In those days rubber solution was dirt cheap, and when it started to go off you could roll it into little pellets which made perfect missiles. Us lads used to have great games…in fact if you looked up at the ceiling of the Salhouse Road factory, you could see all these little blobs stuck to it. We were also a bit naughty because between the clicking room and machine room there was a 40-foot corridor, made by partitions, which led to the loos. When anyone walked down it, they were perfect target practice for us. I am sorry to say that we treated it a bit like a coconut shy!'

By the end of the 1950s Florida was flourishing, and in 1959 was able to purchase Chittock & Sons Ltd and Chittocks (Norwich) Ltd. In so doing they also acquired their large factory premises in Dibden Road, known as the Eagle Shoe Works. Over the next two years all Florida's departments were moved across to Dibden Road, a site the firm still occupies in 2013. Following the move, output more than doubled to around 8,000 pairs of shoes a week.

Janet Metcalf worked in the factory in the 1960s. She remembers it having a lovely atmosphere which was very much engendered by the Goodmans: 'Especially in those early years the camaraderie in the factory was marvellous. The Goodman family always used to get involved and join us at special dinners and lunches. At Christmas we had great celebrations...which included the odd lunchtime drink.' She also recalls that the owners took a very flexible approach to management, one that really paid off: 'I couldn't believe it. I was earning really good money but not only that, if we wanted extra time off we were given it. I remember on one occasion I had Friday afternoon off just to get my hair done, I thought it was great. That said there was a lot of give and take. The Goodman family were very fair to us and allowed us time off if possible, but at the same time if we had lots of extra work to do, and needed to work on a Saturday, we would all go in.'

In 1972 David passed away and Lionel took over as chairman. In the same year Lionel's son Simon, a qualified accountant, joined the family business. As the 1970s progressed and a number of its competitors folded Florida continued to prosper. Simon attributed its success largely to its shoe designs which were popular but could not be copied: 'We were protected because we had a niche. Our styles weren't replicated for a number of reasons. Most importantly competitors didn't know what we were doing. We had a way of designing lasts so that the resultant shoe didn't look as though it was wide-fitting. For example we pointed the toe in a certain way, and as a result the shoes looked elegant even though they were wider than average.'

Janet Metcalf dressing up, c2000

Simon Goodman, 2012

In 1983, in a difficult market, Florida made the decision to invest £700,000 in new machinery and to expand the range. In the following year Lionel died and Simon took over as chairman. One Saturday in January of the same year (1984) a fire in the roof could have had disastrous consequences, although it was caught before it caused too much damage the factory was in disarray. Despite it being the weekend Joan Goodman observed: 'Help appeared from all directions, sweeping and cleaning up all Saturday and Sunday, and astonishingly production continued on Monday morning. No one needed to be laid off,'

In 1987 Florida purchased Edwards & Holmes. Following the takeover the intention was for Edwards & Holmes to continue to operate independently in the Drayton Road factory, producing a range of narrow and medium-fitting shoes for ladies. Unfortunately in 1990, in the face of very difficult trading conditions, the Edwards & Holmes factory was closed down and all production was transferred to Dibden Road.

In the 1990s, despite growing pressure to move abroad, Florida continued to manufacture shoes in Norwich. However, real changes were being made to working practices, as observed by Janet Metcalf: 'In many ways the factory was becoming a lot more professional. When I started in 1959 you just did what you thought was right, but then management started to introduce procedures that we all had to follow, which did improve productivity. At the same time the machinery we were working with changed completely. It became more expensive and then of course, from around the 1980s, the machines became computerised. Not only was the company having to pay for expensive equipment, it was also having to pay to have everyone retrained.'

Van Dal shoes, 2012

Simon Goodman (left) at Florida's fiftieth-anniversary party, 1986

Simon Goodman, takes shoes to the Queen Mother, 2000

Despite Florida's commitment to its Norwich factory it became increasingly obvious that, for the company to survive, it had to transfer at least part of its production abroad. Peter Metcalf, who was the factory manager at Dibden Road in the 1990s, observes of the time: 'I fought tooth and nail to try and avoid work going to India. I constantly tried to prove that we could make shoes in Norwich as cheap as they could there; even though I knew that it was impossible. But I was trying to save people's jobs.'

Eventually in 2001 the firm established operations in India and in 2005 they expanded into China. Florida do not own any factories overseas but work with firms there on a partnership basis. As explained by Simon Goodman: 'We design the shoes and do all of the technical planning here. The shoes are made on our lasts to our specifications. In factories that produce higher volumes we have a quality controller in the factory, otherwise we have quality controllers who regularly visit them. We also have an agent there and send people out from Norwich visiting the manufacturers, so there's somebody visiting each factory at least every other month.'

Lorraine Rodwell, Florida, 2012

Mark Cannell, Florida, 2012

Although Florida have transferred a large proportion of their production overseas, in 2012 they still made between 12% and 15% of their footwear at their Dibden Road factory. Here, using a highly skilled workforce, they produced over 1,000 pairs of ladies' shoes a week using traditional methods. Simon has no doubt why Florida remains as one of the few firms making footwear in Norwich: 'We have survived when so many of our competitors have failed because we found a niche market in ladies' wider-fitting footwear and then "stuck to our last"...'

Ray Carpenter, Florida, 2012

Florida, works outing, Cromer Pier, 1986

Arthur 'Bunny' Baldwin (centre), who worked in the industry for many years and wrote an unpublished history of it, presents his collection of shoemaking tools to Lionel (left) and David Goodman, 1967.

The collection is still displayed in the entrance hall of the Florida factory.

Steve Hewitt (left), 1992

Van-Dal float, Lord Mayor's procession, 1982

Freed of London Ltd

Magdalen Shoes Ltd, so called because of its location on Magdalen Street, was started around 1979 by Sam Thompson. They specialised in the making of hand-crafted dance shoes. After Sam's death in 1990, the firm was taken over by Freed of London and transferred to a new factory on Mason Road (off Mile Cross Lane) where they are still based.

Michael Martin, who had previously worked at Norvic, joined the firm in 1983. He recalls: 'We transferred over one weekend. The new factory was much better and larger than the Magdalen Street premises. When we moved we doubled our staff, to around 50, and also started to make a much bigger range of shoes.'

Freeds has an international reputation for making dance shoes. The firm was founded by Frederick Freed and his wife Dora in 1929. More than 80 years later the firm continues to produce handmade shoes in the style originally adopted by its founder. Norwich is one of three factories in England owned by Freeds, which together produce over 90% of the footwear sold by the firm.

The Norwich factory makes all types of dance shoes for men, women and children, which are sent to London for distribution. They manufacture around 2,000 pairs a week using traditional methods. Apart from closing leather uppers, which is done in Leicester, all procedures are undertaken in Norwich.

One section of the factory is given over to the manufacture of pointe shoes, which are made using traditional turnshoe methods. All are handmade to order by craftsmen who make around 100 pairs a day. Gary Colby, who stitches the shoes, explains: 'Generally a ballerina visits our London shop where our footwear is on display. She can tell who made the shoe, because each operative has their own individual mark which is imprinted on the sole, and so she can choose who she wants to make her shoes. Generally the same craftsmen will make a ballerina's pointe shoes throughout her career. We know when a ballerina is about to go on tour because we'll get an order for 30 pairs at a time.' The team at Norwich make pointe shoes for many prestigious companies including both the Royal and Northern Ballets. In 2010 they made the shoes for Natalie Portman when she appeared in the film 'Black Swan'.

Like Michael, the majority of the staff in the Norwich factory worked in the shoe trade prior to joining the firm: 'Many of my colleagues had similar backgrounds to myself and learned their trade at companies such as Bally, Start-rite or Norvic. We haven't trained any youngsters new to the trade yet, but I would take them on because shoemaking is a dying art, and as us old timers retire we need new blood to ensure the skills aren't lost in Norwich for ever.'

Staff at Magdalen Shoes celebrate their move to Mile Cross. Michael Martin rests his arm on the table, 1990

Made in England

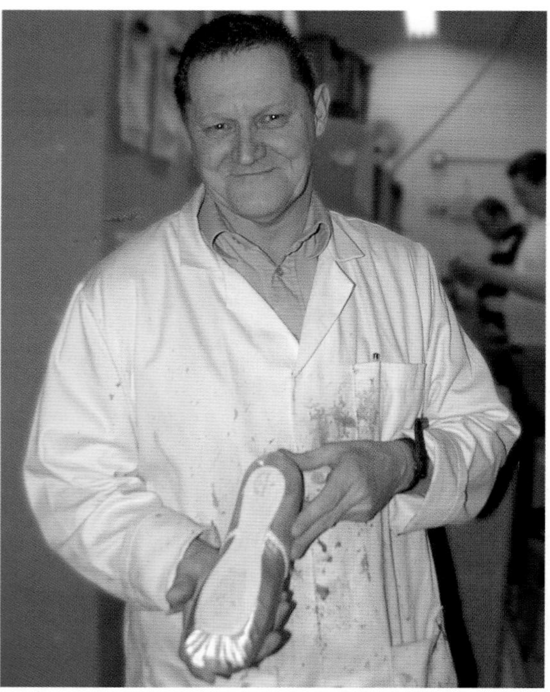

Michael Martin, 2013

Picture Gallery - Freed of London, 2013

The factory floor

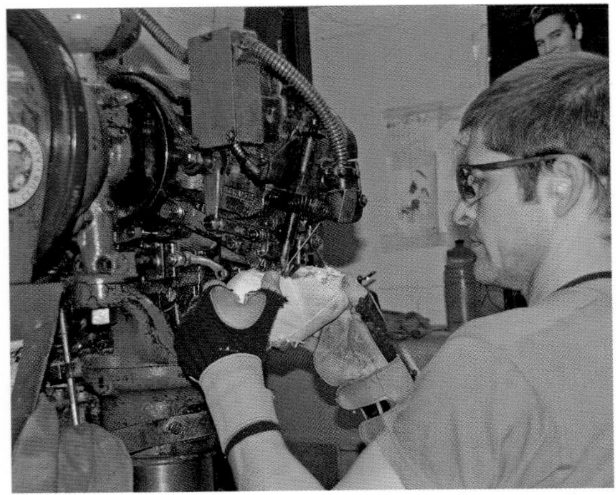

Gary Colby, stitching turnshoes

Skilled craftsmen make pointe shoes

Press clicking

Smoothing the pleats of a ballet shoe

Machinists at work

John F. Kirby Ltd

John F. Kirby, c1910

On the 3 April 1879, at the age of 14, John F. Kirby was apprenticed to the Norwich firm of Howlett & White. In the five years that followed John was trained as a clicker, over which time his wage increased from 6 shillings to 14 shillings a week, and he had to agree 'neither to marry, haunt taverns nor play unlawful games'. At the end of his apprenticeship he was not offered a position at Howlett & White but 'would have been continued in his employment if trade permitted'. As a result he moved to London where he married Julia, his landlady's daughter. Later he returned to Norwich, and in August 1894 started his own business as a master shoemaker in Calvert Street. To establish the business John borrowed £18 from a building society and raised additional loans of around £44 from unknown sources. John used the capital to purchase such items as a cutting board, lasts, an eyelet machine and punches. His family were very supportive and not only loaned him a press and cutting board (valued at £9 10s.) but also provided additional loans. Julia worked with her husband as both bookkeeper and trimming-room supervisor.

In 1898 the business transferred to 65 Pitt Street, and around eight years later John and Julia's son John Richard Kirby joined the family firm. In 1916 it was advertised: 'Mr Kirby has always given great attention to a good medium class of ladies' machine-sewn boots and shoes. He specialises particularly in maids', girls' and boys' school footwear.'

John F. Kirby Ltd, Pitt Street factory, 1936

John F. Kirby, works outing, c1924

After the death of John F. Kirby in 1948 his younger son Francis Allen Kirby took over the running of the factory.

In 1956, when John St Quintin joined Kirbys as a designer, the business was still located on Pitt Street. By then it had the reputation for making fashionable, high-quality shoes for ladies. He recalls: 'The factory was lovely. They employed around 160 people and it was spread over three floors. Downstairs was the office and from there you went through to the shoe room, finishing room, the making room and the heel covering room. On the first floor was the clicking

Sample room, John F. Kirby, c1950

(L to r) Mr John Francis Kirby and James David Kirby with their wives, c1960

room and a superb, ultra-modern sample room which was fitted out in chrome and glass to show the finished shoes at their best.'

By now John Francis Kirby junior (founders' grandson), better known as Mr Jack, was at the helm. His preparation for a career in the shoe trade was very different to his grandfather's. He initially trained as a chartered accountant before travelling to France and Germany to learn how they made shoes. His daughter Janet Abbott recalls how her parents often went to Europe looking for ideas for shoe designs: 'Once in Paris my mother copied down what she thought was the name of a street where she spied shoes that she thought my father would like to see. He roared with laughter when he read the French for "stick no bills or posters here".'

In 1963 the family sold the business to the Liverpool Shoe Group, who in 1962 had also bought the Norwich firm of Batson & Webster. At the time of the purchase it was announced that both Mr John and Mr James Kirby would continue to work within the business and that no staff would be affected. In July 1965 the firm made their last batch of ladies' fashion shoes and instead started to concentrate on men's shoes, slippers and handmade sandals for women. Subsequently all of Kirbys' production was moved to the Batson & Webster factory in Fishergate which was closed down in June 1967.

Trimming room, John F. Kirby, 1966

P. C. Croxford (designer), John F. Kirby, 1966

Meadows Bridal Shoes Ltd

The company was launched in 1984 when John Barrett bought machinery owned by Shorten & Armes Ltd from the receiver. He subsequently located production in factory premises previously occupied by Trimfoot on Starling Road, where he employed 12 of Shorten & Armes' former workforce.

John recalls why he decided to start a new company: 'At Fishergate we [Shorten & Armes and Meadows Shoes] had made ladies' ballroom shoes. I became aware that one of my customers, who did shoe repairs, used to take off the special non-slip sole and replace it with a normal sole, which meant that the shoes were then suitable for weddings. That planted the idea that there was a real market for such shoes and so I started Meadows Bridal Shoes Ltd.' Initially he sent bridal shops across the country a brochure that generated so much interest that he never needed a sales force. At the time wedding-dress shops didn't tend to sell footwear, but were finding that customers increasingly asked for shoes, and so they started to stock them.

Although specialising in wedding shoes the company has always been prepared to be flexible, as illustrated when they made ladies' shoes for men. At one point they even opened a shop in Sydney, Australia, where demand tended to be high because of their annual Mardi Gras festival. John explains some of the challenges he faced: 'Ladies' shoes tend not to fit men because they aren't wide enough, and so we, in effect, made ladies-style shoes for men's feet. To sort out the fittings I tried them on my feet which were the sample size. My office staff weren't very impressed. They made such comments as: "I don't like that pink satin shoe with your black sock Mr Barrett!"'

After a few years it proved too difficult to manage a shop in Sydney from England, and so John brought his stock of around 200 shoes, together with matching handbags, back to Norwich. They included a beautiful shoe made of red satin with a diamanté buckle called Dorothy...well what else could it have been called? Eventually the stock was sold to a Norwich businessman who traded on the internet, where they proved so popular that Meadows made him another 2,000 pairs. John explains: 'I quite enjoyed the challenge of designing the shoes but we don't make them any more. I even made a pair for a friend who's a very keen Norwich City supporter. The front of one shoe was yellow and the back green, whilst the other had the colours in reverse.'

The company continued to make shoes in Norwich until about 2000. After that it became impractical, as explained by John: 'We stopped because we were not only having problems getting components, but as staff reached retirement age it became impossible to replace them. So like many other firms we continued to design and market in the UK but started to manufacture abroad.' In 2013 the firm still successfully trades on the same basis.

(L to r) Ruby and Dorothy, ladies-style satin shoes made for men, Meadows Bridal Shoes, 2012

Meadows (Norwich) Ltd

(L to r) Dennis Gilbert, John Meadows, Percy Meadows and Paul Meadows with their wives, c1948

It was in 1948 that Percy Meadows set up Meadows (Norwich) Ltd. Percy's career in the shoe trade had started before WWI at Howlett and White. Here, as a young apprentice, he earned five shillings a week. After serving in the war he joined Southalls as a factory manager, later moving to Leicester. He returned to Norwich in the 1930s when he became a manager and director of W. H .H. Clarke.

Meadows' first factory, which was located in the old St Paul's schoolroom (St Saviours), was loaned to the firm by Arthur Howlett through Batson & Webster. By 1951, when output had grown to around 600 pairs of shoes a week, the firm was relocated to the Comet Works on Peacock Street. Jean Smith recalls leaving Edwards & Holmes to work there: 'The factory was much smaller than I was used to. It was all on one floor and each room was partitioned off. You could lean over the boards and talk to the chaps in the other departments. We had about 30 in the closing room.'

Percy's two sons, Paul and John, worked in the family business as explained by Jean: 'They were there every day. They talked to us and we called them by their Christian names. This was very different to Edwards & Holmes where I hardly saw the owners, and if I did I'd call them "Mr".' Both Jean and Betty Barnard, who also worked at Meadows in the 1950s, liked working there particularly because of the outings and social events. Betty remembers: 'We often went on a

Percy Meadows holding hat and coat (centre left), Meadows' works outing, Comet Works, Peacock Street, c1952

Meadows' factory, Fishergate, 1968

coach to the coast and then got taken to a show in the evening. We looked forward to going all year. We worked together closely so when we had the trips we were like kids out of school.'

At the Peacock Street factory output grew to 3,000 pairs of shoes a week. Despite extending the building it was not large enough. Fortuitously the area occupied by the factory was needed by the City Council to enable them to build the Magdalen Street flyover. In exchange the company was offered a site on Fishergate which had previously been a vehicle depot. In August 1964 the new factory, which had the capacity to produce up to 6,000 pairs of shoes a week, was officially opened.

In 1968 Percy Meadows died, and the business was continued by his sons. Initially the firm continued to be profitable, but from 1969 to 1972 over £85,000 of losses were generated, which led to Barclays Bank appointing a receiver in June 1972. It was bought from the receiver by a company owned by Geoffrey Barrett and his son John (who owned Shorten & Armes Ltd) and Eric Sexton (whose family owned Sexton, Son & Everard). From then on it operated as an associate company to Shorten & Armes. As John Barrett explains: 'My father considered it to be a good company to buy because of its reputation and the opportunities it gave us to share facilities.'

For further details see: Shorten & Armes Ltd.

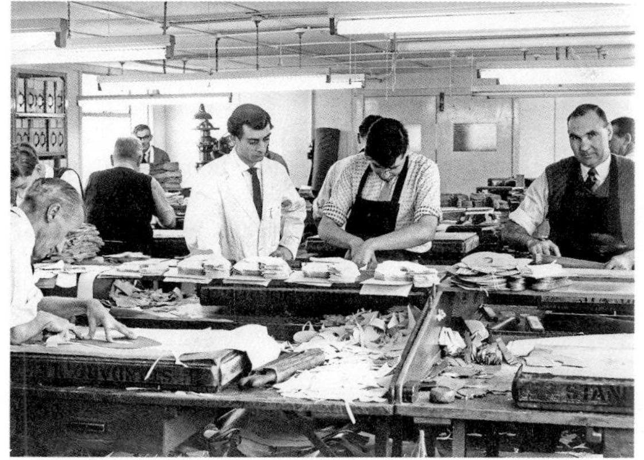

Clicking room, Meadows' factory, Fishergate,1968

Making room, Meadows' factory, Fishergate, 1968

The Norvic Shoe Company Ltd

The Tillyard & Howlett factory, St George's Plain, 1846

The Norvic Shoe Company Ltd can trace its foundations back to 1846 when it is reported that James Warnes Howlett (a farmer) invested £10,000 in Robert Tillyard's leather currying business. There is no proof that the investment was as high as £10,000, a huge sum which today would equate to around £1 million, but there is evidence that money did subsequently become available to the partnership. In particular, around 1856 the partners built a large factory on the site of a former coal yard between Claxton Lane and Water Lane, off St George's Plain, in Norwich. There is evidence that before this the partnership of Tillyard & Howlett, curriers and leather sellers, was located on Pottergate.

It is not clear when the firm became a large-scale boot and shoe manufacturer, but it is generally assumed that footwear production was gradually introduced, as part of the overall business from the late 1840s. Furthermore F. W. Wheldon (author of the book 'The Norvic Century') speculates that manufacturing footwear would have been given impetus by the joint effect of the Great Exhibition of 1851 and the growing demand for British goods abroad.

In 1857 James Howlett's son, John Godfery Howlett (note the unconventional spelling of Godfrey), joined the business. Within two years he was 'put on the road', i.e. he became a travelling sales rep. It was during this period that John met his future business partner, George White, the son of a respected customer. On John's recommendation, George joined the business as a junior clerk. In the years that followed George worked his way through the business and eventually rose to the position of general manager. In 1876 he became a joint partner with John Howlett and the business was renamed Howlett & White.

Almost immediately afterwards a major extension, designed by local architects Edward Boardman & Son, was added to the factory on St George's Plain. The new building took up all the frontage onto St George's Plain between Claxton Lane and Water Lane (see plan on page 174). Meanwhile, in 1882, the neighbouring property on Bridge Street (now St Georges) was also designed by Boardman and built for Robert Fisher, a wholesale grocer and baking powder manufacturer. This was later acquired by Howlett & White.

George White, 1904

In the years that followed George White was responsible for expanding the boot and shoe manufacturing side of the business, a growth which required an even larger factory. In 1893 this was achieved, not by moving to larger premises, but by acquiring the property on St George's Plain which lay between Water Lane and Fisher's grocery (see page 174). Designs for a further extension, which almost doubled the size of the existing factory, were drawn up by Boardman in 1895. These incorporated an arch that was built over Water Lane to join the two developments. The piecemeal nature of the development meant that the factory lacked natural light. To offset this Water Lane was clad in white tiles, which are still there today.

Around 1900 ill health forced John Howlett to retire from active participation in the business. At the same time George White was elected a Member of Parliament for the North-West division of Norfolk (he was re-elected in 1906 and 1910). As a result, their sons Arthur Godfery Howlett, J. Warnes Howlett and G. Ernest White, all of whom had entered the business in the 1880s, took more responsibility. In 1905 the firm continued its expansionist policy with the purchase of a block of buildings, adjacent to their factory, between St George's Street and Water Lane. This block was redeveloped in 1909, again to a design by Boardman.

By now the factory covered a huge area and led to an article in the *Illustrated London News* on 30 October 1909, which described it as having 'long outgrown its original premises and absorbed neighbouring sites, so that the extensions carried out during the last 12 months have made it the largest boot and shoe factory under one roof in the Kingdom'. It further reported that the firm employed 1,200 people who at any one time were working on between 150,000 and 200,000 pairs of boots and shoes.

The firm produced a vast array of designs and sizes of boots and shoes. Amongst their trademark brands were 'Diploma' and 'Mascot', whilst by 1909 a new brand called 'Norvic' was being marketed. In this range alone they made 20 different styles of boots and shoes, each in 13 sizes, with four fittings for each size.

Both George White (senior) and John Howlett were considered to be good employers with philanthropic leanings. David Jones, who wrote a history of the company, in particular observed of George White: 'He represented a Victorian ideal that through hard work, religious observance and temperance he was able to achieve both wealth and political power.' In 1907, in reward for such endeavour, he was awarded a knighthood.

Norvic Shoe Company Ltd
St George's Plain Factory Development

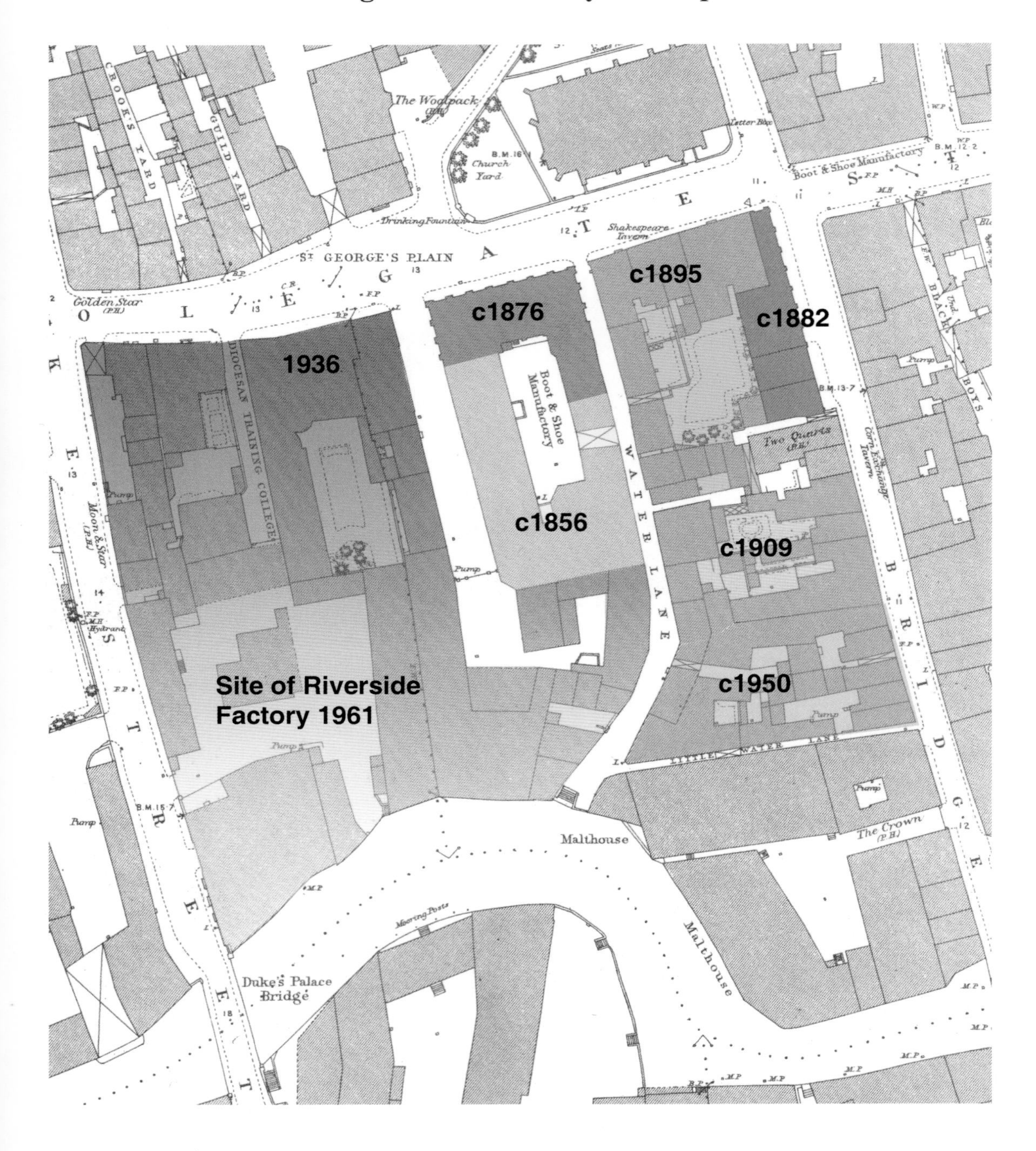

Plan of Norvic Shoe Co. Ltd factory site, see text for details. Compiled by David Jones, 1986 using OS map, 1884

Picture Gallery - Howlett & White factory, printed in their Jubilee booklet, 1896

Scouring shop (Leather preparation)

Stove drying room (Leather preparation)

Rough-stuff cutting room (Press room)

Heel making room

Cutting room (Clicking room)

Machine-sewn lasting room (Making room)

Upper closing room

Finishing room

In 1920 Arthur and Warnes Howlett, and Ernest White clearly showed that they shared their fathers' ideals, when on 13 July they inaugurated the Norvic Pension Fund. To launch the event they held an assembly of 1,300 people, mostly workers from the factory, at St Andrew's Hall, where they also welcomed home soldiers from WWI. Under the terms of the pension fund, men of 65 who had worked for the company for ten consecutive years would receive £52 per annum, whilst ladies of 60 who met the same qualification would receive £30. At the time it was the only non-contributory pension scheme in the shoe trade. In the words of F. W. Wheldon: 'The foundation of this fund....would have had the firmest support of the original partners, who would have congratulated their sons and their colleagues.'

After WWI, the UK shoe industry lost much of its export trade, which made it imperative for producers to secure as much of the home market as possible. To do this many needed to update their marketing techniques. In this respect Howlett & White were ahead of the field and even before the war had been advertising in the national press. However, after the end of hostilities they decided that in the light of new trading conditions they also needed to review their manufacturing and retail policies.

Like many other Norwich manufacturers Howlett & White had specialised in the production of high-quality shoes for ladies. After the war they decided that they also needed to produce footwear for both men and children. They achieved this by taking over firms that could fill gaps in their range:

The Mansfield Shoe Company Ltd

In 1919 Norvic started buying the share capital of this Nottinghamshire-based company. Similar to Norvic, Mansfield specialised in the production of ladies' shoes, but they catered for the cheaper end of the market. By 1929 Howlett & White had purchased the remainder of their share capital.

Oakeshott & Finnemore Ltd

Based in Northampton, Oakeshott & Finnemore specialised in the production of high-quality shoes for men for the export market. Founded in 1902 they experienced financial difficulties in the early 1920s. In 1922 they were taken over by Howlett & White, who in the same year started selling men's 'Norvic' and 'Mascot' branded shoes to complement their ladies' ranges.

S. L. Witton Ltd

In 1934 the Norwich firm of S. L. Witton, whose factory stood opposite Howlett & Whites', was added to the group. Following the takeover Howlett & White started to make children's shoes under the brand name 'Kiltie', which had previously been used by Wittons.

Inauguration of the Norvic non-contributory pension fund, St Andrew's Hall, 1920

In 1935 these companies were formed into a group called the Norvic Shoe Company Ltd, the brand name that had first been used by Howlett & White in 1909. At the time it was the largest footwear manufacturing group in Britain.

The directors knew that expanding production without increasing their share of the home market would make the firm unviable, and so they took the opportunity to expand the 'Norvic Concentration Plan'. This marketing technique, which originated in America, involved the firm either buying shops, or providing a comprehensive scheme for shoe-shop proprietors, who would then trade under the name 'Norvic' – a little like a franchise. Around the same time the company expanded their Norwich base. Details were contained in the firm's in-house magazine, 'Norvic Way', where in 1937 an article announced that a further extension was being built to the factory which was to run westwards along St George's Plain towards Duke Street. The new building contained showrooms and stockrooms capable of holding 250,000 pairs of shoes for immediate delivery.

During WWII much of the company's manufacturing capacity was taken up, as it had been in WWI, with the production of footwear for the forces. Unlike many of its competitors, the St George's factory escaped the war undamaged, and in the 1950s it was still one of the major footwear manufacturers in the country.

During this decade the firm clearly put the same effort into marketing and selling their footwear as they did to producing it. Thus in 1956, in the 'Norvic Way' it was reported: 'Two-day courses have been held for agents and sales staffs in the Midlands and Northern areas. Many of our retail friends attended these functions, and wonderful welcomes were extended to the visiting Norvic Directors and Training School staff.' By then the firm was advertising on television, quite an innovation at the time as the Independent Television Authority (later ITV), with its capacity to show commercials, had only been launched in the previous year.

Around the same time Norvic discovered that, on average, teenage girls bought five pairs of shoes a year, twice as many as the average woman. In response, in their 1959 annual report the directors announced they needed help from teenagers and had formed the Teenage Council, which was described as: 'A group of seven alert young women with just the right mixture of intelligence, wit and fashion-sense.' To add 'authority', and no doubt a bit of star quality, to the Council, it was headed up by Judy Grinham who had won a gold medal in the 100m backstroke at the 1956 Olympic Games.

These initiatives contributed to the success of Norvic, which generated annual profits generally in excess of £500,000 well into the mid-1960s.

Range names of the NORVIC group of companies

Kiltie
Wonder Girl
Devonshire
Knightsbridge
Topflite
Squire
Young Idea
Flitemaster
Footlike
Waukeezi
Charles H. Baber
Chamberlain Slippers
Italia
Sir Herbert Barker
Sheba
Honey Girl
Alfresco
Happy Girl
Colorfit

Norvic brands and advertising, c1955

Judy Grinham (second from left) with the Norvic Teenage Council, 1959

Despite its size and success there is no doubt that by the early 1960s the St George's Plain factory was somewhat dated. Jean Smith recalls: 'It was a big place with lots of rooms. It was dark and in the winter it was very cold. We had benches in a row where we worked. It looked exactly like you imagine an old-fashioned factory to look…there was no lightness to it. I always said that it was a heavy factory.'

In 1961 the firm opened a new plant in the area behind the main factory leading down to the River Wensum, known as the Riverside factory. The company used it as a pilot experiment in new methods of production. Amongst other things they introduced updated conveyor belt systems in both the making and closing rooms.

The Riverside plant was a precursor to the company's new Heathside factory, which was located on Vulcan Road in Mile Cross. The new factory modernised and streamlined the production process, and was designed to replace the complex on St George's. The Heathside plant, which opened in 1964, contained around 40,000 square feet of factory space. Learning from the experience gained at Riverside, one of the most impressive features of the new factory was described in the *Eastern Evening News*: 'Shoe experts are impressed by the bold use of conveyors to establish a "flowline" covering the entire operation of the factory.' The belts not only operated in a conventional manner but also carried work in progress between floors. Unlike the City-centre factory, Heathside was light. In fact its north wall, which formed one end of the clicking room, was virtually all made of glass. New methods of heat setting were introduced, which, when coupled with the innovative conveyor system, resulted in the company reporting that 'the time the shoes spends on the tracks at the moment is about 90 minutes, which compares with days, or even weeks, in making not so long ago'. At the time it was estimated that improved production methods would result in savings of around one shilling per pair. Jean Smith transferred from St George's to Heathside: 'Vulcan Road was an open-plan factory and really, really noisy. Our machines were behind each other and in the middle was a conveyer belt. The work was put in boxes and sent up the conveyer belt to each operator. I think this was done so we didn't have to get up off our seats to get jobs, as they were called. If you did that it took time. I didn't mind working in the new factory. The spirit was better. It was getting more into the modern way. I made lots of friends, some of whom I still see today.' The St George's site was retained for, amongst other things, offices and warehousing.

Machine room, Norvic, 1952

Picture Gallery - Howlett & White, Riverside factory, 1961

Freeman die machine, closing room

Conveyor belt, closing room

OMIC back moulder, making room

OMIC machines, making room

Conveyor belt, making room

The most important machines in the factory!

Heathside factory, Vulcan Road, 1964

In the latter years of the 1960s, although Norvic reported profits of around £202,000 in 1968 and £386,000 in 1969, these figures hid UK trading losses of £210,000 and £125,000 respectively. The losses were partially attributed to the firm holding increased stocks and in particular the cost of financing them. Additionally the company reported: 'Establishment costs have also grown to an uneconomic level and staff are currently being reduced accordingly.' In 1969, as part of a programme of rationalisation, the Heathside factory was subject to a sale and leaseback deal with the Norwich Union. The company seemed to be turning the position around in the second half of 1970 when they managed to generate a trading profit of £105,000 in the UK.

Then in July 1971 the *Eastern Evening News* carried the shock headline: '£3.5 million takeover bid made for Norvic Shoe'. The article disclosed that Drakes, the London-based investment group, had bought a block of 10% of Norvic shares, which increased its stake in the company to almost 20%. On the back of this Drakes had announced that it would make an offer for the balance of the company's shares. Although the directors rejected the bid, by 10 August 1971 Drakes controlled over 30% of the shares, a situation which led Christopher Selmes, Drakes' joint managing director, to comment that Norvic shareholders were voting with their feet. By 18 September 1971 Drakes held almost 90% of Norvics' ordinary shares and were in control of the business.

£3½ m. takeover bid made for Norvic Shoe

DRAKES, the investment Group last night put in a surprise £3½ million takeover bid for the Norvic Shoe Company of Norwich.

But later the chairman of Norvic, Mr. R. A. Parker, said he had not seen the offer and asked for the details released to newspapers by the Press Association, to be read over the telephone to him.

BUSINESS

Mr. Parker added that until the offer arrived and had been examined, he felt unable to comment.

Ken Holmes, our Industrial Editor, writes: When the offer is received it will be considered by the Norvic Board together with the advice of their financial experts and merchant bankers.

Norvic will undoubtedly look at the offer against the background of the fine business recovery the company has made in the last two years.

Norvic has turned a U.K. trading deficit of £180,000 for the six months June-December, 1969, into a profit of £105,000 for the same period in 1970.

When these figures were announced, Mr. Parker was optimistic that this rate of progress would be maintained. With the shoe trade doing well there is little reason for thinking that his forecast is at all wide of the mark.

SHARE STAKE

The P.A. City Correspondent wrote: Disclosing that it has bought a block of 10 per cent of the Norvic shares to boost its stake in the company of almost 20 per cent., Drakes announced it would now make an offer for the balance of the shares.

Eastern Evening News, 28 July 1971

John Lincoln, sales manager, recalls hearing about the takeover: 'I was up with others at the London showroom for the Shoe Fair. One evening Brian Shaw, who was a director, joined us for an evening meal, and he was distressed because of the major changes he envisaged. The new owners turned up and we found that they were very different to their predecessors. The old directors were polite and gentlemanly.' At the time Selmes and his joint MD at Drakes, Charles Metcalfe, stated emphatically that they intended to run Norvic as a manufacturing concern, but rather ominously reported that they were going to take 'a very close look' at Norvic's chain of shops.

In March 1972 the outcome of that 'very close look' was revealed with the announcement that Norvic's estate of over 140 shops was being sold to William Timpson Ltd. Under the terms of the sale Timpson were required to take the same value of Norvic shoes for three years. This was a period of high inflation, and so over those three years the real value of sales fell. Nevertheless it still represented a large part of the company's overall output. John Lincoln explains: 'At Norvic Sales we knew that we needed to persuade Timpson shops to keep selling our shoes after the agreement expired. We worked hard and I remember training Timpson sales people on how to fit children's shoes. Sadly after the end of three years they stopped stocking Norvic footwear. This gave us a big problem, as around 25% of our total output had been sold through the chain.'

Norvic £2.9m. shoe retail deal

By Ken Holmes, Industrial Editor

THE Norvic Shoe Company is in the process of being taken over for the second time in six months — but this time it is only a re-arrangement between the financial and manufacturing interests of Drakes, the parent company.

Drakes, who announced yesterday a net profit increase of 125 per cent. last year (see page 2), also said that agreements were signed yesterday for the sale to William Timpson Ltd. of the Norvic Retail Division for £2.9 million in cash.

Negotiations are also in progress for the transfer to Barker Ellis Silver Company Ltd. of Norvic's manufacturing interests which, said Drakes, had on December 31st, 1971, an approximate value of £3 million.

To conform with Stock Exchange requirements application has been made to suspend the quotations for the preference and ordinary share capital of Barker Ellis on the Midlands and Western Stock Exchange.

On completion of the quotation for Barker Ellis Mr. Charles L. Metcalfe, who is also the chairman of Barker Ellis, will resign from Drakes to become chief executive of the reconstituted Barker Ellis group.

Mr. Christopher Selmes will become chairman of Drakes.

Drakes, who will retain a substantial interest in the Barker Ellis Group, say that the reorganisation of the Norvic Group has been substantially completed since the end of their financial year.

The Norvic fixed assets were valued in June, 1971, at £4,811,000 and the price paid by Drakes was said by one of their representatives to be in the region of £4.9 million.

They have sold Norvic overseas interests for about £1.1 million, and the retail shops for £2.9 million in cash — a total of £4 million.

CONFIDENCE

If their valuation of the remaining Norvic manufacturing assets at £3 million is correct the Norvic deal has been a good one for Drakes, who are buyers and sellers more than manufacturers.

This knowledge has been a factor in any consideration of the future of Norvic, and the steps now being taken should give confidence to the Norvic staff who have, in recent months, been maintaining the improved position of Norvic in the country's shoe trade.

The Barker Ellis Silver Company is one in which Drakes bought a majority interest some months ago. When negotiations are completed it is expected that it will be quoted on the London Stock Exchange, and that Norvic will provide the cornerstone of its manufacturing interests.

The Norvic shops, although bought by Timpsons, will continue to trade under the name of Norvic and so will the manufacturing company.

Eastern Evening News, 23 March 1972

Reg Kilbourn, who was working at the factory recalls: 'After the company was taken over the staff got a very good bonus which made everyone feel secure. Later on we found out that the profit the company had made was not from the manufacture and sale of shoes, it had come from the sale of every high street shop that was owned by the company. In March 1975 we were called to a staff meeting and told that the future looked bleak. We were now in direct competition with every other ladies shoe manufacturer and that a reduction of 10% of the workforce across the board was being looked at.' Drakes also sold many of the company's overseas assets including factories in South Africa and Ireland.

Norvic's former Heathside factory, c1987

By 1981 this once mighty company was in a dire position. In February of that year the local press ran the headline: 'Norvic Crisis: Jobs at Risk'. It went on to explain that nearly 700 Norwich jobs were under threat as the company was facing a £750,000 cash crisis. In the months prior to the announcement the company had taken a number of steps to increase efficiency. These included transferring production in Norwich from Heathside back to St George's, closing factories in Northampton and Derby and halving the size of the Mansfield operation. Then in July 1981 a receiver was appointed. Three days later half of the workforce was made redundant. The Mansfield factory was saved by a management buy-out, and rivals Ward White bought assets, including the children's fitting division, which was moved to Leicester. However, no saviour was found for the Norwich operation, and at the end of September the receivers announced that the St George's factory would completely close. On 1 December 1981 the auctioneer's hammer hit the final nail in the coffin of the factory when over 3,000 items from the building were sold. Although some blamed the collapse of the business on cheap imports, a few years after its demise the business featured in an article in *The Observer* which stated clearly why the business failed: 'Asset stripped by Drakes in the 1970s of 143 shops, never really recovered.'

Norvic's former Heathside factory, c1987

Norvic's former Heathside factory, c1987

In February 1985 the *Eastern Evening News* ran a story announcing a 'New Role for St George's'. They explained that the old Norvic site, which occupied nearly four acres (stretching from St George's Plain down to the river and from Duke Street to St George's Street), was in the process of being redeveloped for mixed usage to include offices, shops, homes, a wine bar and even an indoor market, somewhat similar to London's Covent Garden. The aim was to regenerate this area of the City, now known as Norwich Over the Water, which had degenerated after the closure of the factory. The development was completed gradually, and throughout efforts were made to retain many of the factory's decorative features, although less attractive parts of the site, including the Riverside factory, were demolished. Alas the indoor market has not materialised, nevertheless today the area is both prosperous and attractive.

The scheme was the brainchild of Roger Gawn who was not able to complete his grand design but did succeed in creating a unique and vibrant City-centre environment. The history of the area is still recalled in names adopted throughout the site, including 'Leather House' and of course the 'Last Wine Bar'. Unlike other old factories which have been totally demolished, here the factory's imposing façade has been preserved to give real character to the area.

During the lifetime of the company the streets around St George's were a hive of activity and noise, today it is much more tranquil. Yet despite all the changes it is rather pleasing to think that if John Godfery Howlett and Sir George White could visit St George's Plain, they would still recognise the magnificent factory they developed so many years ago.

The former Norvic factory, St George's, 2012

P. Segger (Norwich) Ltd

Philip Segger founded his 'wholesale and export, boot and shoe manufacturing' business c1898. By 1914 the firm occupied 14 Whitefriars' Street, which it rented for 35 shillings a week. In 1919, when they moved out, the building was taken over by another footwear manufacturer, Cook & Taylor, who named the factory the Palace Works.

From 1919 Seggers was based at 53 Botolph Street, eventually moving to Sultzer's Court in 1937. Philip's two sons, Philip and Ernest, succeeded their father in the business, and it was they who closed it down in 1969. At the time they had 24 employees, mostly women, and made children's shoes and men's slippers.

The Palace Works, Whitefriars' Bridge, c1920

Seggers' factory, Sultzer's Court, Botolph Street, 1938

Pell Footwear Ltd

Pell Footwear Ltd was established in 1965 as a wholly-owned subsidiary of the Norwich handbag manufacturing company D. MacLaren Ltd (MacLaren).

MacLaren was launched in 1946 by D. MacLaren and John Pellegrini to make handbags in small premises on Sprowston Road. The company, originally employing just four people, quickly expanded. By 1960, 3,500 handbags a day were being produced by the 240 members of staff based in their extensive factory on Mousehold Lane, with the assistance of another 140 outworkers. Although the majority of handbags produced were made out of plastic, other materials used included leather, fabrics and even straw!

At their well-equipped factory, they became expert in the use of electronic high-frequency welding equipment, which they used to diversify into the production of footwear accessories, such that in 1961 they produced over one and a half million pairs of bows a year.

From here it was a short leap for the firm to begin making plastic uppers for shoes. In 1963 John Pellegrini proudly reported of their new product: 'These plastic tops mean that a girl can wash her shoes under the tap instead of polishing them!'

The discovery that the straps made for handbags could be adapted to make sandals, led to the production of a whole new range and the formation of Pell.

Until 1970 Pell shared MacLaren's factory on Mousehold Lane, but in 1970 they moved to a two-and-a-half acre site on Mile Cross Lane. By then footwear production amounted to some 30,000 pairs a week and their range had been extended to include slippers and mules.

Making room, Pell Footwear, Mousehold Lane, 1968

Dual-rail track, Pell Footwear, Mile Cross Lane, 1974

In 1972 Steinberg & Sons Ltd, a public company with interests including handbag manufacturing, acquired the whole share capital of both MacLaren and Pell for £195,000. The intention at the time was for both companies to continue trading under their own names with John Pellegrini acting as managing director.

Despite the *Eastern Evening News* running articles in 1973 with headlines proclaiming that 'Steinberg's Aim is Expansion', three years after the takeover officials at Pell announced that the firm would cease trading on 12 September 1975. The failure of the business was blamed on its inability to compete with cheap imports, and resulted in the loss of over 80 jobs.

Although Pell had been closed down, MacLaren continued to make handbags. Then in December 1978 over 90 employees were made redundant, production ceased and only ten members of staff were retained to dispatch handbags made at other factories in the Steinberg group.

It is interesting to note that with growing demand for vintage items, MacLaren handbags are again popular, with some carrying price tags considerably higher than those of the 1950s. Although few examples remain of the footwear produced by Pell, the rather splendid pink mule and platform shoe pictured below have been retained by the Bridewell Museum – small reminders of a once successful company.

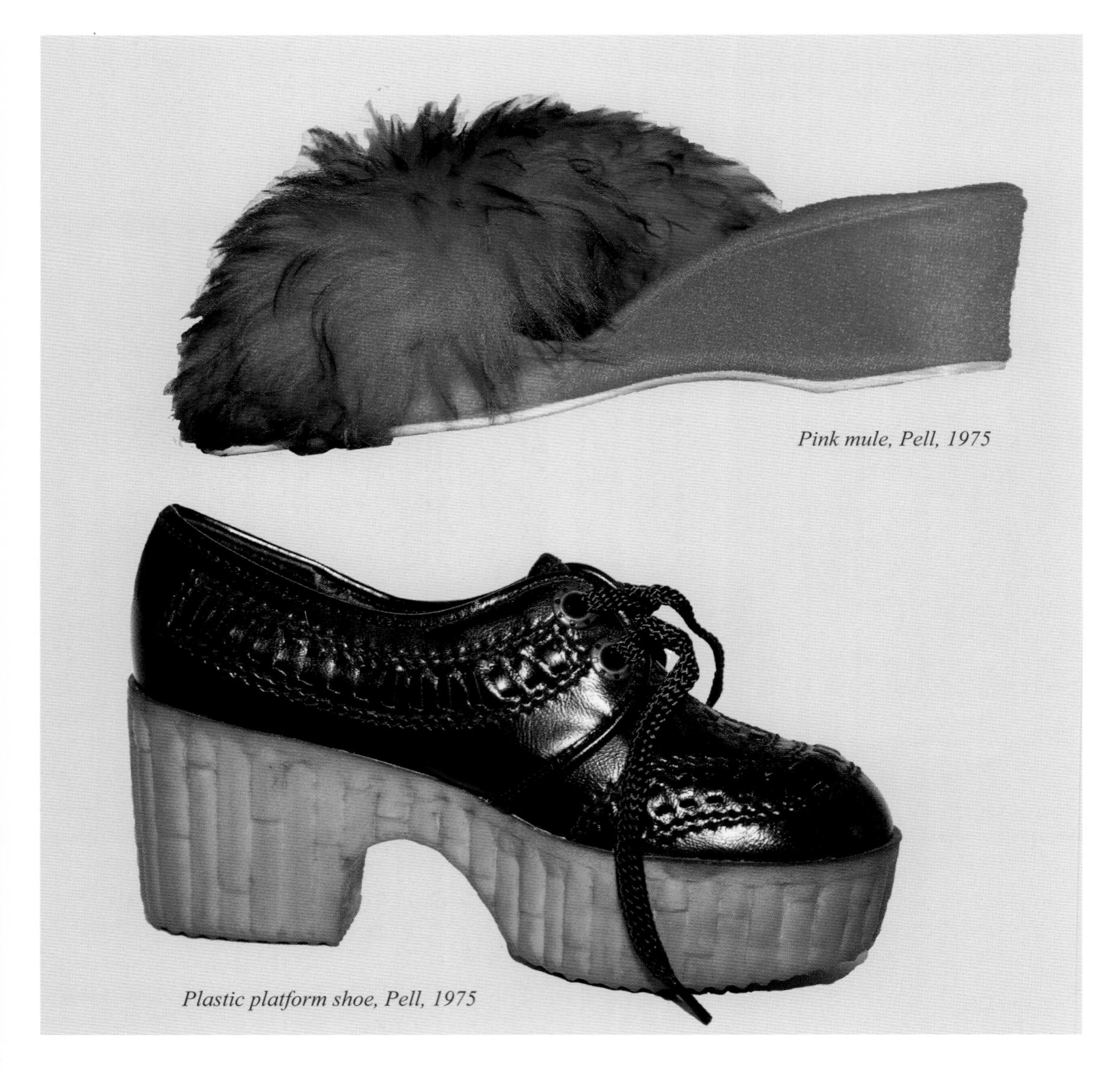

Pink mule, Pell, 1975

Plastic platform shoe, Pell, 1975

Ramsbottom Brothers Ltd

Arthur Ramsbottom with wife Mary Ann and children, c1914

The firm, founded in 1892 by Arthur Ramsbottom, specialised in the production of high-quality shoes for ladies and children. By 1916 they were located in the so-called Progressive Shoe Works on Calvert Street. Arthur came from a working-class background and took a keen interest in the welfare of his workers, which of course included organising a works outing. His son Cecil (who is standing behind his mother in the photograph) used to tell of the occasion when Arthur hired a train to take the workers on a day trip from Norwich to Windermere in the Lake District! As a boy he joined the trip, which left from Norwich at four a.m. and returned well after midnight.

After the end of WWI the firm moved to 106/108 St George's Street. Here they built a new factory employing around 400 people on land behind the houses fronting the thoroughfare between St George's Street and Pitt Street. Albert Garnham worked in the factory in the early 1920s. He recalled that: 'Ramsbottoms was a small factory and the bosses were very nice. The Ramsbottom brothers were keen bowls players, and I remember that there was a bowls green beside the factory where we used to play, workers and management together, on Saturday afternoons.'

Unfortunately, building the new factory stretched the firm's finances and c1925 when a large order for shoes from India failed, so did the business. Arthur's grandson Richard understands that the business never went bankrupt, but had to close so that the creditors could be paid off.

108 St George's Street (left-hand doorway), 1936

R. Roberts (Norwich) Ltd

Robert Roberts moved his family from Leicester c1915 to work in the City's shoe trade. Cecil, the youngest of Robert's six children, was only three at the time and on the day of arrival disgraced himself by falling into the River Wensum.

By 1923 Robert was working at S. L. Witton's factory on St George's. Three years later Robert established his own factory on Fisher's Lane (off Pottergate) where he manufactured children's shoes. His standard shoes were sold wholesale at 2s. 11d. and at 3s. 11d. retail, whilst quality shoes sold wholesale at 3s. 4d. and retail at 4s. 6d. One of the firm's main lines was the 'Doggy-Toe' range, thus called because on the sole it had a semi-circular rubber plate with a pattern of small spirals, resembling a dog's paw, which had been designed to give children a better grip. Later, Robert was joined in the business by his sons Cecil, who looked after sales, and Leslie, who acted as general manager.

During WWII Roberts shared Start-rite's Crome Road factory. After the end of the conflict they returned to their own factory, and in 1950 Robert's grandson Bob (Lesley's son) also joined the family firm.

In 1974 Start-rite bought all of the firm's issued share capital, although Bob Roberts continued to manage the factory. However, in the following year Start-rite began to consolidate their operations. Initially the Roberts' factory played a part in the rationalisation process, and in 1975, when the Start-rite Sonnet factory in Duke Street was closed, production was transferred across to the Fisher's Lane factory. Then in 1981 the Roberts' factory was closed and its 100 workers were transferred to Start-rite's Crome Road factory, enabling the freehold factory premises to be sold.

The former Roberts' factory still stands on Fisher's Lane and has now been converted into residential dwellings.

Robert Roberts, c1934; Fisher's Lane factory, 1981

Christmas party, c1960

Fisher's Lane factory, 1958

Former Fisher's Lane factory, 2012

S. L. Witton Ltd

Originally Sidney L. Witton, known to his friends as Sid, specialised in buying and reselling children's shoes from small manufacturers. In 1903 he founded his own business on Raglan Street, and by 1907 he controlled three factories which annually produced around 500,000 pairs of shoes for children. By 1912 the firm's registered office was located on Muspole Street. In 1926 he amalgamated all production into a new factory which was erected behind a collection of small properties on St George's Plain. This impressive building faced the Norvic factory and stretched back along Muspole Street. Here children's shoes were produced under the trade name 'Kiltie'.

S. L . (Sid) Witton, c1916

In his book, 'A Norvic Century', F. W. Wheldon describes Kiltie shoes as being: 'Good, solid, honest-to-goodness articles, made as the American phrase goes, "to wear like a pig's nose".' Such properties made the shoes particularly popular in the industrial north, and there is some speculation that Sid called them Kilties because of their great success in Scotland. He considered his shoes to be 'keenly costed and reasonably priced'. Unlike many of his competitors, who often sold their branded shoes through a limited number of outlets, Sid aimed to sell his shoes in large quantities in as many shops as possible. Despite this approach, sales were insufficient to keep the vast factory consistently working on a full-time basis. In a bid to increase production lower-grade ranges of shoes, including 'Tartan' and 'Rob Roy', were introduced.

The strain of commercial life proved too much for Sid, and in 1934 he sold his business to Norvic. After re-equipping the factory and introducing improved lasts, Norvic continued to produce their own children's Kiltie range until the company went into receivership in 1981.

Today Sid Witton's huge factory has been sub-divided into offices and workshops. Although no longer the hive of activity it once was, it continues to dominate the City skyline and contribute to its commercial life.

The former S. L. Witton factory, overlooking Muspole Street, 2012

Picture Gallery - S. L. Witton Ltd, St. George's Plain, c1926

Leather store

Bottom-stock department, sole-cutting section

Bottom-stock department, heel-building section

Bottom-stock department, making section

Machine room

Dispatch department

All images reproduced by kind permission of the Bridewell Museum

S. Thompson & Son Ltd

It was around 1920 that Sydney R. Thompson set up a small shoe-manufacturing business in Fellmongers' Yard on Oak Street. Subsequently he relocated to a workshop at 17 Golden Dog Lane. In the early 1930s Sydney was joined in the business by his son Sydney H. Thompson.

Throughout its lifetime the firm was run as a small-scale concern. Although they manufactured shoes for Scottish country dancing, they built their reputation making exclusive shoes, by hand and to order. In this capacity the Thompsons not only supplied leading West End shops but many of their shoes were also exported to the United States. It is amazing, and a tribute to the quality of their work, that in 1956 this tiny Norwich firm was chosen to make the shoes worn by the two pages at Grace Kelly's marriage to Prince Rainier in Monte Carlo. They also gained much kudos when they made shoes for the children of both President Kennedy and President Carter. Other stranger commissions included making thigh boots for the figures of Peter the Great and William III for Madame Tussauds!

Sydney H. Thompson did not retire until 1990, by which time he was in his 70s. By then he was making two pairs of shoes a day which sold for between £20 and £50 a pair. At the time he told the press: 'You have to love the job to do it because you're not going to make a lot of money, and I've loved every minute.'

Black suede shoes, S. Thompson, 1951

Brocade evening shoes, S. Thompson, c1965

Sexton, Son & Everard Ltd

The firm of H. Sexton & Sons was founded c1886 by Henry Sexton, who was assisted in the business by his five sons: Henry, Jesse, Arthur, Fred and Alfred. Prior to setting up his business, Henry (senior), together with three of his sons, worked for Howlett & White. The story goes that Henry set up his new enterprise after George White refused him an advance of 2s. on his wages. Despite this Mr White showed great magnanimity when he gave Henry his first order, which was for satin dance pumps.

The firm's original factory was located in two small buildings in the City centre, but within ten years it had moved to St Edmund's Mills. For many years this six-storey building with its 300-feet river frontage, located in the vicinity of St Edmund's Church, had been used for spinning yarns. However, the Sextons refitted it as a modern footwear factory where they installed the most up-to-date equipment of the time, including some of their own patented machines. By constantly updating machinery and manufacturing techniques, Sextons soon built a reputation as being highly competitive. In these early days they made a large range of footwear, but were best known for their dress and court shoes.

Henry Sexton died in 1897, but his sons continued to expand and develop the business. By the turn of the century the firm employed up to 900 workers, with constant employment being given to around 500 hands. But then on the night of the 15 – 16 January 1913, disaster struck the company when their factory at St Edmund's Mills went up in flames. It was reported at the time that 'people shook their heads in dismay at the spectacle of the accumulated work of more than a quarter of a century reduced to ashes in a few hours.' Subsequently the original firm was liquidated and two firms were immediately created from the ashes of the old, another Henry Sexton Ltd and Fred Sexton (Norwich) Ltd.

The fire at Sextons' shoe factory, Fishergate, 16 January 1913

After the fire, Henry J. Sexton, grandson of the founder, who had worked in the family business, considered quitting the trade. However, after a conversation with a certain Mr Everard, in February 1913 a third business, Sexton, Son & Everard Ltd, was incorporated. Initially they exclusively produced turnshoes in Southalls' old factory in Wounded Hart Lane near the market, but by 1916 they had built a new factory, with around 40,000 square feet of floor space, known as the St Mary's Works (on Oak Street, in the vicinity of St Mary's Plain). Here they installed modern machinery which enabled them to produce high-grade goods, which they advertised 'combined the best characteristics of British workmanship with the elegance of the most fashionable Continental styles'. Already their turnover exceeded that of the original firm.

Site of Sextons' first factory, Wounded Hart Lane, c1930

After the war the business was hit by a number of problems. Firstly, in 1919 Mr Everard died in the influenza epidemic that swept the country, and then in 1921 the entire industry was hit by a slump that claimed over 20 Norwich shoe manufacturers. Yet whilst others failed Sextons flourished, after Henry Sexton shrewdly unloaded his leather store. Speaking in 1952 he recalled: 'As I cleared out my leather stocks into shoes at competitive prices, it left me with cash to buy more material at ridiculously low quotations, and this placed me in a strong position to compete with other manufacturers who had held on to their stocks. I also had the great advantage of receiving substantial orders from New Zealand and Australia from samples whose prices were based on high-priced leather, and in many cases when the order arrived I could buy the material at half the prices for which I had quoted.' In fact orders received over this period were so substantial that in 1921, despite prevailing market conditions, Henry was able to build a new, modern factory on St Mary's Plain opposite his existing factory. Together the two premises had a floor area in excess of 120,000 square feet.

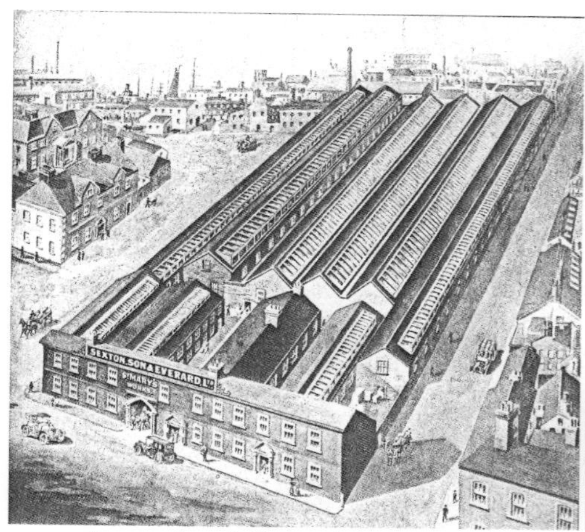

Sexton, Son & Everard, St Mary's Works, 1916

A. A. Everard, c1916

H. J. Sexton, c1916

Picture Gallery - Sexton, Son & Everard, St Mary's Works, c1925

General view across the factory floor

The shoe room

The making room

All photographs reproduced by kind permission of Archant

Around the same time Sextons was one of the many Norwich firms who responded to the increased demand for high-legged boots and fancy, Louis-heeled shoes. Originally these were produced by turnshoe makers who, realising that their skills were in high demand, took full advantage of the situation. Henry Sexton recalled: 'My office was then on the opposite side of the yard to the turnshoe room, and the thing I dreaded most was to hear a loud bang on a bench which meant a stoppage. This happened several times weekly.' Unsurprisingly, as soon as new methods were devised which enabled light, machine-sewn shoes to be manufactured, Henry closed his turnshoe department. Using new techniques, it was easier to make the shoes which also cost around a shilling less to produce.

Between 1924 and the early 1930s Sextons, along with other Norwich manufacturers, gained a reputation for making beautiful ladies' shoes, but then other centres started to copy Norwich designs, which they could produce at significantly lower prices. Initially Sextons tried to compete by making cheaper shoes using the conveyor-belt system, a move which Henry Sexton later described as 'the biggest mistake of my life'. Soon realising that he was on the road to ruin, Henry Sexton reversed this trend and again started making high-grade shoes which he now did in multiple widths. Alongside his own lines he also bought the licence to manufacture 'Joyce of California' casual shoes. By the time WWII broke out, the firm employed around 1,750 people and produced in excess of 25,000 pairs of shoes a week.

Bar shoes with Louis heels, Sexton, Son & Everard, 1927

Leather store, Sexton, Son & Everard, c1950

Works outing, Sexton, Son & Everard, 1941

During the war Sextons was badly hit by enemy action. In April 1942 the smaller Oak Street factory together with a storage facility on Westwick Street were destroyed. Then during the August Bank Holiday blitz of the same year the main factory was hit, leaving the company with an operational floor space of some 30,000 square feet.

Despite the devastation, in later years Henry considered himself to have been very lucky, as during the same raid a further incendiary device, which penetrated his only remaining building failed to explode. Only 11 weeks after the raid the firm was again manufacturing shoes and meeting targeted production levels, including their government service contracts.

After the war the firm built a new factory on the site of its St Mary's Plain factory (originally built in 1921). Continuing the strategy set before the war, the firm specialised in the production of high-class fashion footwear for ladies. Their range included brands made under licence from America, together with unbranded shoes sold under their own label. The latter were sold to outlets such as Saxone and Lilley & Skinner.

St Mary's Works, Sexton Son & Everard, 1952

Bob Drake, seat lasting, Sextons, St Mary's Works, c1965

Henry Sexton (who died in 1954) was succeeded by his son Eric. In the 1960s, under Eric's leadership, Sextons developed into a volume business which needed to maintain high levels of sales. Bob Drake recalls first entering the huge factory which literally churned out footwear: 'In the main part of the factory the shoes were transported on three tracks which went around in a circle. Each track was around 15 metres long. The shoes were on hangers. They'd clank around and stop at every operation. Each week between 5,000 and 6,000 pairs of shoes were made on each track. It was mass production on a huge scale. I'd never seen anything like it'.

By now many of Sextons' customers, such as Lilley & Skinner, had been absorbed into the vast British Shoe Corporation, which had huge buying power. Additionally Sextons had started to manufacture a large number of shoes for Marks & Spencer, which could similarly dictate both price and quality. To meet these requirements Sextons had even created a Marks & Spencers' room. Despite their efforts the company still ran into difficulties with the contract. In fact Reg Kilbourn, who worked for Sextons at the time, recalls that the company were so concerned about meeting standards, that the staff in the factory were told that if they went into Marks & Spencer and saw a faulty shoe they should buy the pair and the company would refund the cost of purchase. This was necessary because the company's profitability had become very dependent on this large order. But in the mid-1960s a catastrophic announcement was made, as recalled by Bob Drake: 'One day we were inspected by Marks & Spencer. Two days later Mr Sexton and all the big-wigs came up and asked us all to gather round. They then told us that we'd lost the Marks & Spencer contract across all of the ranges. Later on I heard on the grapevine that it was because we were undercut on price. We then found out around 100 of us were being made redundant.'

In 1969 Sextons joined the John James Group of Companies, after the group bought a large portion of the shoe company's shares. At the time Sextons employed a workforce of 900 and the *Eastern Evening News* commented: 'There was considerable relief in Norwich shoe circles last night when the news was released. The fact that Sextons has been in some difficulties had been known, and it was felt that there was no shoe firm in Norwich able to step in and help.'

Despite the new investment, on Tuesday 29 February 1972 Sextons called in the receiver – an announcement that sent shock waves around the City. The unions immediately moved into action and on 1 March 1972 they held a meeting for employees at St Andrew's Hall, where by a vast majority (the vote was 646-6) they gave their committee the power to order a range of actions, including the occupation of the Norwich factory, refusal to allow machinery, leather, boots or shoes to be moved from the factory and the refusal of redundancy notices.

On the following day, the firm's 700 employees received termination notices, which were returned unopened the following Monday. In response, as expected, the receiver confirmed that he was giving workers the requisite notice under their contracts of employment, but more surprisingly he also announced that an offer had been made for the purchase of the business. Then on 8 March a bulletin was issued confirming that Jack Taubman, a property developer and manufacturer, had negotiated an agreement with the receiver whereby the company's assets would be transferred to a new company, Sexton Shoes Ltd, which would continue manufacturing footwear thus safeguarding around 400 jobs at the Norwich factory.

Dereham & Fakenham Times
The Norfolk Chronicle and Journal
No. 4800 FRIDAY, MARCH 3, 1972 Price 3p

SEXTON JOBS: WORKERS WAIT TO HEAR

Dereham & Fakenham Times
The Norfolk Chronicle and Journal
No. 4803 FRIDAY, MARCH 24, 1972 Price 3p

WORK-IN WOMEN'S PETITION TO QUEEN

The deal made with Jack Taubman excluded the firm's closing rooms, which were located in Fakenham and Beccles. In response the staff at Fakenham, led by forewoman Nancy McGrath, commenced a sit-in which lasted 18 weeks. The ladies eventually formed themselves into a co-operative called 'Fakenham Enterprises' producing leather goods. It lasted a few years as a co-operative but by 1976 had become an outpost of a local clothing manufacturer.

Meanwhile in Norwich, the reorganisation of the St Mary's factory resulted in redundancies being higher than anticipated, and by July the staff had been reduced to around 360. However, there was optimism that the restructured firm was now a viable concern. Sadly this was far from the case, and in June 1976, when the number of employees had fallen to around 240 and output was below 6,000 pairs a week, the board of directors of Sexton Shoes Ltd called in the receivers. Within a few weeks the business was closed down, thus marking the end of this once illustrious firm.

St Mary's Works, decorative feature, 2012

The imposing St Mary's Works still stands on St Mary's Plain, where it has been converted into individual units comprising: office space, leisure facilities, light storage units and workspace for artisans.

St Mary's Works, St Mary's Plain, 2012

Shingler & Thetford Ltd

(L to r) Albert Shingler and Charles Thetford, 1930

Albert Shingler moved to Norwich in 1901. Originally brought up in Leicester, he had some experience as a pattern cutter and was invited here to work at the Hales Brothers' shoe factory on Westwick Street. The invitation was not driven by Albert's shoemaking ability, but by the fact that he was an excellent cricketer and Mr Hale was a cricket enthusiast. Once established in the county Albert went on to play for Norfolk.

Albert subsequently moved to Southalls where he met Charles Thetford, the finishing-room foreman. In 1919 these two men formed their new company and established a factory at Salmon's Court (off St Stephen's Street). From these early days the firm specialised in the production of ladies' shoes made from fabrics, particularly satin and crepes.

In 1923 they moved to larger premises on Willett's Court (Ten Bell Lane) which had previously been occupied by W. H. H. Clarke. By now output had reached some 1,000 pairs a week. Production continued to expand and in 1925 part of the factory was moved to 54 Pottergate. Meanwhile George and Edwin Shingler had joined their father in the business.

In the 1930s the footwear industry was hit by the depression, but it was also a time of shorter skirts and ladies who demanded elegant shoes to complement the changing fashions. In response George Shingler produced a last, which was unique at the time, to make a court shoe which could be fitted with three to four inch heels. This led to their footwear being in high demand and enabled them to survive this turbulent period.

Colman House (63a Pottergate), prior to acquisition by Shingler & Thetford, 1936

In 1947 a second storey was added to the Pottergate factory enabling the Ten Bell Lane premises to be totally vacated and production to be amalgamated on one site. Around the same time George Shingler took over control of the family business. At the time the firm continued to produce high-class footwear for ladies using a variety of fabrics, including suede, reptile, white satin and brocade.

By 1955 the firm had expanded into 63a Pottergate, known as Colman House, another Georgian property standing opposite number 54. The new premises were mainly used for the production of components. Additionally the clicking room was located on the site, in a building originally built for use by the Home Guard during WWII. By the end of the 1950s production had reached around 6,500 pairs a week.

In 1964 Edwin Shingler retired from the business. In the same year, with no clear family successor to take over, his brother George sold it to Bank & Commercial Holdings Ltd, a property group from Bradford. George himself continued to run the business until 1969 when he handed the reins over to Mr Ron Carr.

During the late 1960s and early 1970s the evening-shoe trade done by Shinglers was expanded at the expense of other types of footwear, and the firm built a reputation for manufacturing such shoes. It was during this period that John Thain worked here, and he can still remember the factory buildings on Pottergate: 'On the left-hand side of the road, as you left the City, were the main offices where you'd find the directors, whilst on the first floor were the pattern cutters. It was a funny sort of layout. You used to go through the Georgian building which fronted the road to reach the back. On the first floor they had the machine room and on the bottom floor was the making room. On the right-hand side of the road there are now new buildings at the front, but if you look through you can see the yard where we used to park the cars and bikes, and behind that is a Georgian building that housed the rest of the factory. On the ground floor they used to make and prepare all the soles. Above that you'd find all the heel coverers and the ladies who did trimming, whilst next door was where we did the pattern making. Outside to the right was a Nissen hut which housed the clickers.'

In 1973 the firm was bought by the British Shoe Corporation (BSC), who at the time were taking 70% of the factory's production of 10,000 pairs a week. By this time Shinglers were one of the leading makers of evening shoes in the country, having developed a considerable expertise in the use of fabrics. In the years that followed the market for evening shoes contracted. In response, the company rapidly and successfully diversified into the production of shoes for day wear.

During the 1970s the firm had purchased buildings adjacent to their site on Pottergate which enabled them to build a new shoe room and dispatch department. But by the end of the decade it was decided that the City-centre site had outlived its usefulness. Rebuilding the factory presented many planning problems, and so in 1981 the firm relocated to Coslany Street, where they converted an old warehouse into a shoe factory. At the end of May everything was transferred to the new factory which opened on 1 June 1981. Russell Abbott, who had worked for Shinglers since 1970, recalls how lovely it was to transfer from the hotchpotch of buildings on Pottergate to a purpose-built factory on one floor: 'It was like moving into heaven!'

In 1988 Shingler & Thetford was one of the BSC factories taken over by the footwear giant the Burlington International Group, leading many to assume that its future was secure. Then in autumn 1991 Burlington closed the Coslany Street factory with the loss of 150 jobs. Burlingtons themselves went into receivership the following year.

Although this marked the end of the company, all was not lost. Behind the scenes, factory manager Gordon Walker, supported by three of his management team (Russell Abbott, Bob Taylor and Chris Fisher), secured financial backing from Katz Dancewear Ltd (a leading manufacturer of dancewear in the UK) which enabled a new company to be formed from the ashes of the old. Called Norwich Shoes Ltd, the firm was initially based in part of the old Edwards & Holmes factory on Drayton Road (which by then was owned by the Florida Group) where they manufactured ladies' and children's wedding and ballroom shoes. Subsequently they relocated to a new factory on Havers Road. When the company moved to its new premises, Russell Abbott, who was financial director of the company, took over as MD from Gordon Walker. Russell recalls that the company's motto was to 'make the right product at the right price to deliver at the right time'. At Havers Road the company employed 40 people and made around 2,000 pairs of ladies' and girls' wedding and ballroom shoes, together with around 1,500 pairs of ballet pumps. Russell retired in 2003 since when the business in Norwich has significantly contracted. In 2013 it operates as part of Katz Dancewear in a small unit at the rear of the Florida factory on Dibden Road.

Shingler & Thetford shoes, 1972

Vic Thompson, Burlington, 1990

David Hawes (white coat), Norwich Shoes Ltd, 1992

The buildings that housed the Shingler & Thetford factory on Pottergate remain largely intact. It is unlikely that many people would suspect that these elegant houses were the home of one of Norwich's pre-eminent shoe factories.

54 Pottergate, 1968

54 Pottergate, 2012

Colman House, 63a Pottergate, 2012

Shorten & Armes Ltd

The firm was founded in 1918 by Harry Shorten, a clicker, and George Armes, a maker. They originally located their enterprise in premises just off St John Maddermarket where they installed a few machines in a disused shop. In 1919 George Barrett, chief clerk with a firm of solicitors and friend of Harry, noticed a factory for sale in St Stephen's Church Lane. Shorten & Armes relocated here and George made the decision to join the firm full time.

Geoffrey Barrett (George's son) initially trained as an accountant before undertaking a two-year course at Northampton Technical College (1923-25), after which he joined the firm, eventually taking on the role of Managing Director. In a career spanning 50 years Geoffrey was both forward looking and supportive of the trade. Not only was he chairman of the Norwich Boot and Shoe Manufacturers Association four times, but was also national president in 1959 and 1960.

When Geoffrey joined the business, one of the excitements of the day was the discovery of a new material, sheets of raffia, which it was thought could be successfully made up into shoes for the South African market. Speaking in 1968 Geoffrey recalled the occasion with wry amusement: 'We had some lovely orders, but the trouble was that when the shoes were worn the raffia cracked, and we had a lot of returns. But our agent out there was equal to anything. He sold them to the locals who tied them together and hung them round their necks as a sort of ornament.'

From its early days the firm made elegant evening shoes, and by 1928 they were advertising themselves as specialists in the production of silver-kid shoes. Geoffrey Barrett was one of the first manufacturers to see the possibilities of using reptile skins. The firm could cut a pair of shoes from a Java python skin for which they could charges 30 shillings a pair, which was three times the amount charged for a similar pair made out of conventional leather. By the early 1930s, a large proportion of their footwear was made from reptile skins.

In 1931 the firm moved to new premises in Esdelle Street, which had originally been Edwards & Holmes factory. Betty Barnard recalls working here in the 1940s: 'It was a very old building. The mice used to run around and you'd hear the girls scream. But it was a lovely place to work because the atmosphere was so good and we made beautiful shoes…they were really first class.'

During WWII the factory was taken over by a Luton clothing firm under the government's rationalisation of production scheme, and Shorten & Armes operated as a unit within the Howlett & White factory on St George's Plain. After the war they returned to Esdelle Street where they purchased additional land allowing them to extend the site. In 1953 a subsidiary company, Trimfoot Shoes, was formed to produce shoes which sold slightly below regular Shorten & Armes prices.

Geoffrey Barrett, c1960

George Barrett, 1958

In 1963, John St Quintin joined Shorten & Armes as a designer, when he recalls they still produced beautiful footwear: 'Even in the late 1960s the firm was renowned for selling shoes made from a range of leathers and fabrics, with ladies high-quality evening shoes being their speciality. We made a lot of snake-skin shoes and of course snake skins at their widest were only four inches wide. As a consequence we had to piece them together, which was a really skilled intricate job.'

John Barrett (Geoffrey's son) became involved in the business in the 1960s. He recollects: 'When I left school I didn't really know what I wanted to do but my father said: "Why don't you try the shoe trade and see if you like it?" I did and 50 years on I find that I still like it.' His training included a course in shoe design at the Ars Sutoria School (which is still an international technical institute of art, footwear and leather goods based in Milan) and a time in the design department at K Shoes in Kendal. He then returned to Norwich and did an evening course at Norwich City College and Art School on St George's. In the meantime he had joined his father at Shorten & Armes, where he specialised in sales, and was appointed to the board in 1962.

In 1972 Geoffrey and John Barrett, together with Eric Sexton (whose family owned Sexton, Son & Everard), bought Meadows (Norwich) Ltd from the receiver. From then on Meadows operated as an associate company to Shorten & Armes.

The Shorten & Armes factory on Esdelle Street had been built in 1896, and inevitably by the 1970s it was old fashioned. In fact John St Quintin thought it almost had a Dickensian feel to it. The decision was therefore made in 1975 for Shorten & Armes to relocate to Meadows' modern premises on Fishergate. At the time both companies produced their own ranges, but eventually Shorten & Armes started to trade under the name of Meadows of Norwich.

In January 1984 the firm joined forces with the Northamptonshire footwear firm William Green of Rushden (which still makes high-quality shoes for men, under the trade name of Grenson) where the directors wanted to produce a ladies' range to complement their existing production. John Barrett retained an interest in Shorten & Armes and was appointed chairman whilst Neil Pettit, who at the time worked for the Ward White organisation, came in as the new managing director. In June of the same year a receiver was called in. Despite what had happened John Barrett was sure that there was still a market for the company's shoes and therefore bought equipment from the receiver. He then took over the old Trimfoot factory on Starling Road, which he and his sisters owned, and launched Meadows Bridal Shoes Ltd.

For further details see: Meadows Bridal Shoes Ltd.

Shorten & Armes factory, Esdelle Street, 1967

Picture Gallery - Shorten & Armes, Esdelle Street, c1968

The factory entrance

Sandals from the Fiesta range

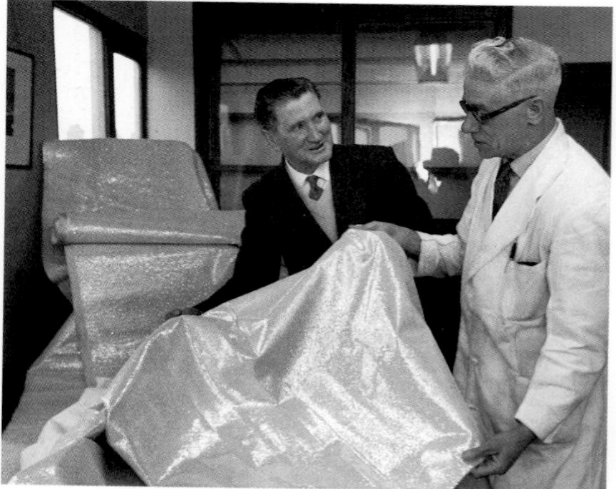

(L tor) Albert Hannant and A. W. Sayer, material store,

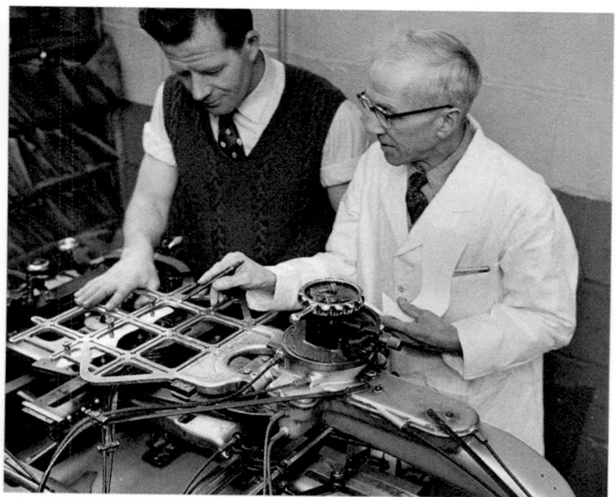

Ron Sheldon (left), pattern room

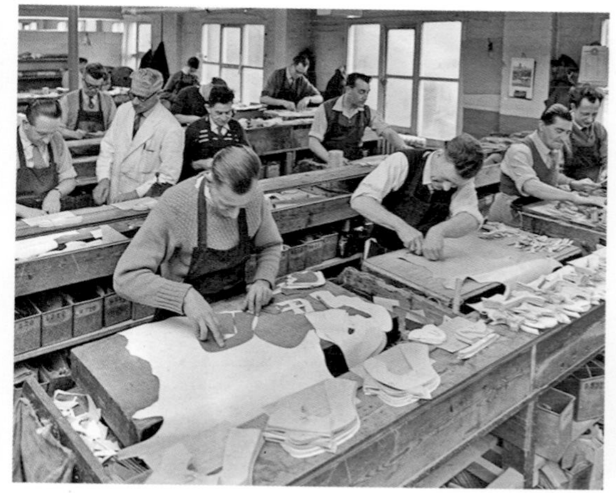

Clicking room

Mrs Cullum (white coat), machine room

All photographs in the gallery reproduced by kind permission of the Norfolk Record Office

Picture Gallery - Shorten & Armes, Esdelle Street, c1968

Machine room

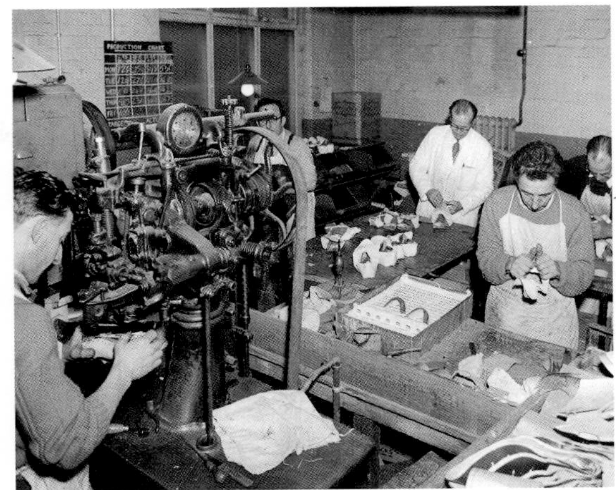
Making room

Fred Culyer, bottom-stock preparation department

Shoe room

'Show time' for Shorten & Armes shoes, c1960

Shorten & Armes shoes on display, c1960

Start-rite Ltd

Site of James Smith's St Peter's Street factory, c1890

Start-rite can trace its history back to 1792, when James Smith established a shop and factory in the Upper Market on St Peter's Street where he made and sold ready-made shoes. At the time the vast majority of shoes were produced on a made-to-measure basis. Instead James produced a series of lasts from which standard, off-the-peg footwear was made. He thus became one of the first shoemakers in the country to offer an alternative to expensive bespoke footwear. By the time of James' death in 1818 the business was flourishing.

For the nine years after James' death the business was briefly run by his son, Charles Smith. After Charles' demise his executors appear to have held the fort until Charles Winter (the founder's young grandson) was of sufficient age and experience to take the helm, which he did from 1827 until 1867. Charles clearly inherited his grandfather's entrepreneurial flair, and under his leadership the business prospered. When he took control the vast majority of the City's shoe trade was in the hands of the garret masters, yet he had the vision to base workers in his expanding factory, whilst employing homeworkers where necessary. Around 1856 Charles was the first Norwich manufacturer to use the sewing machine for closing uppers in his factory. As one straight-sewing machine could produce 3,000 stitches a minute, the incentive to mechanise, and hence base more workers in a single premises, was enormous. By 1860 Charles' business occupied numbers 7, 8 and 9 Upper Market. Over the following decade the business employed between 800 and 900 people, based both in the factory and in their homes.

Charles Winter, undated

In 1857 James Southall, who at the time was an accountant living in West Hackney, had married Charles Winter's niece, Marianne. Approximately three years later he started work in her uncle's thriving enterprise. Marianne was a beneficiary under Charles' will, which allowed James to stake a claim in Winter's business after his death in 1867. However, before he could take control James also needed access to additional capital. This, along with shoemaking experience, was provided by a John Willis, who is believed to have come to the City from Gloucestershire. From 1868 the firm was renamed Willis & Southall. Although few records survive from this time, an 1871 catalogue lists almost 1,000 different styles of footwear produced by the firm. The 54-page booklet showed that the firm produced an extensive range of footwear for children, ladies and men.

James Southall, c1920

Crome Road factory, James Southall & Co., c1910

Following John Willis' death in 1888, the firm passed into the sole ownership of James Southall. Subsequently James Southall & Co. Ltd was incorporated as a private company in 1900. James Southall was a formidable character, as noted by Ken Holmes in his book about Start-rite: 'James Southall's sons, Charles and Frederick, born respectively in 1866 and 1874...became directors when the company was formed. But there is not the slightest doubt that James Southall was very much at the helm all his life. He knew exactly what he wanted, and got it.'

Early in the 20th century it became clear that the City-centre factory was obsolete. The Southalls recognised that to produce shoes of a consistently high quality on a large scale, they needed a single-storey factory where they could install the latest machinery and provide good working conditions for their operatives. The site chosen was on Crome Road, where in 1907 they built a 25,000 square feet shoe factory incorporating offices and a warehouse, to a design by the architect Ernest Buckingham. In the years that followed the directors acquired additional land which enabled the factory to expand, and by 1949 it covered 62,000 square feet.

Arthur Holmes, the firm's cost accountant from 1950 to 1986, recalls the factory layout: 'My office was on a little bridge which overlooked the clicking room. I could see out, but from the outside you couldn't see in. On the right-hand side was a pattern-cutting office and then there was a big closing room which led to a finishing room. Further down were the making room, press room and preparation room for the soles. The factory was all on one floor which meant it was very noisy, although it wasn't too bad where I was as the clicking room was fairly quiet. The noisiest rooms were the making room, where they were attaching soles to the uppers, and the press room, where soles were cut with knifes.'

The City-centre, factory was retained by the firm, although parts were leased to other organisations. In fact the press room was still located there in 1935, when the building was one of many demolished to make way for the new City Hall.

St Peter's Street factory, James Southall & Co., c1930

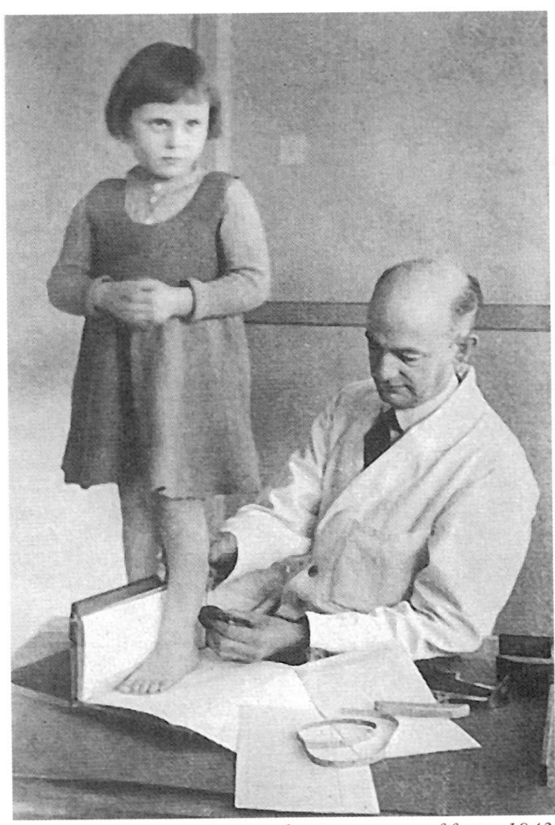

William Peake, conducting survey of feet, c1943

The original drawing for the Start-rite twins, c1936

Although James Southall took little part in public affairs, he was one of the prime movers in the formation of the Norwich Footwear Manufacturers' Association. In 1891 he became their first president, a position he held until his death in 1920, when he was in his ninetieth year and still at the helm of the company that bore his name.

James was succeeded as company chairman by his 46-year-old son Frederick (James' elder son Charles having predeceased his father). Frederick took control immediately after WWI, when the British shoe industry lost a significant portion of its export trade, leaving manufacturers in a precarious state. In response to this crisis Southalls' directors realised that they needed to concentrate on promoting and selling their shoes in the home market. One of the strategies they adopted was to purchase the exclusive use of the trademark 'Start-rite', which had first been used by Quant & Son, a shoe retailer in Bury St Edmunds, to sell certain boots and shoes manufactured for them by Southalls. Once the board realised that the public were concerned about healthcare, and particularly children's fitted footwear, they put extra resources into promoting the brand.

In 1927, Bernard Hanly, James Southall's son-in-law, succeeded Frederick as company chairman. Bernard's role in ensuring the survival of the firm through turbulent years cannot be underestimated. Ken Holmes writes of him that 'he was as equally decisive and single-minded as his father-in-law had always been'. Additionally Wilfred Sparks gives him the credit for 'piloting the firm through the trade depression of the late twenties and thirties', a period that claimed many Norwich firms. Under Bernard's leadership the firm's commitment to providing healthy footwear for children grew, and in 1928 the company commissioned an investigation into schoolchildren's feet to confirm their belief that children should be catered for differently to adults. Then in 1936 the iconic Start-rite twins first made their appearance. Amazingly they still feature today as the Start-rite logo and are recognised as the hallmark of well-fitted, quality shoes for children. Stocked by agents throughout Britain, and with a range of 120 fittings, by the outbreak of WWII Start-rite had become a household name. Their reputation was such that during the hostilities the Board of Trade decreed that 85% of Southalls' output should be children's footwear.

James Hanly, undated

Meanwhile, in 1925 Bernard's son, James Laffan Hanly, still remembered by many today simply as Mr Jim, joined Southalls as a 20-year-old management trainee. Jim was given a thorough grounding in how to make shoes, following which he was sent to a Northampton factory for six months before being put 'on the road' to gain some idea of selling. The story goes that early in his career Jim requested an increase in his salary, which was referred to his uncle, Fred Southall. In turn his uncle spoke to Fred Jex, one of the leaders of the shoe trades union in Norwich, about the merits of his nephew. The reply was positive so it is not surprising that when both his father and uncle died in 1942, Jim succeeded as company chairman. Despite being given minimum authority whilst his father was alive, Jim immediately began to make a positive contribution to the company. In 1943, with the aid of medical research experts, schools and health authorities, he commissioned a nationwide survey of children's feet. The results proved that whilst Start-rite shoes were better for children's developing feet than other brands, there was still room for improvement, including the need for the shoes to be fitted by trained people. This, amongst other things, led to the firm introducing an intensive course for shoe fitters. To give the course kudos, successful students were awarded the Start-rite Diploma.

Shoe exhibited in Turin show, James Southall & Co., 1911

In the years immediately following WWII Southalls were still producing ladies' fashion shoes under the brand name 'Lightfoot', and were also one of the few remaining shoe factories in Norwich where turnshoes were made. Then in 1952 they made the decision to stop manufacturing adult footwear and instead to put all resources into producing the Start-rite brand for children.

The firm subsequently received a huge accolade in 1955, when it was first granted a Royal Warrant for supplying shoes for Prince Charles and Princess Anne. In the years that followed the firm fitted hundreds of pairs of children's shoes for members of the Royal Family including Prince William and Prince Harry. They retained the warrant until 1993 when there was no further demand for children's shoes among the members of the Royal Family who could grant the Warrant, namely the Queen, the Queen Mother, the Prince of Wales or Prince Philip.

James Hanly was known for his wit and humour. His nephew David White, who succeeded his uncle as chairman (of Start-rite in 1978 and of James Southall & Co. in 1985), recalls an occasion when James, accompanied by Start-rite's fitting consultant Bill Peake, visited the Royal Family: 'Jim loved to tell the story about one of the first times they went to Buckingham Palace to see Prince Charles. After they'd finished measuring and Prince Charles had decided which shoes he was going to have, the Queen walked in. He was introduced and she was very gracious and there was a bit of small talk. Eventually the Queen said: "We're just going to have tea. Have you had your tea Mr Hanly?" He said no he hadn't whilst thinking: "This is marvellous, here I am selling shoes and I'm going to have tea with the Queen." That was until she said: "Oh dear, we mustn't keep you... Good-bye."'

Boys' shoe, Start-rite, c1955

The Royal family at Sandringham, c1988

By 1966 the Start-rite brand had become so important to Southalls that the decision was taken to officially adopt Start-rite as its trading name. Today both the business and brand are known as Start-rite although the parent company remains James Southall Ltd.

Meanwhile the demand for Start-rite branded shoes seemed insatiable. As recalled by David White: 'The 1960s and early 1970s were an absolute boom time; the company simply couldn't make enough shoes to meet demand. The birth rate was going up and fashion didn't really play a part in the trade. We only made black and brown shoes, and if they didn't sell one year you'd put them back into stock, increase the price and sell them the following year.' In line with other major Norwich firms Southalls had additional closing rooms at locations that included King's Lynn, Wymondham and even Ireland, but even this was not sufficient.

The firm couldn't expand further at Crome Road, where they were limited for space, so instead they contracted production out to other Norwich firms, and also started a programme of acquisition. This resulted in them taking over the Ward Shoe Company Ltd in 1957, Thomas Bowhill and Hubbard in 1961, Arthur Howlett Ltd in 1973, and R. Roberts (Norwich) Ltd in 1974. Additionally in 1962 a new firm Start-rite Sonnet was formed which made colourful shoes for young children, in which Southalls held 75% of the shares.

Stock room, Start-rite's Crome Road factory, c1975

By the early 1970s the total output of Start-rite branded shoes from all of its factories plus those bought-in, reached two million a year. With approximately 1,400 employees, Start-rite had become the biggest Norwich shoe manufacturer. Then in the mid-1970s the market changed, as explained by David White: 'Not only did the birth rate considerably slow down, but fashion became important to buyers. At the same time retailers began to import more from overseas producers and price competition became stronger...These factors all combined to adversely affect sales, not least because children's shoes are very price sensitive.'

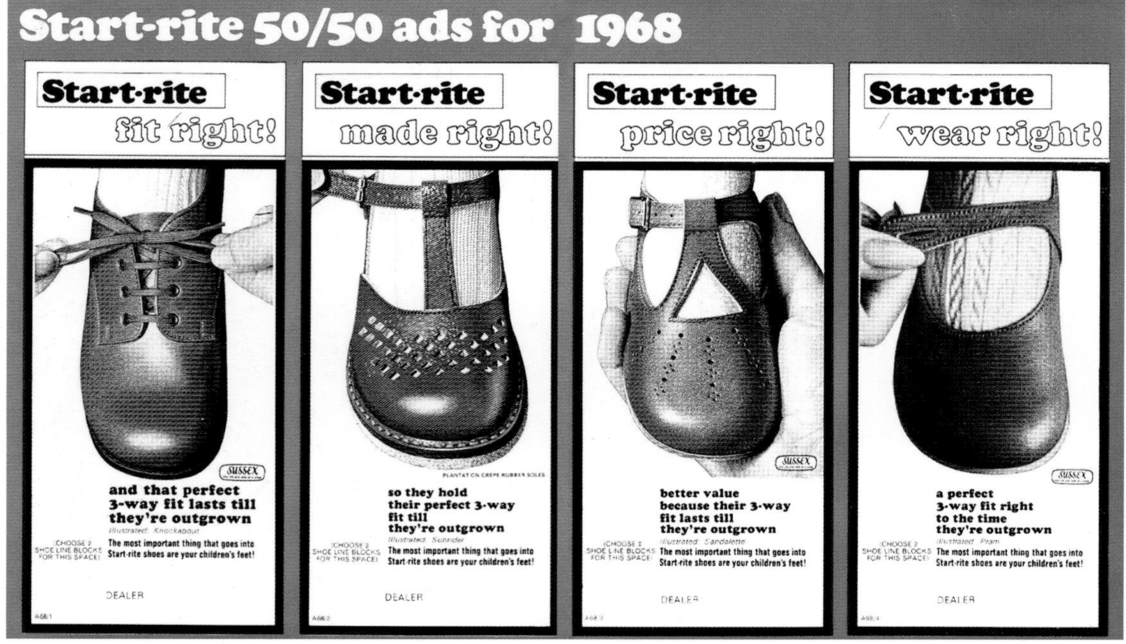

Start-rite shoes, 1968

The firm had no choice but to reduce output. One of the first things they did was to stop contracting out work, without which some smaller firms could not survive, e.g. Trimfoot Ltd failed in 1975. They also introduced a four-day week for many of the workforce, in preference to redundancies, hoping that jobs could be saved and skilled labour retained to meet an anticipated future increase in demand. However, it soon became obvious that both production levels and the number of employees needed to be reduced, and so the board made the difficult decision to start closing its subsidiary outlets, including the Start-rite Sonnet factory in Duke Street at the end of 1975, the Ward Shoe company in Magdalen Street in May 1977 and the R. Roberts Ltd factory on Fisher's Lane in 1981.

David White, c1992

In 1985, following the death of James Hanly, David White was appointed group chairman. By taking drastic action Start-rite had survived whilst many of the major shoe manufacturers in the City had failed, but the directors were under no illusion that they could now relax. If they were to remain in business they knew that they had to continue to adapt to changing market conditions. It was in the late 1980s that the firm started to outsource abroad. Nigel Brown who had worked at Crome Road since 1974 recalls: 'When we started to bring in uppers from abroad, we had to wrap them in wet rags because they were so hard. At the time in the factory we were quite pleased it wasn't working too well, because we thought our jobs would be safer, but obviously processes got better.'

Start-rite's Crome Road factory, c1965

Start-rite news

AUTUMN 1992 **BICENTENNIAL SOUVENIR** **EDITION 9**

A year to remember!

The Bicentennial Souvenir edition of 'Start-rite News', 1992

In 1992 Start-rite celebrated its bicentenary year. This was a huge achievement, all the more impressive when one considers the fate of so many of their competitors, and also the fact that it was the oldest shoe-manufacturing company in England. Two years prior to this Peter Lamble, David's nephew, joined the group as finance director. In 1997 he became managing director at first jointly with David, and on his own from 2002, when he also took on the role of chairman. Since starting he has overseen extensive changes in the company's structure: 'When I first arrived we made around 80% of our shoes in Norwich. The vast majority were made at our Crome Road factory but some were still being produced at a small factory on Fishergate, previously occupied by Arthur Howlett Ltd. At the time we also had a warehouse on Mousehold Lane. The big adaptation has been to move from essentially being a manufacturer to being a design and marketing business, which is what we are now.'

The company first outsourced in the 1980s in a minor way to Thailand, but in the years that followed more and more procedures were transferred abroad. Avis Brown, who worked at Crome Road at the time recalls: 'In the late 1980s they started shipping work out, and that was the first time we thought the factory might close. But we didn't really believe it. We never, ever thought that they'd make everything abroad.' But the directors were faced with a stark choice, they knew that to secure the future of the company production had to be transferred overseas. It was done as a gradual process, with the machine and clicking rooms finishing on 9 September 2001 and the factory finally closing on Thursday 25 September 2003. On that date the last 28 people working on shoe production were made redundant. Amongst them was Avis: 'The last day was awful. There were a lot of tears. There was such emptiness. Everyone was so hurt. We knew each other like family but didn't know if we'd see each other anymore. To think that all of the skills we all had were just going to go. On that day we felt just like a number, something we'd never been before.'

In the years leading up to the factory closure Start-rite had reinvented itself from being a company that manufactured footwear to one that designed, developed, distributed and marketed footwear, in each case 'for the developing foot of a child'. After the factory closed, the company moved to their new distribution centre on the Broadland Business Park on the outskirts of Norwich. For Nigel Brown, who had transferred from the shop floor into an administrative job, this was one of the saddest times: 'Several times I'd wander into the old, closed-down factory and just stand there in the empty room and imagine what it used to be like. In my mind I could see everyone I used to work with. To others it was just an empty room...but to me it was full of people.'

Members of the Richardson family who worked at Start-rite with David White, c1992

During the transformation the company retrained many factory staff, such as Nigel, and many still work for the company. For example, John Thain who was a pattern cutter now works in the shoe development department as head of fitting, whilst Keith Richardson, who trained as a clicker, now works on the resourcing side of the business. Today Start-rite has around 100 people working in Norwich, but instead of clickers, skivers, machinists and passers they now employ warehouse operatives, sales and telesales people, designers, marketing and IT specialists.

Start-rite no longer owns any factories, but to ensure that shoes are made to a high standard of workmanship, they only work with firms where Start-rite products are important to the factory's output. As explained by Peter Lamble: 'It would be impossible for us to work with large, impersonal, mass producing factories. We are very pleased that a large portion of our shoes are made in India where we largely work with smaller, family-run businesses. Our aim is to build a long- term relationship with the manufacturers. We visit them a lot. Sometimes we announce our arrival, sometimes we don't. In any case as part of the product-development process we visit at least every other month.'

Start-rite continues to apply rigorous standards to all of their new styles. The process starts at their head office in Norwich where footwear is designed. Subsequently one of the factories makes a prototype. If that meets the company's standards one shoe is made in every size and fitters, such as John Thain, will go into local schools and nurseries to ensure that they fit the appropriate youngster's feet. As explained by John: 'We then bring them back and make sure everything is alright, and tweak them as necessary. We then liaise with our overseas partners and get a pair made in every size and we go through the same procedure again. If we start to use any new materials or buckles or anything like that, we give the kids free pairs so that we can thoroughly test them. There are some schools in Norwich where most of the kids are wearing Start-rite shoes, which the parents and kids love. They swamp us when we go to the schools. Once we're satisfied we'll put in an order for a few thousand pairs, which we'll spot check to ensure that everything meets our standards.' Such rigorous procedures mean that the firm often discards around half of its initial designs, whilst it takes approximately a year from the time the first sketch is made to the shoe appearing in the shops.

Start-rite produces around 150 designs of footwear in any season, each in different lengths, widths and colours, giving an astonishing 7,500 permutations. Retailers could not stock such a vast range and many will only hold one or two shoes in each variation of size/colour/design. In response to this challenge, Peter Lamble explains: 'We spend a lot of time working with retailers' EPoS (Electronic Point of Sales) Systems to ensure we get automatic replenishment up and running very quickly. We hold between 200,000 and 350,000 pairs of shoes in our Norwich warehouse at any time. It is a complex system which is a key element of our business model. It is essential that we know our level of stock, because if we are short of a line it takes us three months to do anything about that. When we made shoes at Crome Road it took three weeks.'

During its long history Start-rite's directors have made many difficult decisions to ensure its survival. It is still trading today, supplying high-quality, attractive footwear because it has adapted. In the words of David White: 'The company has now been in operation since 1792 making it England's oldest shoe manufacturing business... something to be very proud of.'

Start-rite head office, Broadland Business Park, 2012

Picture Gallery - Start-rite's former Crome Road factory, 2012

Start-rite's former Crome Road factory has been developed as a residential site. Reminders of its earlier use are retained in the archway: 1792, is the date James Smith established a shop and factory in the Upper Market on St Peter's Street; 1907, is the date that the Crome Road factory was built; J. S. Co. Ltd, is of course James Southall & Co. Ltd.

All photos taken by Mike Dixon

Thomas Bowhill & Hubbard Ltd

The firm of Thomas Bowhill & Hubbard was established by Thomas Bowhill and William Hubbard in 1890. Between 1896 and 1923 their factory was based in the Bridewell on Bridewell Alley (which is now occupied by the Bridewell Museum). In 1916 they advertised that they also occupied the Victoria Hall Works, 'another manufactory in the same thoroughfare'. At the time they employed around 450 staff split between the two locations. The firm specialised in the production of high-grade footwear for children. The business was incorporated in 1915 when the factory manager, Walter Griffiths (pictured right), became one of the first shareholders and directors.

Walter Griffiths, c1897

In 1924 the firm relocated to the Endura Works on Heigham Street. The factory was badly damaged by enemy action in 1942 and was subsequently rebuilt in 1947. The firm continued to be based on the same site until 1959, when they moved their equipment and 100 staff to smaller premises on Pitt Street, where they occupied part of John F. Kirbys' factory. Following the move they continued to make footwear for children together with adults' slippers.

In 1961 the firm was taken over by Start-rite, at which time all of Bowhills' plant and machinery were transferred to Start-rite's Crome Road factory.

The Bridewell, 1934

Trimfoot Shoes (Norwich) Ltd

Trimfoot Shoes (Norwich) Ltd was founded in 1953 as a subsidiary of Shorten & Armes. Geoffrey Barrett oversaw the operation whilst Len Waspe, the MD, ran the business on a day-to-day basis. The firm started in a small factory in a lane that led to Mousehold Heath. Then in 1954, when Barfield & Richardson closed, Geoffrey bought their factory on Starling Road and Trimfoot relocated there. At the same time they took on many of Barfields' staff.

It was quite a homecoming for Len, a skilled designer, who had started work in the Starling Road factory in 1931 as 'the boy' and had only left there to become a director at Trimfoot. His father Fred Waspe, a clicker, also moved to Trimfoot. Len's daughter Margaret Brawn Meek remembers: 'I often visited them both at the factory. I particularly remember the lovely smell from all the rolls of leather. On a Friday afternoon after the workers had been paid they all used to bring out sweets that they called "Rosies".'

Avis Brown worked in the Trimfoot factory in the mid-1960s. She recalls: 'The factory was very small. Upstairs, before I went there, must have been used for machinists but in my time it was just used for storage. The room we worked in was at the back. It had been an old courtyard over which a roof had been built. They'd also put in two big brown wooden doors which could be opened to take the work out. In the room we still had drainpipes and drains, which before the conversion would have been outside. Because it was below street level, to get in you'd open the door and go down six steps. If it was a foggy morning outside, you'd open the door and find that there was also fog in the room!'

Trimfoot was originally formed to produce shoes which sold slightly below regular Shorten & Armes prices. Later it became one of a number of factories in the City that had a contract to make Start-rite shoes. Although they also made beach sandals and slipper mules, for the summer and winter markets respectively, and Len made some specialist dance shoes, they relied on the Start-rite order to keep the factory running. Hence in 1975 when Start-rite withdrew their order they could not survive, and in the following year the factory closed.

Len Waspe, 1951. Trimfoot factory in background, 1960

W. H. H. Clarke Ltd

W. H. H. Clarke, 1916

In 1898 William Clarke left the firm of H. Sexton & Sons, where he had been bound as an apprentice, and established his own shoemaking business in modest premises in St Margaret's Plain. After two years he moved to a small factory on Ten Bell Lane, which was later enlarged. The business was so successful that by 1916 the firm operated from three factories: the Ten Bell Lane Shoe Works, the Pottergate Street Shoe Works and a small additional factory on Pottergate. Each week from these factories they produced around 8,000 pairs of children's and girls' better-class boots and shoes.

Further expansion of the business had been halted by the start of WWI, but once hostilities had ceased the firm continued to grow, and in 1922 they moved into a new modern factory on Northumberland Street. Four years later the founder's son W. G. Clarke (Bill) joined the family business.

Over the following years the firm continued to prosper, and then came WWII. During the course of the hostilities Clarkes suffered so badly from enemy action that the *Eastern Evening News* dubbed it 'probably the worst-bombed firm in Norwich'. Their problems started in April 1942 when their Northumberland Street factory was completely destroyed in the Baedeker Raids. Undeterred they took up space with box manufacturers Mansfields (Norwich) Ltd at their factory on St Saviours. Sadly a few months later Mansfields was also burnt out. At this time Clarkes relocated to Sextons' factory on St Mary's Plain – that is until the August Bank Holiday (1942) when the same fate befell them. It says something for William Clarke's fortitude that he never gave up and instead moved across to Dibden Street, where the firm was taken in by Chittock & Sons Ltd, Here they remained until the end of the war.

St Margaret's Plain, Westwick Street, c1925

Once hostilities had ceased Clarkes were given the opportunity by the Norwich Corporation to purchase the old A.R.P. (Air Raid Precaution) site on Sussex Street, which had previously been a shoe factory. This was on the understanding that the Northumberland Street factory would not be rebuilt for five years.

By the end of October 1946, Clarkes' new Apex Works on Sussex Street was producing 6,000 pairs of high-quality shoes per week. As was observed in the *Eastern Evening News*: 'The place has been modernised in every way, with the latest methods of air-conditioning and heating installed. Messrs Clarkes claim to be the only factory in Norwich at present in which every machine has an individual motor.'

At this time plans were already underway to rebuild the Northumberland Street factory, which it was envisaged would perform at double the capacity of the Apex Works. In April 1955 these plans came to fruition, and the firm started to move operatives into their new, modern factory.

W. H. H. Clarke's Apex Works, Sussex Street, 1987

Similar to the Apex Works, care had been taken at the Northumberland Street factory to provide good working conditions. As Bill Clarke said at the time: 'We have set out to produce for our operatives, conditions in which the fashioning of shoes can be the really pleasant occupation it deserves to be.'

W. H. H. Clarke's Northumberland Street factory, 1955

Following its opening the *Evening News* ran a glowing article on the high standards set in the factory, which included a reference to the top-floor machine room with its 'spacious glazing...blue and cream decorations...parquet floor...and [outstanding] view of the City; use of high-efficiency dust extraction and air purification; and the use of thermostatically controlled heating.' The premises had a floor area of some 54,000 square feet, and was devoted to making intricately-styled shoes for ladies. To achieve this it was decided not to introduce a conveyor belt system to the factory. Instead metal strips were laid between the work benches in the closing room, which acted as tracks for the trolleys that transported the work backwards and forwards between the company's 230 machinists.

In the years that followed the firm continued to operate from both sites, and in 1959 they announced that they would be re-equipping the Sussex Street factory and extending it to some 34,000 square feet. In 1960 the firm had around 700 employees and were producing approximately 500,000 pairs of shoes a year. Their two largest customers were Dolcis and Saxone, who were in competition with each other in the High Street of every large town. The company's success was very much due to the drive and innovation of Bill Clarke, who was so open-minded that his company was one of the few Norwich firms to employ a woman shoe designer, Miss Shirley Thaxton.

In 1961, with no natural successor for the family business, Bill Clarke actively sought a merger with a public limited company. Bill was approached by K shoes where it was considered that a merger with Clarkes would not only strengthen their interest in the fashion business, but also add the expertise of the Norwich shoemakers to their skill set.

The subsequent merger, which resulted in Clarkes becoming a wholly-owned subsidiary of K Shoes and Bill Clarke joining their board as a director, took place in October 1961. The takeover cost K Shoes £806,000, equivalent of around £15m today. From Clarkes' point of view the timing of the merger was perfect, as almost immediately afterwards Dolcis and Saxone were taken over by the British Shoe Corporation. This meant that Clarkes' two largest customers came under one control, and a complete ban on buying was imposed by the new owner whilst stock levels were sorted. Around the same time the government doubled purchase tax, which put a damper on retail sales. In response to the crisis both of the Norwich factories switched to the manufacturing of K Shoes.

Derek Rye (front), W. H .H. Clarke, Sussex Street, c1975

It was in 1964 that Derek Rye joined Clarkes: 'I started in the factory in Northumberland Street, which was relatively modern having been rebuilt after WWII. It was a very good factory, the managing director always made sure it was relatively safe. The finishing room was located on the bottom floor, and then you had the making room on the middle floor and on the top floor were the clicking room and machine room. At Sussex Street there was some machining but there they mainly did finishing. The building was a lot older.'

In 1972, when Clarkes was producing between 17,000 and 18,000 high-grade K and Gold Cross shoes (both K Shoes' brands), the Norwich operation was restructured. Following the reorganisation all clicking and closing was done at Sussex Street, whilst the making room, shoe room and finishing room were located at Northumberland Street. At the time it was estimated that following the changes output would increase by around 25%. This was very good news for the local shoe industry. John Thain joined the firm in 1973 after the restructure, he recalls that he was very pleased to get a job: 'You could earn more money at Clarkes so everyone wanted to work there.'

In the years that followed the K Shoe group started to experience difficulties, and by 1975 could not generate sufficient sales to keep its factories at full production. In response, on 1 January 1976 all manufacturing activities were put under the control of a new company, K Shoemakers Ltd, which also gave its name to the Norwich operation – until then it had always traded as W. H. H. Clarke Ltd. Over the following months demand for Gold Cross Shoes continued to fall. This was disastrous for the Norwich factories where many of the shoes were manufactured, and in September 1976 it was announced that the Northumberland Street factory would be closed at the end of the year and all production was to be concentrated in the Sussex Street factory. The closure resulted in 350 redundancies.

The announcement was accepted by the National Union of Footwear Leather & Allied Trades 'with regret', but representatives of the Association of Scientific and Managerial Staffs (ASTMS) resolved to fight the closure, and at 5 p.m. on 5 October they took over the control of both the Norwich factories. During a ten-day sit-in production continued. At the end of this time officials realised that there was no hope of keeping the Northumberland Street factory open and the dispute was called off. The factory was closed at the end of 1976, after which it was sold to Horne Bothers to be used for the manufacture of suits and uniforms. Parts of the premises have now been converted into residential flats.

Subsequently both output and employment at the Sussex Street factory fell, and from April 1985 workers were on almost permanent short time. By February 1986 only half of two floors in the three-storey building were being used for production, and just 6,000 pairs of shoe a week were being manufactured in a factory with a capacity for 30,000 and a break-even target of 10,000. Inevitably K Shoemakers made the decision to close the Sussex Street premises, and production was transferred to a smaller factory on Beech Drive (off Mile Cross Lane). As a result the workforce shrank from 150 people to 70, and at the same time output halved to 5,000 pairs a week. Despite the challenges, Derek Rye recalls: 'You have to say that K Shoes did invest in the new factory and tried to make it work. It was just that everything was being done on a smaller scale. We still had the clicking and making rooms, but after this the uppers were transported to their factory in Kendal to be made up.' Following the move the Sussex Street factory was taken over by the Norwich Union Insurance Company (now Aviva), who converted it into offices. The building has since been demolished.

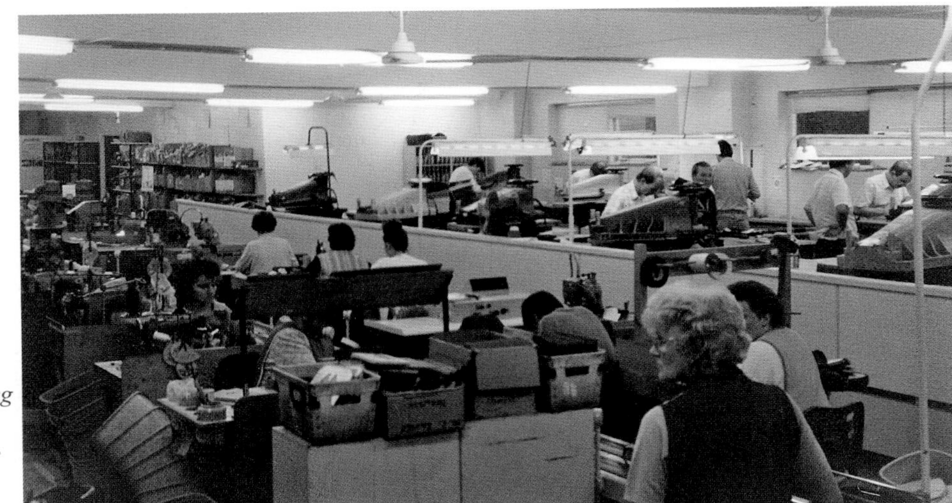

Making room (left) and clicking room (right), W. H. H. Clarke, Beech Drive, c1990

In 1987 K Shoes achieved a record profit for the third year running. However, as inflation, rents and interest charges climbed in the UK, complete shoes were increasingly bought in from abroad, where manufacturing costs were significantly lower than in this country. In response to these challenges in 1990 K Shoe Shops and K Shoemakers ceased to trade as separate companies, and the first of a steady stream of redundancies in their factories and offices began. In Norwich the factory was put on short time, and despite the efforts of local directors it became clear that the factory was failing. Then in February 1992 the directors of Clarks International, K Shoes' parent company, announced that the Norwich factory would be shut down. It was a time that Derek Rye will never forget: 'A Mercedes drew up in the car park. We could all see it through the windows. Once the managing director got out we all said, "Oh no", because we knew what was coming. We all switched the machines off and were gathered together and we were given two-weeks' notice. The women stopped work more or less straight away, but the men helped pack up the factory because anything useful was being transferred to Kendal. Under an agreement made with the unions we were paid three-months' redundancy money, which was obviously very welcome. I have to say that K shoes didn't try and avoid their responsibility in this respect.'

Looking through this brief history of the firm which will always be known locally as W. H. H. Clarke, one is struck not only by the resilience of its founding family but also by their paternalistic attitude towards their employees. It therefore seems appropriate to end this section with a comment made by Lenford Laband: 'As a sales rep I spent hours sat in Clarkes' foyer and to this day I can remember the wording on a plaque they had on a wall. It said: "W. H. H. Clarke, our founder, whose wise counsel and warm understanding continues to inspire us."'

Former Apex Works, Sussex Street, 2012

W. Hurrell Ltd

W. Hurrell, Phoenix Shoe Works, Magdalen Street, 1906

The firm of William Hurrell & Son was established in 1875. By 1906 the firm's factory was located in the Phoenix Shoe Works on Magdalen Street, where they specialised in producing children's footwear under the brand name 'Cinema'. The factory was destroyed during enemy action in 1942, but rebuilt during 1947.

The firm continued to make children's shoes and sandals for the medium-priced home market until 1956, when the managing director, William Hurrell (grandson of the founder), decided that increased foreign competition was making the firm unviable. He therefore started making high-grade, fashion shoes for women. As part of the change in strategy William introduced machinery that was more widely used on the continent than in Britain. At the time he told the local press: 'We have done this because we are convinced that shoe manufacture is now an international business and we can only keep up our standards if we compete with other shoemaking countries.' By 1960 ladies' footwear made up around 20% of the firm's output, much of which was exported. Two years later William took his strategy one step further when he decided to move production from Norwich to Oporto in Portugal. He explained: 'We have for some time been considering the expansion of our ranges of women's fashion shoes, maintaining the quality and styling and at the same time offering the increased mark-ups which are now so necessary. With the rapidly changing events in Europe we have decided that this will be achieved by moving our manufacturing unit abroad.'

W. Hurrell, Phoenix Shoe Works, Magdalen Street, 1938

In December 1962 the firm's machinery was transported from Great Yarmouth's South Quay to Portugal. Then in 1964 the factory itself was demolished ending the firm's long links with Norwich.

W. Hurrell post-war factory, Magdalen Street, c1963

Walter Edwards & Son Ltd

Although we know very little about the firm of Walter Edwards & Son, a wonderful photograph album is held at the Norfolk Record Office which we have used throughout this publication. Between these and other documents we have gleaned the following.

By 1900 the firm of Edwards & Son was located at 52 Colegate. A year later they were the first Norwich shoemaker to install the Consolidated pulling-over machine (used for lasting). This suggests that the firm was innovative and forward looking. By 1908 it had expanded sufficiently to occupy both 52 Colegate and 56 Pitt Street.

In 1922 the firm, which by then was named Walter Edwards & Son, was still located at 52 Colegate and had also taken on the Castle Shoe Works on Duke Street. In the same year they exhibited at the British Industries' Fair (an annual exhibition first held in 1915 with the aim of encouraging British firms to produce goods which had traditionally been imported). At the fair they were listed as manufacturing children's boots and shoes, together with dancing pumps and slippers.

From the photographs taken at the Castle Shoe Works in 1925 we can see that the firm employ over 200 staff in a well-developed factory which contains the traditional rooms. Both ladies' and children's shoes are pictured on the racks, suggesting that they had extended their ranges. This is substantiated by the fact that in 1929 the firm again exhibited at the British Industries' Fair when they were listed as being 'manufacturers of ladies' and children's boots, shoes and sandals for walking and dress wear, in all leathers'. By then it would seem that they no longer occupied the Colegate premises.

In 1935 they were still located at their Duke Street premises, but by 1937 were no longer listed in local directories, and so it can be assumed that they stopped trading during this period.

The land occupied by the factory was taken over by Norvic and the site was eventually used for their Riverside factory which was opened in 1961.

Walter Edwards & Son, Castle Shoe Works, Duke Street, 1925

Picture Gallery - Walter Edwards & Son Ltd, Castle Shoe Works, Duke Street, 1925

All photographs of Walter Edwards & Son Ltd reproduced by kind permission of the Norfolk Record Office

Pattern room

Bottom cutting

Clicking room

Machine room

Making room

Shoe room

Ward Shoe Company Ltd

The Ward Shoe Company was founded at the turn of the 20th century when it produced children's hand-sewn shoes. The Howes family first became involved with it c1933 when Richard Howes senior bought the business, incorporated it, and took on the role of managing director. Previously they had operated their own small business, Howes Bros Ltd, at the St Miles' Shoe Works, which was located on Oak Street. Howes Bros specialised in making shoes for children which were marketed as 'All Time Shoes'.

Following the closure of Howes Bros (c1932), Richard James Howes (Richard Howes senior's son) moved to Chingford where he continued to work as a pattern cutter and designer in a shoe factory based in Hackney. In 1945, Richard junior returned to Norwich and took on the role of director and factory manager. On completion of his National Service, Derrick Howes joined his father in the business.

From the early 1930s Wards' factory was situated at 122 Magdalen Street. Mollie Howes, Derrick's wife, recalls the building well: 'It was up a short alley behind the shops fronting the street and behind what was then the Mayfair Cinema and the Blind School. It was, in the main, a newish building with an outside staircase to the top floor, but built on much older foundations reputed to be an old 18th-century brewery. This was discovered when heavy machinery was to be installed on the ground floor, and the cellar had to be shored up to take the additional weight. At that time they discovered an old D-shaped well and, I believe, an old window.'

In 1957, when they employed around 80 people, the firm was taken over by Start-rite. Prior to the takeover they had made high-quality shoes for children, many of which were produced on behalf of Start-rite, together with men's dress shoes and men's Albert slippers. As explained by Jim Hanly, managing director of Southalls at the time: 'The Ward Shoe Company will continue to supply the home trade through its normal outlets and, through Start-rite purchasing raw materials in larger quantities, it should now be more competitive.' At the time of this reorganisation Richard senior retired and his son continued in his role as director in charge of production.

Magdalen Street factory, Ward Shoe Company, 1977

(L to r) Mollie, Richard and Derrick Howes, 1991

Although the firm continued to concentrate on the production of children's shoes they still manufactured both high-class slippers and dance shoes for men. The slippers, which sported gold embroidered motifs sewn by local firm Harmers, were mainly sold through Bowhill & Elliott (London Street). In 1959 they made a pair for Sammy Davis junior in black velvet piped with gold leather with a fox head embroidered in gold. It was just before Richard junior retired in 1973, that he had a chance meeting with world ballroom-dancing champion Peter Eggleton. As recalled by Mollie: 'The talk naturally turned to dancing shoes...Richard suggested making a pair for Peter to try. They were produced with the extended heel like the Start-rite brand. They proved so successful that the factory then made these shoes in quantity for sale by Peter in London.'

After his father's retirement Derrick became managing director until 1977, when Start-rite closed the Ward factory. Derrick continued to work for Start-rite until his retirement in 1991.

Although Ward's factory has been demolished, the lasts used to make their Albert slippers were passed on to Bowhill & Elliott who still make slippers to a similar design today.

Albert slipper, Ward Shoe Company, 1970

9. Support Industries

Plastic lasts, 2012

The story of the City's boot and shoe trade would be incomplete without mention of the firms that developed in its wake. These included organisations making lasts, boxes, heels and trimmings, together with others that provided services as diverse as tanning leather to leasing machinery.

Many of the firms had their head offices in either Leicester or Northampton, from where they serviced their Norwich branches, whilst other companies were founded and based in Norwich. During the shoe industry's heyday the contribution made by the support companies to the City's prosperity cannot be underestimated, but it was a symbiotic relationship. Inevitably as the shoe industry contracted the firms that supplied them slowly closed down. In the pages that follow we look at a small selection.

Tannery, believed to be William George & Sons (Norwich) Ltd, Barrack Street, c1960

The British United Shoe Machinery Co. Ltd

The formation of the British United Shoe Machinery Company Ltd (the B. U.) can be traced back to the 19th century. At this time shoe manufacturing had become more mechanised, and as a result a number of British shoe-machinery manufacturers had amalgamated. Eventually the firm Pearson & Bennion was formed, which by the mid-1890s had become a leading supplier of UK shoe-manufacturing machinery. In 1899 Pearson & Bennion merged with the US company United Shoe Machinery and formed the UK-based B.U., which established its headquarters in Leicester.

The B. U. leased machinery, which had the advantage of minimising entry costs for new manufacturers to the shoe trade. Additionally as noted by Walter Moll, director at Bally: 'Leasing meant that we didn't have to invest huge sums in machinery, and it also meant that when a new machine came on the market we could swap it for our out-dated equipment.' However, there was some criticism that the firm acquired a monopoly status which enabled it to apply lease restrictions and also dictate how machinery evolved. Notwithstanding this, the firm built a reputation for technical innovation and between 1898 and 1960 it developed and marketed around 800 new and improved machines and patented more than 9,000 inventions. By the 1960s it had more than 4,500 employees in Leicester and a further 5,000 worldwide.

By 1908 the B. U. had premises in Norwich. At this time they were based on Colegate, in close proximity to Howlett & White. They then briefly moved to Magadalen Street before establishing themselves in Starling Road. From here the firm not only marketed its machinery, but also gave the manufacturers additional technical support, a service which they provided in all of the major shoemaking centres. Early in his career, John St Quintin undertook such a role: 'In the 1950s I worked for the B.U. in their shoemaking quality-services department in Leicester. Here we had around six people who specialised in different aspects of making shoes. We were employed to go into factories and advise the management how to get the most out of the machines that the B. U. supplied.' The firm were also responsible for mending their machines when they broke down, but Brian Lambert recalls that the service had its deficiencies: 'Many of the Norwich factories leased machinery from the B. U., and so their engineers were often busy and we [Bally] had to wait quite a time for them to arrive.'

The B. U. started to decline in the 1970s as a result of a combination of factors including the invention of less complex machinery and increased foreign competition. At the same time demand for their services in Norwich all but disappeared as factory after factory closed, until eventually the company left the City. Today the B. U. is no more. Following a series of complex international take-overs the company went into receivership in October 2000. However, in Norwich the building it occupied for so many years on Starling Road, and which still bears its name, survives as a small reminder of Norwich's industrial past.

British United's former premises, Starling Road, 2012

The Standard Engineering Company Ltd

The Standard Engineering Company Ltd (the Standard) was founded in Leicester in 1894. The family business manufactured a wide range of shoemaking equipment, machinery and accessories, including pincers, embossing machines, benches, abrasives and knives. The Norwich branch, located on Fye Bridge Street, was opened in 1919. Within the same building was an outlet of their subsidiary company, F. H. & H. S. Pochin Ltd who were 'boot findings manufacturers', i.e. they supplied the trade with small tools and supplies such as inks and adhesives.

In 1946, at the age of 16, Lenford Laband started a five-year apprenticeship at the Standard. As an engineer he split his time between Norwich and Leicester where he went around the factories fitting machinery. Although most was supplied from Leicester some items, such as the skivers, were made from scratch at the Norwich depot.

Lenford recalls the layout of the premises on Fye Bridge Street: 'The stables were our original workshop. We had the showroom on the ground floor until we started manufacturing. The petrol store led down to the river.' In 1959, Lenford was appointed manager after which he sold both companies' merchandise and services: 'The products supplied by the two companies complemented each other so we did a lot of cross selling. For example, we sold hand-clicking boards and dressing through the Standard and resurfaced them with hand-clicking oil which was sold by Pochins.'

Lenford supplied many of the major Norwich manufacturers, often introducing them to innovative, labour-saving devices: 'All Start-rite logos were created as transfers, and eight girls would manually transfer them onto the shoe socks [linings]. I persuaded them to use a sock-stamping machine which produced a gold impression of the Start-rite twins which did away with all those jobs.' He still remembers that attempts to automate the lasting process didn't always go down too well: 'The chaps always put tacks in their mouths so that they were ready to tap in a tack manually if the machine missed. We started to supply waxed tacks, which were more suited to the machines but the men complained because they didn't like the taste.'

In the 1970s the Standard was taken over by Halma (an industrial holding company). The Norwich business diversified, although it still dealt in shoe-related products. Around the end of the 1980s it moved from the City centre to Hall Road. Although the business has long since closed in Norwich, following a management buyout in 1999 a new company, also called Standard Engineering Ltd, was formed in Kettering. Today it sells a range of products and services, including equipment to make and repair shoes.

The Standard's former premises (centre), Fye Bridge Street, 2012

Mansfields (Norwich) Ltd

Mr Dan Mansfield had many friends who were garret masters. From discussions with them he realised that once they had been made, shoes needed both protection from the outside elements and also a means for being distributed to customers. As a result in 1904 at his house on St Saviour's Lane he brought together workers with paper skills and started manufacturing cardboard boxes specifically for the footwear trade. In the early days the boxes were invariably covered in white enamel paper, i.e. high-gloss heavy-weight paper. This changed when larger companies requested that their own designs and logos should be printed on their shoe boxes, so that in shoe shops their footwear could be easily distinguished from their competitors.

In 1919 the business was incorporated, after which it was owned collectively by the Norwich shoe manufacturers. As a result Mansfields' board of directors was drawn from the shoe industry.

One firm that did not invest was Haldinsteins, who did not want to rely on Mansfields and instead set up their own business, the Norwich Box Company, in Soman's Yard on Fishergate. The Norwich Box Company continued to operate until 1972 when Bally (who had taken over Haldinsteins) closed it down. Subsequently they bought their boxes from Mansfields and also built up a 15% stake in the company.

Mansfield (Norwich) Ltd, 37 St Saviours Lane, 1937

The firm's St Saviour's Lane factory was destroyed in enemy action in 1942. When it was rebuilt after the war the extended factory covered an area stretching from Peacock Street to the rear of the shops at the junction of Magdalen Street and St Saviour's Lane. Following the rebuild the firm had the capacity to significantly extend the range of boxes it produced. Further investment and expansion meant that by 1960 Mansfields was producing ten million rigid boxes per year for a huge range of goods, including chocolates, radios, toys and of course shoes. Additionally they had a large letterpress department where all wrappers and labels were printed and a screen- printing department which made such items as placards and posters.

Despite the diversification, shoe boxes still made up a large portion of the company's output. Ken Cutting who worked there at this time recalls: 'The production of shoe boxes was based totally on the demand from the shoe factories. On an average week we made between 60,000 to 100,000. We had a daily shuttle service to most factories using two vans. Daily deliveries were essential as most factories had limited storage space.'

By 1976 the firm was facing difficulties. Mr W. G. Hill, their managing director, blamed the slow down on falling demand from customers who were letting stocks drop. However, as reported in the local press at the time: 'The economic blow has been cushioned by their good connections and daily service of shoe-box supplies to local customers.'

In the years that followed the Norwich shoe companies continued to contract and Mansfields had little choice but to follow suit. Eventually in 1982 they downsized and moved to new premises on Raynham Street (off Heigham Street). Peter Holmes, who was the company's final chairman, recalls 'We tried to diversify by making boxes for other products such as toothpaste and the like. In the end we printed almost anything.' Despite such action, in 1987 the firm was subject to a management buyout and renamed the Mansfield Group. In 1991 it was purchased by Amalgamated Packaging, a division of Remploy.

Mansfields' factory, St Saviour's Lane, c1970s

In the 1990s the building became Hi-Tech House, it has since been demolished.

John Culyer & Son Ltd

John Culyer founded a tannery in 1860 on Duke Street, where it remained for over 100 years. It was an independent firm until after WWII when it was purchased by Frecknall, Barnard & Scott Ltd, leather manufacturers and exporters, who were based in Northampton.

By 1960 the firm worked mostly on East Indian goatskins and sheepskins which were delivered to them in a half-tanned state. At their Norwich depot Culyers dressed the skins, preparing them for use in the shoe and fancy-leather trades. About 25% of their output was exported to countries including Canada, New Zealand and Holland.

In 1974 Culyers' premises was subject to a compulsory purchase order to allow the widening of Duke Street, and the firm moved to Waterworks Road. Around the same time staff were being sent to India to train local workers on how to finish the leather. Once this was achieved, with so much shoe production being transferred from the UK, the business became unviable, and Frecknall, Barnard & Scott Ltd was liquidated.

Interestingly Culyers premises were not destroyed and the factory reverted to private housing. The smell in the factory was atrocious so one hopes that it was fully fumigated before its change of use!

Culyers' former premises, 43 Duke Street, 1989

Bobcol Components: A Success Story

In 1995 Bob Drake and Colin Gibson took over a small Norwich firm, Alpha Lasts, to form 'Bobcol'.

Bob started in the trade in 1960 when he joined Mobbs & Lewis Ltd who were one of the major last makers in the country. The national firm, whose head office was in Kettering, had a branch in Norwich on the corner of Magdalen Street and Fishergate, and this was where Bob underwent a thorough training in the manufacturer of wooden lasts. At the time he did not think the job suited him but that it would tide him over until he found something better.

Subsequently Bob worked in the making room at Sextons. Then in 1970 he started work at H. B. Cares Ltd, a firm owned by Bally that only made lasts and heels for Bally themselves. Bob recalls that whilst working there wooden lasts were replaced by plastic: 'The main problem with making plastic lasts was that unlike wood when you filed them down the plastic went everywhere. The shavings came off in flakes that, despite us having extractor fans, flew around like flies. Unlike wood the shavings never compressed. However, plastic was a better material to work with, especially as we could do away with a number of operations, including sanding and polishing. We were even able to use the same machinery that we'd used for making wooden lasts.'

In 1976 Bally's closed down Cares as they could get the lasts made at half the price by Mobbs Miller Ltd, the firm created by the amalgamation of Mobbs & Lewis Ltd and O. A. Miller Ltd, another national last-making firm. After a period away from the industry, Bob worked for a small local last maker, Alpha Lasts, until 1995 when he and Colin took it over and renamed it Bobcol. Despite the challenges they faced the firm is still flourishing. This is their story, as told by Bob:

'The first year of being self-employed was terrifying, but we had one huge advantage...I knew the major customers and they knew me. Almost immediately I got a phone call from George Cleverley who makes high-class bespoke shoes for men. I had been making his shoe trees and lasts before I'd taken the company over, and he wanted us to continue supplying him. This was followed by a big order to produce wooden wedges for Vivienne Westwood's 'rocking-horse' sandals, thus called because of the distinctive shape of the wedged soles.

'When we started we discovered a huge gap in the market. You see most of the shoe factories had started to use plastic heels, and as a result most of the wooden-heel manufacturers went out of business. Now

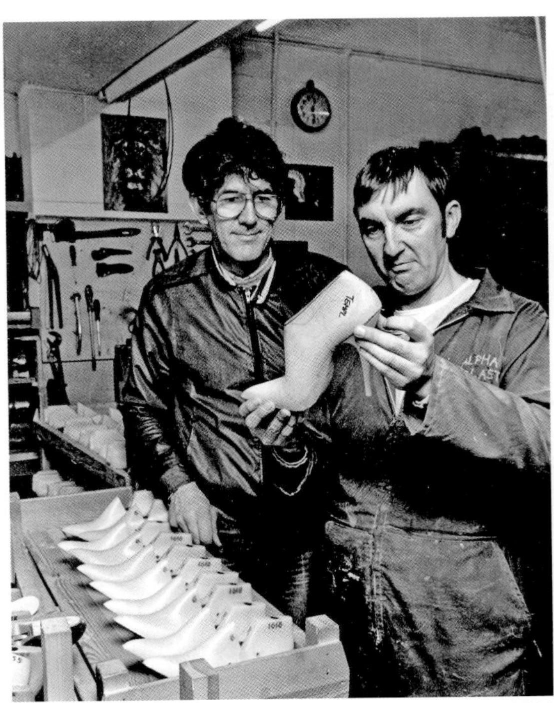

Bob Drake (right), Alpha Lasts, c1993

Bob Drake making plastic lasts, Bobcol, c2000

there are drawbacks with plastic heels. Firstly the manufacturers wouldn't accept orders for under 250 pairs at any one time and the mould could cost an additional £2,000. So we started to accept smaller orders for wooden heels and, although the unit cost was higher, the purchaser didn't have to pay for the mould. The first pair may cost £60 but any subsequent heel cost around £4. The second disadvantage was that plastic isn't a suitable material for making really high heels, as it just isn't strong enough without reinforcement. We now make more heels than lasts.

'We've never had to advertise...it all happened through word of mouth. A lot of business comes through pupils on the Cordwainers course at the London College of Fashion. George Cleverley used to have a lot of their students work with him who'd ask where he got his supplies from.

'The vast majority of our customers are small shoemakers who make bespoke, high-quality footwear, these include Anello & Davide, who not only make shoes for the Queen but in the 1960s designed the 'Beatle Boot' for the 'Fab Four', G. J. Cleverley, on Bond Street, who make bespoke shoes for gentlemen, Andy Burke, a historical shoemaker who makes shoes reproduced from different periods often for the stage and iconic designer Vivienne Westwood. For the majority of these customers I make heels. Most would go to Spring Line, who are based in Northampton, for their lasts. They are the only major last manufacturer still based in England and they can make bespoke lasts or give access to their huge model store.

'Another market which emerged in the 1990s was for fetish shoes, which are characterised by having huge heels and platforms which we are able to supply.

'Making lasts and heels has changed considerably over the years. The guys who used to make the wooden heels were really skilled. Now you don't need a model-maker you just put your drawing into a computer and a lathe automatically cuts the shape. But there is a big but...the machine is very expensive.

'It still amazes me that I'm still in the industry. So much for my intention of only "sticking it for a while" in 1960!'

Hand finishing lasts, Bobcol, c2000

10. Avis Brown : A Life in the Shoe Industry

Avis' career in the shoe industry spanned 46 years. Here she shares her memories, and in so doing brings to life many of the themes, people and subjects covered in this book.

Avis, 1959

Avis, 2013

'I left school in 1957 when I was 15, and went into Caleys' chocolate factory. After a few months someone said that they were paying more money at Harmers clothing factory, so a group of us went over there, but I only lasted two weeks because I was put on the hot press, which I really didn't like. I knew about the shoe trade because my mother was in it. So I left Harmers and walked up the road to Edwards & Holmes on Drayton Road and found myself at the age of 15 on my third job! From the beginning I absolutely loved it.

'The Edwards & Holmes factory was modern when I was there. It had just been rebuilt after the war. There were lots of windows. Downstairs was the press room and the finishing room, and upstairs we had the clicking room at one end and the machine room at the other. All those in my age group were asked if we wanted to go to City College, which at the time was on St George's. I was paid to go there one day a week. It was a general course and I learnt all about the leathers and how to make shoes. I found it really interesting.

'I started in the shoe room where I learnt how to clean the shoes, which we did before they were boxed. We had a special wash and then used a piece of crepe and went around the edges of the sole and upper to make sure as much solution as possible had been removed. Then someone would apply paint, which was the same colour as the leather, over any white solution which you couldn't wash off. From there on in I graduated to bigger things and put bows on shoes and sewed diamantés onto the vamp. The diamantés were tiny, just like diamonds in a ring, but they had a piece of mesh behind them that matched the shoe and it was the mesh you sewed on. When we did that sort of work we were on a flat rate. You couldn't sew on the diamantés until you'd graded right up and proved your worth doing less skilled trimming jobs. It was fiddly work and if we had an order for 12 pairs of diamanté decorated shoes it would take forever for one person to do it, and so we were asked if we wanted to take a pair home to work on overnight. You'd be lucky to do one pair in the evening as it took a good half a day. We did a lot of fancy work like this because at Edwards & Holmes we made really high-class ladies' shoes.

'I was always buying shoes. I particularly remember we had a special order from America for pointed, sling-back green-suede shoes. Even in 1959 they cost £42 a pair. When one pair was made up the left shoe was a different shade of green to the right which meant they were rejected. So I asked if I could buy them at the reject price. They said I could but not until the rest had left England. I probably paid about £5 for them, which would have been a week's wages, but I loved wearing them.

'From there I learnt how to put the socks in the shoes. I then went on to do slashing, in fact I still have my slashing knife which was shaped a bit like a little scythe. You had to sharpen it until you had a lovely little fine point then you cut off the excess leather inside the shoe We also made trimmings. At Edwards & Holmes we cut strips and flowers, for the fancy shoes. I was always nicking my fingers. I did that for quite a few years, until they got a machine in.

'So in those first few years I learnt many skills, which meant that when I moved factories I could do all the jobs in a trimming room.

'When I was there Mr Forrest, who was a big stout man, was the managing director, and the factory director was Mr Johnson. At that time all the bosses were always called "Mr". One day Mr Forrest decided to have a new office built for Mr Johnson on the bottom floor. At the time you had the trimming room, where I worked, on one side then a gangway and the men's press room on the other. He ended up with a big glass office with six steps up into it. So when he was in his office it was like he was in a big, glass tower looking down over everybody. In the mornings Mr Forrest didn't come through the front door, like you'd expect a boss to do, he'd come through our back door and then walk all the way up the gangway looking to make sure everything was in order. As he walked through the factory a tiny lady who worked on the socks burst out singing, "Jesus wants me for a sunbeam", and every day he looked straight ahead and ignored her. We all looked on and tried not to laugh – I'd love to have known what he was thinking.

'Around 1958 Mr Forrest decided he was going to build a new ladies' toilet – we even had an opening ceremony. I think that he must have been on holiday somewhere posh because when it was unveiled, hand painted in pastel colours across the top of the door, was written the word "Boudoir". Well of course it was something new to us. We were quite excited. We all went in for a look. In the first section across one side there was a full length mirror with a shelf. I remember him telling us that it was for us to put our handbags on. There were seats all around and ashtrays on stilts, so that we could sit and have a smoke. In the next piece there were the hand basins and then the loos. I can tell you now that in all of the factories I've ever worked in I've never seen such posh toilets!'

Bill Forrest, c1965

Howard Johnson in his new office, c1965

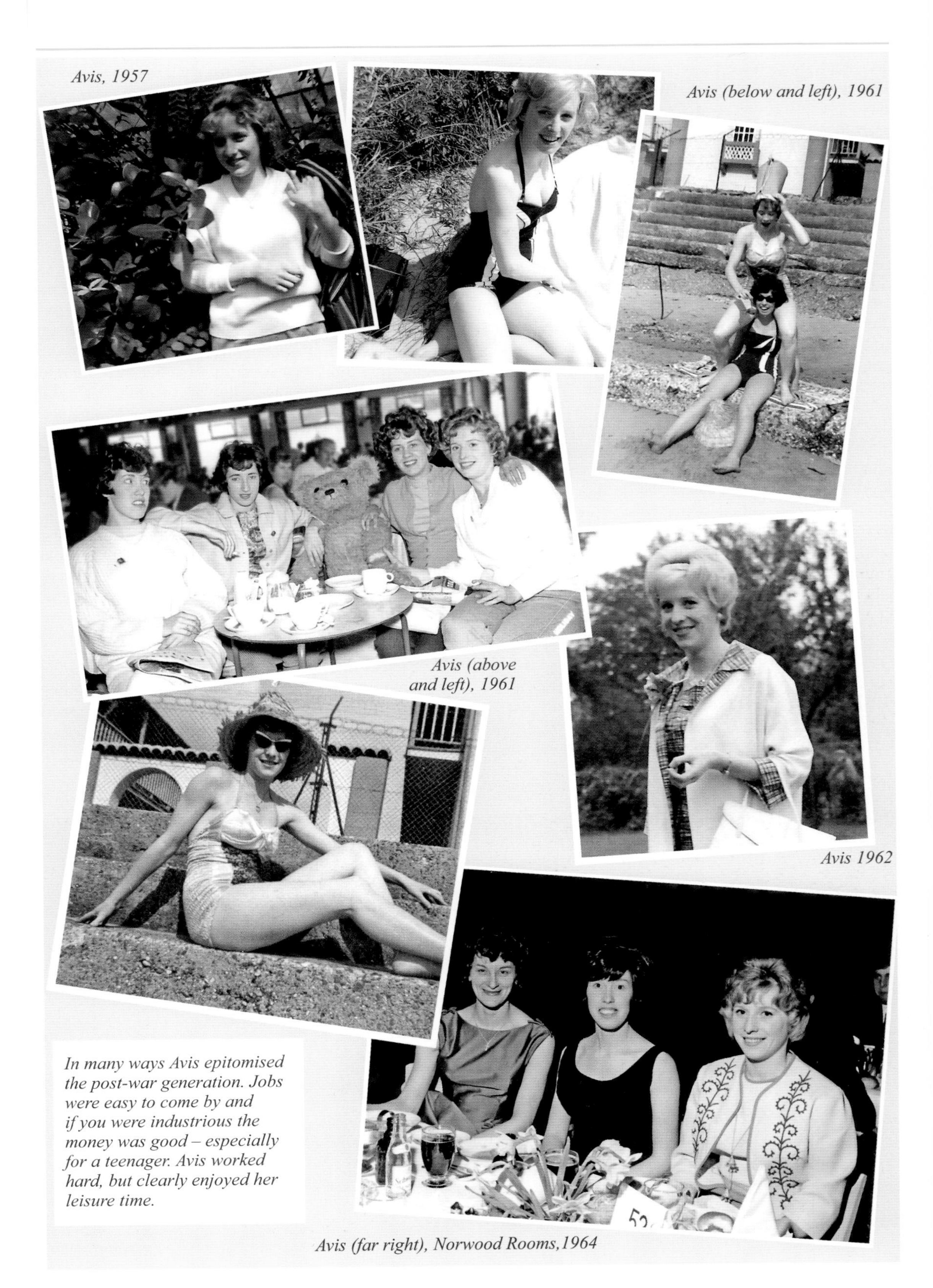

Avis, 1957

Avis (below and left), 1961

Avis (above and left), 1961

Avis 1962

In many ways Avis epitomised the post-war generation. Jobs were easy to come by and if you were industrious the money was good – especially for a teenager. Avis worked hard, but clearly enjoyed her leisure time.

Avis (far right), Norwood Rooms,1964

'At lunch times we went out into our yard at the back. If it was a lovely day we used to put our feet in the River Wensum because there was no fencing. At 10 a.m. to 10.30 a.m. in those days the radio played "Workers' Playtime" and everybody sang. All the men and all the ladies joined in. Upstairs were the machine and clicking rooms and you could hear them up there as well. The atmosphere was electric. Everyone would be doing their work and singing away. It was absolutely lovely.

'On our last day at work before Christmas we had an extra half an hour for dinner, so we all used to go over the road to the Ropemakers' Arms. It was really tiny, so after buying a drink we all stood outside. When we got back to work we were a bit squiffy, but it didn't matter because it was Christmas time. We weren't supposed to have alcohol in the factory, but on the day we broke up some people had a secret drink under the benches. As we didn't do a lot of work on the last afternoon it wasn't really a problem. Of course we had food and we sang and nearer home time we'd all do the conga. The managers just used to say: "Let them get on with it." Looking back they were happy days.

'We were treated fairly. Most of us were on piecework. I always wanted to learn as much as possible and whatever I learnt I wanted to do as quickly as I could. You see I was young and wanted to earn as much as possible because I liked going out at weekends to pictures and to dances. They call them discos now, but we went to "record hops". We used to go to the Samson & Hercules on Tombland and all of the picture houses down Prince of Wales Road. You didn't leave off work until six and the last bus home was at half-past ten, which didn't give you a lot of time. So I used to eat my tea while I did my hair.

'Health and safety was very different to today. I remember there being fire extinguishers but that was about it. We always had four Bunsen burners lit in the finishing room and thought nothing of it. Then one day, in the late 1950s, I saw a lady catch fire in front of my eyes. We had a special flammable liquid which was needed sometimes to do repairs on shoes. At this particular time I was on the boxing and she was on passing, which meant that she was doing the final check on the shoes before they left the factory. She put some wax on her knife and took it over to a Bunsen burner, to heat it up. She then accidentally dripped the hot wax into the flammable liquid and it blew up into her face, hair and clothes. She was completely alight. She just ran around until someone caught her and threw a coat over her. Her daughter worked upstairs and she came down screaming. It was horrendous, but there was no question of compensation because she knew that the liquid was highly inflammable and she shouldn't have taken the boiling-hot wax near it. Although she recovered her face was badly burnt. She never returned to work. It was lucky that the whole factory didn't burn down because all four tables were alight. Everyone was obviously trying to help the poor lady. Luckily a young man called Roger grabbed a fire extinguisher and managed to put the fire out.

'We didn't think about hazards in the same way as today. We knew that Bunsen burners were dangerous and didn't put our hands near them. We applied common sense.

Avis (second right), 1961

'I left Edwards & Holmes in 1963 because I was annoyed when one of the boxers left and I ended up doing her work as well. I asked for an extra half a crown a week and they wouldn't give it to me so I told them what they could do with their job. That dinner time I walked to Sexton, Son & Everard and got a new job. I didn't even work my notice.

'At Sextons I did passing and repairing. Passing was the last thing that happened to the shoe. The passer's job was to make sure that everyone had done their work properly. If there were any little repairs to be done I'd do those as well. In later years the job was called quality control. I worked in a nice little room which made satin mules with fluffy bits on the front for Marks & Spencer. They cost quite a bit. When that room closed I worked in the office printing work tickets for the jobs.

'At Sextons there was no yard. It was built on the pavement and all you had was a pathway around the factory. Many of us went to work on a bike and, because there was no land, we had nowhere to put them. Luckily the landlord at a nearby pub let us park them in his yard for a shilling a week. In the evenings he'd be there to make sure we all took the right bike.

'Sextons was a very big factory and I found there was no atmosphere. You weren't allowed to walk about the same way you were at other factories that I worked in. At Edwards & Holmes they were strict, but the rules made sense. At Sextons they seemed to make unnecessary rules. For example at Sextons they had a doorkeeper who had a little office just inside the entrance. At eight o'clock in the morning he would lock the door from the inside and so if you didn't get in there on time you had to stand outside until a minute to quarter past. He then opened the door again so that you just had time to run to your room and clock in by quarter past. But by then you'd already lost 15-minutes work. I didn't really like Sextons much and had been working there for less than a year when I bumped into my old foreman, who asked me to come back. I said: "What even after I told you what to do with your job?" He said: "Yes." So I returned to Edwards & Holmes where I worked until 1965 when I had my son. I still needed a job, but they didn't have part-time work there so I went down to Trimfoot, a little factory in Starling Road, which was a very nice place to work.

Sexton, Son & Everard, 1972

'The manager at Trimfoot was Lenny Waspe. Of course we always called him Mr Waspe. He had a sister called Rita who had a shop near where I lived on Woodcock Road. My Mum worked at Trimfoot when I was younger, and when Mr Waspe left off and went to see his sister he gave my mum a lift home in his posh car. At the time very few people had a car, so she felt very grand when she got out and hoped that all the neighbours would see her. The factory was very small. Upstairs, before I went there, must have been used for machinists but in my time it was just used for storage. The room we worked in was at the back. It had been an old courtyard which had been built in by putting a roof on it. They'd also put in two, big, brown, wooden doors which could be opened to take the work out. In the room we still had drainpipes and drains, which before the conversion would have been outside. Because it was below street level, to get in you'd open the door and go down six steps, and if it was a foggy morning outside you'd open the door and find that there was also fog in the room! It was really cold so we were eventually transferred to a room that was at street level. We were given cut uppers and soles by Start-rite and at Trimfoot we assembled the shoes. My job was to pass and make any necessary final repairs. We also made some dance shoes. We had one girl who could cover heels with cloths, such as satin. When I worked there Fred Waspe (Lenny's dad) had retired but he still came in to visit Lenny.

Len Waspe, c1965

'I left Trimfoot early in 1974 when I heard about a passing and repairing job at Start-rite. I was glad to be working at a bigger factory because I thought that the job would be more secure. Within a few weeks I never wanted to leave. It was great because I was doing the work that I loved. I also had the opportunity to do extra jobs, which meant that I could earn more. They liked it because I had so many skills, which meant that if someone else needed a hand, I could nip across and help them for half an hour.

'We actually had a Start-rite song. It was made up years before I worked there. As new people came they taught the women, the men weren't interested. The song went:

We are the Start-rite girls.
We are the Start-rite girls.
We know our manners.
We spend our tanners.
We are respected wherever we go.
We are the Start-rite girls.
We are the Start-rite girls.
And when you hear our foreman shout,
get your blooming finger out…
We know we are the Start-rite girls.

We'd all sing it when we were breaking up for a holiday or having a party, anything like that. One Christmas time we put our foreman, who was quite short, into a box and danced around singing the song. When Roger Hook, who was one of our directors, came out to see what was happening he couldn't stop laughing. That's what it was like being a Start-rite person. You felt like you were one of a big family.

'We had the social club on Romany Road, which was also the works' canteen. We had loads of sections, including football, cricket, badminton and even floral art. We used to work together and also played together. In the end we knew each other so well it was as though we were all in the same family. By the 1980s the relationship between managers and staff was very different. We were all on first-name terms. David White often walked through the factory and if you said hello to him he'd stop to have a chat. He'd look at our work and ask a couple of questions. He really was a gentleman. He always cared about us.'

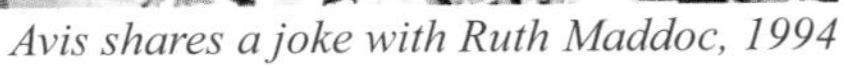

Avis shares a joke with Ruth Maddoc, 1994

Avis meets Prince Charles, 1994

The factories supported many local charities. Avis presents a cheque to Norfolk & Norwich Hospital, 1997

Start-rite's social club even organised holidays abroad. Group (including Avis) visiting Santa Susanna, Spain, 1992

'Shoe-factory work used to go up and down. It happened everywhere. We'd go from being very busy to being quite slack. At Start-rite they did everything possible so that you didn't lose jobs. If things were slow they'd have a meeting with the rooms and we'd be told that they didn't have enough work and we were asked to reduce hours. Then when the work picked up we were put back on full-time. They were very fair with us, but it did also mean that they kept the quality workers. In 1975, when Start-rite started to contract, we just thought it was a normal fluctuation. No one dreamt that eventually all of the shoes would be made abroad. We thought that we'd be alright because Start-rite was the biggest factory in Norwich, but in the 1980s, when so many of the others had closed, we started to be more worried. Then in the late 1980s they started shipping work out, and that was the first time we thought the factory might close. But we didn't really believe it. We never, ever thought that they'd make everything abroad.

'When it started to really hit home that everything was going to finish and we were all going to be out of a job we were absolutely devastated. We thought that we wouldn't be able to get other work. I'd been in the shoe industry for 46 years, and along with others didn't know anything else. Some hadn't even worked in other factories, and had spent all their working lives at Start-rite. We were very upset. We knew about the new place on the Broadland Business Park and were aware that it wasn't a factory.

'The closure was very different to what happened at Norvic where the factory workers walked in one morning and that was it. At Start-rite we gradually closed. So I was very lucky being there right to the end. The machine and clicking rooms finished on 9 September 2001, the same day as the twin towers were attacked in New York. We knew what was happening in 2000, but I never thought we would last so long. I was there until 2003 when the factory closed. The last day was awful. There were a lot of tears. There was such emptiness. Everyone was so hurt. We knew each other like family but didn't know if we'd see each other anymore. To think that all of the skills we all had, were just going to go. On that day we felt just like a number, something we'd never been.

'We had the word Start-rite running through us. We didn't just go to work, we really cared about the company. I still meet many people who worked at the factory. They all have jobs and enjoy themselves, but they all say: "There's nothing like Start-rite is there?"

'That ends the story of my life in the shoe industry, and I can honestly say that I never wanted to work anywhere else.'

The very last day, Avis (ringed), Start-rite's Crome Road factory, 2003

11. The Legacy

In its heyday, the Norwich boot and shoe trade not only generated jobs and wealth in the City, but also gave it a sense of pride. Norwich shoes were admired across the world, as were those with the skill and craftsmanship to make them.

In many ways the contribution made by the shoe industry to Norwich is impossible to calculate. Following the devastation of the once great worsted industry, the three decades after 1815 were years of great depression in the City. By the middle of the century, the coming of the railway gave a real boost to the local economy, and in particular to a range of industries, including engineering, brewing, and of course shoemaking. In the years that followed the boot and shoe trade grew to be the City's major industry and leading employer, at times generating over 10,000 jobs, and even as late as 1971 the numbers employed in the trade exceeded 5,500. In the 1930s its impact on the local economy was such that the Norwich Chamber of Commerce commented that 'the prosperity of the City as a whole seemed to flag with its fortunes'. Which leads to questions such as: Where would Norwich be today if the footwear industry had not flourished? Would another trade have boosted the local economy, or would the City have undergone a long period of decline?

However, what is indisputable is that boot and shoe trade has left Norwich a tangible legacy as proof that the City was once a major footwear-manufacturing centre.

One only has to look at the façade of Norvic's monumental factory on St George's Plain to get some idea of the impact it had on the City. It is hard to imagine that this quiet, attractive area of Norwich was once a bustling hive of activity, where the pounding and screeching of huge presses reverberated. At lunchtimes it heaved with workers, especially in the summer when many bought in packed lunches, whilst others went to the workers' cafes that lined the streets. The area buzzed. Unsurprisingly after the closure of the factory the neighbourhood became dilapidated, and a plan was set in motion to regenerate it. Today the area is known as 'Norwich Over the Water'. Redevelopment started in the 1980s and the old factory site now comprises a mix of offices, shops and residential apartments. Many of the factory's decorative features have been retained, although less attractive parts of the site, including the Riverside factory, have been demolished. In deference to its past glories the history of the area is still recalled in names used in the complex including the 'Leather House' and of course the 'Last Wine Bar'.

The former Norvic factory still dominates St George's Plain, 2012

The former Norvic-Kiltie factory, behind 'The Woolie', 2012

Opposite the main Norvic factory site is the old Kiltie factory, built by Sid Witton in 1926. This once huge factory with its angular roof, resembling a series of pyramids, still rises majestically behind the adjacent pub ('The Woolie'). The factory was closed down in 1982 and has since been sub-divided into offices and workshops.

Moving around to St Mary's Plain, the St Mary's Works stands as a monument to the once powerful firm, Sexton, Son & Everard. The factory, which was rebuilt in the 1940s after the earlier building was devastated during the raids of WWII, again adds much ambience to this area of Norwich. The red-brick façade with its white adornment strangely complements the medieval church of St Mary Coslany, which is its immediate neighbour. What is more surprising is that behind this frontage still stands an area of some 100,000 square feet which now comprises offices, storage units and workshops.

Sexton, Son & Everard's St Mary Works is now offices, storage units and workshops, 2012

The former Haldinstein (Bally) factory building, Queen Street, 2012

Conversely, most of the buildings occupied by the Bally factory between Queen Street and Princes Street were demolished after the firm relocated to Hall Road in the 1970s. However, part of the premises, first occupied when the firm was owned by the Haldinsteins, still stands. This imposing and somewhat solid looking building now houses a mix of commercial businesses, including offices and a bar.

In contrast, few people passing between 54 and 63a Pottergate would suspect that these attractive Georgian buildings, located on either side of this historic thoroughfare, housed one of Norwich's foremost shoe factories. Here Shingler & Thetford produced elegant footwear, but since moving out they have left little evidence of their occupation. The buildings have now been converted into residential properties. Similarly it is hard to believe that the genteel and attractive shop of Bowhill & Elliott, on London Street, fronts a small factory, where skilled craftsmen and women continue to make exquisite slippers that are sold across the world.

This Georgian house at 63a Pottergate was once part of the Shingler & Thetford factory, 2012

Around the City centre other less imposing factory premises such as that owned by R. Roberts Ltd on Fisher's Lane and Arthur Howlett Ltd on Fishergate still stand. Elsewhere, even though the main factory premises have been replaced by residential developments there are still reminders of the buildings' industrial past. So for example:

- Although the CWS factory which stood on Mountergate has been demolished and replaced by residential properties, the impressive wall and gate that marked its perimeter still stand. In memory of the old factory part of the development is named Parmentergate Court (a parmenter being a leather worker)
- More poignant is the plaque on a residential block on Fishergate, that doesn't officially mark the location of an old factory, but commemorates George Smith and Joan Knights 'who were both killed on 5 September 1942 during a German air raid on the Batson & Webster shoe factory that stood on this site'
- Outside the City centre, on Crome Road, the entrance to a newly refurbished residential block is by way of an arch which bears the inscriptions: '1907', 'JS Co. Ltd' and 'Estd 1792'. All clues, of course, to the fact that this was the site of James Southall's factory
- The old Edwards & Holmes' factory on Drayton Road is remembered in the street names of the residential development that replaced it. These include: Clickers' Road and Boot Binders' Road.

Arch, former Start-rite factory, Crome Road, 2012

The City's oldest shoe factory, which is still operational in 2013, is located on Dibden Road. Originally built by the shoe manufacturers Chittock & Sons in 1912, it has been occupied by the Florida Group since 1959. The firm welcomes visitors (by arrangement) to take a tour of the factory and see footwear being manufactured. Making beautiful shoes continues to give Simon Goodman, chairman, and his colleagues a real sense of achievement: 'Our workforce enjoy it when people come on factory visits, they love to show off their skills. We are proud that after 75 years we still make shoes in Norwich. We are very aware of our heritage and consider it an inherent part of the company.'

Parmentergate Court, Mountergate, bordered by the wall of the former CWS shoe factory, 2012

The influence of the shoe manufacturers extended well beyond their factory boundaries. Many were forces for good in the City. Sir Henry Holmes, who was twice Lord Mayor of Norwich (in 1921 and 1932), and Sir George White, MP for the North-West division of Norfolk (1900, 1906 and 1910), are just two examples of those who contributed to the welfare of Norwich's citizens.

Another philanthropist was Henry J. Sexton. In 1944 he became the sole owner of the Assembly House when it was in an extreme state of decay. In the following year he formed the H. J. Sexton Norwich Arts Trust, under whose auspice the building was completely redeveloped and refurbished. In November 1959 the Assembly House was reopened and presented to the people of Norwich as an arts and social centre. The project cost Henry around £70,000 (equivalent to around £2 million today), making it a remarkably generous gift.

However, there is one building in the City which more than any other epitomises the importance of the boot and shoe trade to Norwich, and that is the Bridewell Museum. Not only was the building the factory premises of Thomas Bowhill & Hubbard Ltd (from 1896 – 1923), but in 1925 it was given to the City by Sir Henry Holmes as a museum of trade and industry. Working with other local business men he helped create a museum which he hoped would: 'Provide a source of pleasure and pride to the citizens…inspire the younger generations to realise the greatness of their heritage…and encourage the worker to take pride in the finished product of his workshop…' Unsurprisingly Sir Henry took a particular interest in the displays devoted to shoe making, which he strongly believed should promote and celebrate local craftsmanship. As Hannah Henderson, curator at the museum, commented: 'Henry Holmes and his co-curators left an impressive, inspiring and enduring legacy. Theirs was a pioneering mission of preservation, local patriotism, promotion and education. As a result of their vision we have been able to preserve many fine examples of Norwich's heritage, not least of which is a unique collection of around 3,000 shoes which were made in the City.'

On 3 July 2012 the museum was re-opened after undergoing a £1.5m redevelopment. Magnificent new displays still tell the story of Norwich and its people, and include a revamped shoemaking section which both explores the industry in Norwich and considers what it was like to work in the factories. But the highlight for many will be the sheer beauty of the shoes (a selection of which have been featured in this book) which are on display. They remain as a true testament to the skill of the men and women who designed and made them – a legacy to us all.

Assembly House, Norwich, 2008

Shoemakers' Gallery - Bridewell Museum, 2013

Displays include heels and shoemaking tools

The outstanding displays incorporate machinery, tools, stories, workers' memories...and of course beautiful shoes.

Sir Henry Holmes would have approved.

All photos reproduced with the kind consent of Fisheye Images. (Copyright: the Bridewell Museum)

The display cabinets are part of the original bequest made in 1925

Glossary of Terms

Albert Slipper A man's slipper with a straight top line to the quarters. The vamp is extended upwards to form a tongue resting on top of the foot.

Average An amount calculated over a period of time by dividing how much each operator had earned by the number of hours they had worked. The quicker they worked the higher this sum would be. On piecework it was important for workers to keep their average high because it was used to calculate such things as holiday pay.

Bottom Stock The under part of the shoe encompassing the sole, insole and heel

Bottom Stuff Another name for bottom stock

Boxer (Boxing) The person responsible for putting the finished shoes in a box

Cement An adhesive

Clicker (Clicking) Clickers cut the uppers. Historically, clickers cut leather on boards made of blocks of wood. When they came to the end of a cut they withdrew their knife and a 'clicking' sound was heard …hence the name.

Closing Stitching the upper sections together, may also be called machining

Closing Machine Similar to a domestic sewing machine, used to stitch flat pieces of upper

Coupon Each batch of shoes went around the factory accompanied by a work ticket, a perforated paper list of tasks that needed to be completed. Each perforated section was known as a coupon. When a job was completed the worker retained the coupon which was used by the accounts department to calculate how much each person should be paid.

Cuban Heel A fairly straight-sided heel

Feeder The person feeding work to machinists working alongside a conveyor belt

Finishing Room Where the bottoms were trimmed, made weatherproof and polished

Fitting Process by which the bottom stuff was matched (or fitted up) with the corresponding upper

Folder (Folding) Person responsible for folding and sticking down the raw edges of the uppers before they are stitched by a machinist

Forepart The front of the shoe

Garret Master In pre-factory days the garret masters organised small-scale shoe production, using both their own premises and a team of outworkers who worked in their own homes

Insole The inside part of the shoe that runs underneath the bottom of the foot, usually insoles can be easily removed

Last The block, originally wooden but now normally made out of plastic, on which a shoe is made. Its shape roughly corresponds with that of a foot but incorporates differences to take account of the design of the shoe.

Lasting The operation of shaping the upper to the last

Louis Heel A heel with graceful curves on the side and back where the front surface is covered by a downward extension of the sole

Machining Stitching the upper sections together, may also be called closing

Making Room The department in a shoe factory where the uppers and bottoms (soles and heels) are assembled to make a shoe

Passer Person in the factory who made a final check of the shoe. If it was up to standard it would be 'passed', a similar job today would be in quality control.

Pattern The shapes made out of card, paper etc. used to cut out the upper sections of a shoe

Pattern Cutter In pre-computer days, once a design was agreed the pattern cutter was responsible for devising a pattern based on the design in one size

Pattern Maker	Once a pattern cutter had devised the pattern in one size the pattern maker was responsible for producing working patterns for every size and fitting
Perforating	Making decorative holes in the upper
Piecework	Wages which are paid according to the amount produced
Post Machines	Were used to do final stitching when the uppers were more or less complete and would not lie flat
Press Knife	A steel cutter which was pushed through material (e.g. leather) by the pressure generated by a press. They were produced in different shapes and were eventually used to produce both uppers and soles. They are sometimes described as being similar in function to pastry cutters.
Press Room	Also knows as the bottom-stock room, this was the department where soles and heels were cut using presses
Puttee	A long narrow piece of material wound around the leg from the ankle to the knee serving as both support and protection
Quarter	One side of a shoe between the heel and the vamp
Racks	The name given to the trolleys used to transport partially completed shoes around a factory
Room	A department in a factory were a specific task takes place, e.g. the closing room
Rough Stuff	Another name for bottom stock
Sample Room	Room where the manufacturers displayed their shoes
Seat or Heel Seat	The rear end of the sole (or insole) on which the heel of the foot rests
Shank	A reinforcement placed at the waist of the shoe between the sole and insole to prevent the shoe from bending
Shoe Room	The department in a shoe factory where the shoes were made spick and span and then boxed. Jobs undertaken here included adding ornamentation, correcting faults, and sticking socks into the shoe
Skiving (Skiver)	The term used for reducing the thickness at the edge on an upper where a fold or joint was to be made
Slashing (Slasher)	Trimming off any excess lining, or leather, from the inside of the shoe
Sock	A piece of material stuck inside a shoe to cover stitches etc., which may also carry information such as the maker's trademark
Stiffener	Also known as a heel stiffener, this reinforcement is placed inside the back of the quarters
Toe Puff	A reinforcement under the toe end of the vamp to give it stiffness
Travellers	Salesmen employed by the major shoe manufacturers to sell their footwear to independent shops and stores within a specified area
Trimming Room	Another name for the shoe room
Turnshoes	Shoes which are made inside out then turned the right way out, so that the grain side of the leather is on the outside of the shoe and the upper/sole seam is then inside
Upper	The top of a shoe extending downwards as far as the sole, a normal shoe upper consists of the vamp and two quarters
Vamp	The front section of a shoe upper
Waist	The narrowest part of the sole between the forepart and the heel
Wicket	The name given to the department in a shoe factory where work was handed to the homeworkers and, once completed, taken back from them
Work Ticket	Each batch of shoes was sent around a factory accompanied by a work ticket which told you the name of the shoe and what it looked like, together with a perforated list of the various operations which were needed to make the shoe (also see coupon)

Bibliography

Allen, Rod et al 'The Shattered Dream: Employment in the Eighties', Hutchinson Publishing Group, 1981.

Anderson, A. P. and Storey N. R. 'Norwich, Eighty Years of the Norwich Society', Sutton Publishing, 2004.

Archant Publications including the *Eastern Daily Press* and the *Eastern Evening News*, various dates.

Ayers, Brian 'Norwich, A Fine City', Tempus Publishing Inc, 2003.

Baldwin, Arthur E. B. 'Gentlemen of the Gentlecraft', unpublished, c1972.

Beer, Olive 'A Study of Master and Man in a Norwich Leatherdressers (1860 – 1945), John Culyer and Son Ltd', Unpublished, c1993.

Blake, P. W., Bull, J ., Cartwright, A. R. and Fitch, A. 'The Norfolk We Live In', Jarrold & Sons Ltd, Norwich, 1964.

Brooks, Pamela 'Norwich Street by Street', Breedon Books Publishing, 2006.

Burgess, Edward 'Men who have made Norwich', self-published, 1904.

Central Youth Employment Executive 'Boot and Shoe Manufacture', HMSO, 1949.

Clutterbuck, David and Crainer, Stuart 'The Decline and Rise of British Industry', W.H. Allen & Co. Plc, 1988.

Colman, Richard 'The Development of the Boot and Shoe Industry in Norwich. 1750 – 1850', (no publisher recorded), 2000.

Cozens-Hardy, Basil and Kent, Ernest 'The Mayors of Norwich 1403 to 1835', Jarrold and Sons Ltd, 1938.

Crookenden, Spencer 'K Shoes – The First 150 Years 1842-1992', K Shoes, 1992.

Dunning, J. H. & Thomas, C. J. 'British Industry', Hutchinson & Co. (Publishers) Ltd, 1966.

Fowler, Eric 'Buckinghams - A Hundred Years in the Shoe Trade; 1862 – 1962', Jarrold and Sons Ltd, 1962.

Goreham, Geoffrey 'Yards and Courts of Old Norwich', (no publisher recorded), undated.

Gurney-Read, Joyce 'Trades & Industries of Norwich', Crowes of Norwich, 1988.

Gurney-Read, Joyce Miscellaneous collection of information retained in the Local Studies Section, Norfolk & Norwich Millennium Library, various dates.

Hawkins, C. B. 'Norwich: A Social Study', P. L.Warner, 1910.

Holmes, Ken 'Two Centuries of Shoemaking: Start-rite 1792 – 1992', Start-rite Shoes, 1992.

Hudson, Kenneth 'Towards Precision Shoemaking: C & J Clarke Ltd and the Development of the British Shoe Industry', David & Charles (Publishers) Ltd, 1968.

Industrial Training Service (The) 'Report on Operative Training', British Footwear Manufacturers, c1965.

Johnson, Maggie 'The Norwich Shoe Industry 1850 – 1890', Journal of the Norfolk Industrial Archaeological Society, 1980.

Johnson, Maggie '16th-and-17th-Century Norwich Cordwainers', Costume & Textile Association Newsletter, November 2008.

Johnson, Maggie 'Industrial Structure of the Norwich Trade in the 19th Century', Costume & Textile Association Newsletter, November 2008.

Johnson, Maggie 'Shoemaking in Elm Hill, Norwich 1850 – 1890', Costume & Textile Association Newsletter, November 2008.

Johnson, Paul '20th Century Britain: Economic, Social and Cultural Change', Longman, 1994.

Jones, David 'Business, Tact and Thoroughness: A History of the Norvic Shoe Company', Journal of the Norfolk Industrial Archaeological Society 1986.

Jones, David 'The Norwich Boot and Shoe Industry', Norfolk Museums Service, 1986.

Kelly's 'Directory of the City of Norwich', various dates.

Leeds, Herbert 'Peace Souvenir: Norwich War Record', Jarrold, 1919.

Meeres, Frank 'A History of Norwich', Phillimore, 1998.

Meeres, Frank 'Strangers: A History of Norwich's Incomers', Norwich HEART, 2012.

Mitchell, Louise and Ward, Linda 'Stepping Out, Three Centuries of Shoes', Powerhouse Publishing, Sydney, 1997.

Mottram R. H. 'If Stones Could Speak', Richard Clay and Company Ltd, 1953.

Neve A. F. 'The Principles of Clicking', Youngmans Printers, 1930.

Norwich HEART 'Norwich 12', Norwich HEART, 2008.

Norwich Heritage Projects 'A Market For Our Times', Norwich Heritage Projects, 2010.

O'Keeffe, Linda 'Shoes: A Celebration of Pumps, Sandals, Slippers & More', Workman Publishing Company Inc, 1996.

Owen, Geoffrey 'From Empire to Europe', Harper Collins, 1999.

Rampling, Freda 'Technological Change in the Shoe Industry', Costume & Textile Association Newsletter, November 2008.

Rawcliffe, Carole and Wilson, Richard 'Medieval Norwich', Hambledon and London, 2004.

Rawcliffe, Carole and Wilson, Richard 'Norwich Since 1550', Hambledon and London, 2004.

Reed, Brenda 'The Courts and Yards of Norwich', Norwich Heritage Projects, 2009.

Renton, John 'Shoe Manufacture in Norwich: An Introduction to the Bridewell Collections', Costume & Textile Association Newsletter, November 2008.

Roth, Arnold 'History of Shingler & Thetford', unpublished, 1981.

Start-rite In-house magazines, self-published, various dates.

Sexton, H. J. 'Fifty Years in the Shoe Trade', Journal of the Norfolk Industrial Archeological Society, 1974.

Shoe and Leather Record, 'Elizabeth II, Coronation Souvenir', self-published, 1953.

Shoe and Leather Trades 'Footwear: Shoe and Leather Trades Export Journal', The National Trade Press, 1948.

Shoe and Leather Trades 'Shoe and Leather News: Biographical Directory of the Shoe and Allied Traders', self-published, 1916.

Sparks W. L. 'Shoemaking in Norwich', The National Institution of the Boot and Shoe Industry, 1949.

Start-rite 'Foot Notes', Self-Published, Spring 1950.

Taylor, David 'Mastering Economic and Social History', the Macmillan Press Ltd, 1988.

Thornton J. H. et al, 'Textbook of Footwear Manufacture', the National Trade Press Ltd, 1975.

Van Dal '75 Years of Beautiful Shoes', self-published, 2011.

Wacjman, Judy 'Women In Control', The Open University Press, 1983.

Weber, Paul 'Shoes: A Pictorial Commentary on the History of the Shoe', the Bally Shoe Museum, 1982.

Wheldon F. W. 'A Norvic Century and the Men Who Made It', Jarrold and Sons Ltd, Empire Press, Norwich, 1946.

Wilson, Eunice 'A History of Shoe Fashions', Sir Isaac Pitman and Sons Ltd, 1969.

Acknowledgements

W. H. H. Clarke, 1957

Howlett & White, c1928

We are very grateful to all who have generously shared information with us. Without their help this book could not have been written.

Particular thanks must be given to Penny Clarke for her guidance and help in editing the book.

We are especially grateful to Derek James, Rosemary Dixon, Steve Adams and their colleagues at Archant, who have allowed us both access to their archives and permission to reproduce many splendid photographs.

Hannah Henderson and John Renton at the Bridewell Museum have been exceptionally helpful in allowing us to photograph their wonderful display of shoes and to reproduce images held in their archives.

Philip Armes has given us invaluable help in searching out, and allowing us to reproduce, relevant photographs from his collection. Also thanks to Jonathan Plunkett for giving us permission to use photos taken by his father George.

Both the Norfolk County Council Library and Information Service and the Norfolk Record Office have given much guidance and permission to use materials. Rebecca Shawcross at the Northampton Shoe Museum has also kindly shared her knowledge and expertise.

We extend our thanks to Mike Dixon for taking many of our recent photographs. We are also grateful to Barbara Miller and Maggie Johnson, who have shared their own research material, and to Gordon Smart for his insight into the industry.

The directors and staff at Start-rite, the Florida Group, Broadland Slippers, Freeds and Bowhill & Elliott Ltd were all very welcoming. We are very appreciative of the time they took to talk to us, the access they gave to their premises and their archive material, including photographs.

We are exceptionally grateful to all of our contributors listed on pages v to vii not only for speaking to us but also for sharing photographs. Their help has been invaluable.

We have made much use of printed works, all publications are listed in the bibliography. Further information on photographic sources can be found on page ii.

Finally we apologise if we have inadvertently failed to acknowledge any of our sources. Anyone who has not been contacted is invited to write to the publisher so that full recognition can be given in subsequent editions of this book.

Index

Back cover photographs (left to right):
Top Row
Detail on former factory buildings:
James Southall & Co. Ltd (Start-rite), Crome Road, 2012
Sexton, Son & Everard Ltd, St Mary's Plain, 2012
Norvic, St Georges Plain, 2012
James Southall & Co. Ltd (Start-rite), Crome Road, 2012
Middle Row
(L tor) Miss Esdelle and Lady Holmes, Edwards & Holmes, 1949
Miss Sexton contestants, Sexton, Son & Everard, 1961
(L to r) Actress from Cinderella and Howard Johnson, Edwards & Holmes, c1960
(L to r) Miss Florida contestants and David Goodman, Florida, c1960
Bottom Row
Clicking presses, Norvic, 1952